THE
AMERICAN
FAMILY

GARLAND REFERENCE LIBRARY
OF SOCIAL SCIENCE
VOL. 925

THE AMERICAN FAMILY

A Compendium
of Data and Sources

Josefina J. Card
Evelyn C. Peterson
Sachi Mizuno
Kathryn L. Muller
Elizabeth A. McKean
Eric L. Lang
James L. Peterson
Aaron S. Kaplan
Toni Deser

GARLAND PUBLISHING, Inc.
New York & London / 1994

Library of Congress Cataloging-in-Publication Data

The American family : a compendium of data and
sources / [compiled] by Josefina J. Card.
    p.   cm. — (Garland reference library of social
science ; vol. 925)
    Includes bibliographical references.
    ISBN 0–8153–1492–2 (alk. paper)
    1. Family life surveys—United States.   I. Card,
Josefina J.   II. Series: Garland reference library of
social science ; v. 925
HQ536.A545   1994
306.85'0973—dc20   93–24328
                                             CIP

Printed on acid-free, 250-year-life paper
Manufactured in the United States of America

CONTENTS

PREFACE

This compendium is one of a series of social science research and teaching resources created by the American Family Data Archive at Sociometrics Corporation. It describes 28 data sets chosen by a panel of scientist-experts as having outstanding potential for secondary data analysis on issues facing today's American family. At present, data and documentation in standard form from the following nationally recognized studies can be obtained from the Archive: National Survey of Families and Households, 1988; 1976-1987 National Survey of Children, Waves 1, 2, & 3; National Child Care Survey, 1990: Parent Study and Low-Income Substudy; A Profile of Child Care Settings: Home-Based and Center-Based Programs, 1989-1990; National Commission on Children: 1990 Survey of Parents & Children; National Family Violence Surveys, 1975, 1985; National Health Interview Survey on Child Health, 1988; Marital Instability over the Life Course, 1986-1988; Stanford Study of Child Custody, 1984-1990; Treatment Process: A Problem at 3 Levels, 1988.

This compendium describes these studies, both individually and as a set. Eighteen additional data sets on the American family, available from other sources, are also presented. Each description is aimed at conveying sufficient information for a reader to decide whether a particular data set is suited to address a research or policy question at hand. Included are details on the content of the data set, the sample from which the data were collected, and the instrumentation and data collection procedures that were used to create the data set. Cost and contact information is also included. For example, the individual data sets described in this compendium range in price from $100 to $500; the data and documentation from all the studies listed above as comprising the American Family Data Archive—along with customized search and retrieval and data extracting software—can be obtained for $950 from Sociometrics Corporation in Los Altos, California (see Chapter 30).

The 29 data sets in this compendium address family-related issues such as child care, children and youth, education, health, economic and social issues, labor force participation, violence, family therapy, and marriage and divorce. Embodying the current state-of-the-art of empirical data on the American family, the data sets are an excellent resource for researchers, teachers, and policymakers interested in studying and documenting the current status and well-being of the American family.

J. J. Card, Ph.D.   *November 1993*
Director, American Family Data Archive
Sociometrics Corporation
Los Altos, CA

ACKNOWLEDGMENTS

This publication was produced with funds provided by Contract N44-HD-0-2910 (*Establishment of a Family Data Archive*) between Sociometrics Corporation and the National Institute of Child Health and Human Development (NICHD). Our Project Officer at NICHD, Dr. Jeffery V. Evans, provided encouragement and support throughout the production of this book. We thank him for his help.

The selection of data sets to include in this compendium was made by a National Advisory Panel of scientists: Drs. Brent Miller (chair), Richard Kulka, Theodora Ooms, Douglas Sprenkle, Elizabeth Thomson, and Arland Thornton. The contributions of these individuals are acknowledged, with great appreciation.

We also acknowledge our intellectual debt to a predecessor of this book, the *Guide to Federal Data on Children, Youth, and Families*, edited by Nicholas Zill and James L. Peterson. While we have added new data sets not included in such *Guide*, our description and variable checklist templates represent expansions of those contained in the *Guide*. Indeed the *Guide* was the primary information source for 3 of the 30 abstracts in this book.

Finally, we wish to express our gratitude to the institutions and principal investigators who created the valuable data sets described herein, and who gave us permission to publicize the public availability of their data as well as to publish the enclosed data set descriptions, many of them taken from their own scientific work.

INTRODUCTION

USING EXISTING DATA ON THE STATUS AND WELL-BEING OF THE AMERICAN FAMILY

by Josefina J. Card

Technological breakthroughs in the last decade have brought rapid advances in computing capabilities. Powerful microcomputers the size of a notebook, with speeds of several million instructions per second and storage capacities of several hundred megabytes, can now be purchased for under $2,000. Data analysis software formerly available only for mainframe computers have become available for microcomputers for under $1,000. These technological developments mean that social science research and teaching laboratories with the hardware and software needed to analyze the best data in a given field can now be set up with ease by an academic department or even by an individual professor.

Analogous advances in the development of social science research and teaching resources have taken place. Data and instrument archives are now under creation that allow free and open access to hundreds of the best health and social science data sets accumulated in the last couple of decades. The data available from these archives are clean, the documentation user-friendly, and the software versatile and powerful.

These twin developments have put virtually unlimited and cost-free secondary data analysis within the grasp of the typical researcher, professor, or student. Secondary data analysis refers to the analysis of data for purposes other than the original one(s) for which the data were collected. Generally, secondary data analysis is conducted by scientists who are not the original data collectors or scientific investigators. Secondary data analysis is a relatively inexpensive scientific endeavor, but its potential to contribute to the state of knowledge and the formulation of enlightened policy should not be underestimated.

Outstanding data sets often lend themselves to analyses of topics other than the ones intended and pursued by the original investigators. Appropriate, creative use of secondary data analysis can thus yield rich benefits. The work of the original investigators can be validated and extended by other researchers using the same data. Timely analyses of pressing issues of policy or practice can be carried out without the long delay necessitated by original data collection. Bringing together topically related data sets facilitates quantitative comparisons and meta-analysis across similar studies. The use of the same data by multiple investigators and the use of multiple data sources by the same investigator foster the building of a network of colleagues and strengthen the research community. The ready availability of high quality data sets for secondary analysis expands the number of scholars undertaking research using the best data in the field; the interchange promoted by this network serves to stimulate further innovation and development of the field. Finally, taken together these advantages result in a much greater economy in the use of scarce research funds: given the high cost of original data collection—especially when such collection is from one or more national samples studied longitudinally over time—it is appropriate to view each data set as a public resource to be drawn on again and again whenever it is appropriate to answering a scientific, policy or program question.

One of the greatest barriers to secondary data analysis is the lack of an efficient and cost effective way for an investigator to locate and gain access to data that are suitable for a proposed research project. Another barrier to secondary analysis is the sometimes poor quality of the original data file or its documentation. An investigator interested in conducting secondary analysis of a particular data set does not want to spend hours poring over incomplete or inaccurate documents before determining whether such data set contains the information necessary to the investigation desired. Nor does an investigator want to conduct secondary analysis of data drawn from inappropriately selected samples or collected with poorly constructed, unreliable, or invalid measures.

To address these challenges, federal agencies that fund large-scale research programs are increasingly turning to data archiving and dissemination centers to cull the best of existing data sets in the field of inquiry covered by their research mandate; process and document these data sets in standard fashion; disseminate the public availability of the data sets to the scientific community at large; and provide no- or low-cost ongoing technical assistance to data users. Over the long run, such data archiving and dissemination programs serve to upgrade the standards that will be demanded of scientists by their peers for both the design and execution of studies and the documentation of resulting data.

An Illustrative Success Story: The Sociometrics Data Archives

This book describes 29 data sets chosen by a panel of experts as best able to speak to the current status and well-being of the American family. All the data sets included in this compendium are publicly available for little more than the cost of reproduction, postage, and handling. Many of them have been processed and documented in standard format by the American Family Data Archive, a pioneering data archiving and dissemination center housed at Sociometrics Corporation in Los Altos, California. Others are available from various agencies of the federal government, or from the Inter-university Consortium for Political and Social Research at the University of Michigan.

Investigators who are considering using secondary data to address a particular research or policy question welcome the functions served by a well-thought-out data archive: easy access to a group of topically-related data sets; search and retrieval capabilities that make selection of relevant data sets and variables inexpensive and easy; assurance of minimum technical standards in the data sets archived; prepared program statements for developing pre-labelled analysis files; standard guides that summarize the data set concisely and clearly; and the availability of technical assistance from archive staff. Each of these functions relieves a comparable burden from the shoulders of the potential user of secondary data, thus promoting the use of such data.

In this section we discuss the state-of-the-art data archiving procedures and resources under development at Sociometrics Corporation. Since assuming responsibility for the establishment and operation of the Data Archive on Adolescent Pregnancy and Pregnancy Prevention in 1984, Sociometrics has branched out to form the American Family Data Archive, the AIDS/STD Data Archive, the Maternal Drug Abuse Data Archive, and the Data Archive of Social Research on Aging. Over two hundred premier data sets are currently available from these archives. We describe their common, user-friendly features, designed to facilitate secondary data analysis,. Then we note how these features combine in the American Family Data Archive to form a unique, new research and teaching resource for family researchers, teachers, and policymakers.

Topically-Focused, Best-of-the-Lot Collections

The Sociometrics Data Archives embody the best-of-the-lot in a given topical area. Each data archive is a planned collection, as opposed to an ad-hoc one that is comprised primarily of data volunteered by faculty colleagues and friends. An advisory panel of scientists is commissioned with making selection decisions for each data archive, based on the following criteria for inclusion: (1) technical quality, or the scientific merit of the sampling, instrumentation, and data collection procedures used by the original investigators; (2) substantive utility, or the range of the variables covered by the data set and the scope of the population to which findings can be generalized; (3) program or policy relevance, or the ability of the data set to answer applied questions on how to improve public policy or shape intervention programs; (4) demand or marketability for secondary data analysis, or the extent to which theoretical or applied questions relevant to the data set have not yet been published by original investigators or replicated by colleagues; and (5) disciplinary balance, or the extent to which demographic, psychological, sociological, and economic perspectives are reflected in the collection taken as a whole.

Public Use, Easy Access

A key feature of the Sociometrics Data Archives is that they are public use, available for purchase and analysis by all who are willing to pay for copying and mailing of the data and documentation. Data sets are costed to be maximally affordable—generally $100 for data sets whose raw data is under five megabytes in size, $150 for larger data sets. This purchase price includes free ongoing technical assistance; in addition, quantity discounts are available for those who wish to analyze several data sets simultaneously. Sociometrics publicizes the availability of new data sets in a free semiannual newsletter.*

Focus on User-Oriented, Value-Added Features

Because the market for the data sets is students and scientists who were not part of the team that designed the study or collected the data, Sociometrics' processing and documentation procedures are aimed at producing clear, user-friendly material, with many "value-added," user-oriented features that go beyond the documentation provided by the original investigator. These value-added features represent the state-of-the-art in how to make a data set publicly available to a user community.

      Standard machine-readable files. Five machine-readable files comprise each data set. The first file is the *raw data* provided by the original investigator. The second and third files are the *SPSS and SAS program statements* that give the byte positions, names, labels, and missing value codes for each variable. These program statements serve as machine-readable codebooks for the data set, and simultaneously facilitate data analysis with SPSS and SAS, the leading statistical analysis packages in the nation today. The fourth file is a *dictionary* of variables that presents in organized fashion all relevant information about each variable in the file: names and labels of all variables (questions) and values (responses), read and write formats, as well missing value codes. The fifth file gives *frequencies* or response distributions for each variable. While the machine-readable files are self-documenting, a printed and bound *user's guide to the machine-readable files* is also provided to assist the user further. The user's guide describes the sampling, instrumentation, and data collection procedures that were used in creating the data file. Also included in the guide are: a list of all included variables in the data file, sorted by topic and type; a description of the study sample in terms of two dozen or so "key characteristics" such as age, gender, race, education, occupation, religion, etc.; results of completeness and consistency checks performed on the data by archive staff; and other noteworthy features, strengths, or weaknesses that a user of the data file would find useful. The user's

---

*To receive the newsletter call (415) 949-3282 or write Sociometrics Corporation, 170 State Street, Suite 260, Los Altos, CA 94022.

guide is always approved by the original investigator prior to public release of a data set.

User's choice of operating system, machine-readable medium. Data sets can be acquired in a variety of media formats to suit the user's computer platform: mainframe tape; floppy diskette or CD-ROM for PC or Macintosh microcomputers; tape cartridge for SUN Workstations; or 8-mm videotape for SUN Workstations.

Customized data set collections. Catalogs containing abstract descriptions of each data set are provided free of charge, so that a user can select those data set(s) most relevant to the research or policy problem at hand. Additional power and flexibility are then achieved by allowing the user to "mix and match" data sets within and across the various data archives at Sociometrics. For example a user can request that any combination of two, three, or several dozen data sets be put on a single mainframe tape or microcomputer CD-ROM for personal use or for use as a shared resource within an academic department. All the machine-readable data and documentation files associated with the data sets are put on the custom tape or CD-ROM. Such tape or CD-ROM, along with the user's guides for the included data sets, are produced by archive staff and shipped to the purchaser within a week of receipt of the order.

Teaching and library collections. All the data sets from a given substantive archive can also be purchased on a set of mainframe tapes or CD-ROMs. The richness and sheer volume of information in such collections mean that they are best viewed as resources to be shared by faculty and students of a given college or academic department. Another possible depository for such data collections is in main libraries of colleges and universities. As the price of CD-ROM drives has fallen, and as local area networks (LANs) of shared microcomputer resources have become commonplace, a growing number of libraries have begun to view themselves as data centers, depositories not only of printed materials such as books and journals but also of electronic informational materials such as encyclopedias on CD-ROM or data archives on CD-ROM.

Software to facilitate use of big machine-readable files and use of multiple files within a substantive archive. A typical user or data analyst can become familiar with the contents of a small well-documented data file—i.e., one with several dozen variables—in a week or two. Many data files of national samples, however, are extremely large and complex, encompassing information from several thousand people on several thousand variables gathered over many years. To facilitate perusal of the contents of such large data files, Sociometrics has developed search & retrieval and data extracting software to accompany its data archives. The software is available for single orders of very large data files, for customized orders of multiple data files, and for teaching and library collections containing an entire topically-focused data archive.

Search and retrieval of contents of collection at both the individual variable and study levels. The software enables users to: search for variables in one or more data sets according to user-defined criteria; retrieve a customized set of variables resulting from a search; and construct an SPSS or SAS command file that will create an extract of the full data set that contains only the retrieved variables. Searches may be conducted by any one or more of the following methods: variable topic or type (as classified by Sociometrics during archiving); data set number; keyword in the variable or value labels; and variable name. The program allows the use of "and" and "or" statements (i.e., Boolean logic) to select the intersection or union of keyword sets. Furthermore, the results of different searches may be combined, and/or individual variables may be tagged to create a customized set. Once a satisfactory search has been completed, the researcher may save the resulting set for later retrieval or for use as input into the data extract component of the software.

Data-extracting software. The extract component of the search and retrieval software enables a user to retrieve the raw data for desired variables, along with any associated recodes, variable and value labels, and missing data specifications, and to create a working system file that contains only those variables of interest for analysis. System files may be created in SPSS/PC+, mainframe SPSS, PC SAS, or mainframe SAS.

Toolkits on how to use data sets. To assist in the use of large data sets by first-time users, Sociometrics has developed Social Research Toolkits to accompany several premier data sets in its data archives. Each toolkit consists of a workbook and diskette containing data extracted from the data set of interest. The exercises in the workbook allow novice researchers, undergraduate students, or graduate students to use survey data to answer questions about the real-life experiences of their fellow Americans. In the process, users learn how to prepare data for analysis, handle basic statistical techniques, and use SPSS, one of the most widely-used computer statistical analysis packages. An Instructor's Manual contains the solutions to questions asked in the workbook. The Toolkits are appropriate for use as supplementary textbooks for research methods, statistics, or content courses.

An Application from the World of Family Research: The American Family Data Archive

Data Sets in the Collection

The following steps were taken in choosing the data sets comprising this compendium. *First*, Archive staff identified candidate data bases for the collection, using a combination of literature searches, telephone calls to funders and principal investigators, and published calls for field-instigated nominations. *Second*, project staff prepared brief descriptions and evaluations of each data set. *Third*, these evaluative descriptions were forwarded to the project's National Advisory Panel of outside scientist-experts. *Fourth*, the panel decided, based on the evaluative descriptions and subsequent discussion, which of the data sets to include in the Archive. Previously discussed criteria (technical quality; substantive importance to field; program or policy relevance; marketability; and balance) were used in making the selection. Many of the data sets selected by the panel were already in the public domain or had only moderate relevance to family issues. Others were important data sets of critical importance to family research and policymaking, but in private hands.

All the data sets chosen by the panel are described in this compendium. However, only the latter group of studies (those of critical importance and/or not yet publicly available) were acquired, processed, and documented by Sociometrics. Thus only the following data sets contain all the value-added features described in the preceding section:

National Survey of Families and Households, 1988 (J. Sweet, L. Bumpass, & V. Call);

1976-1987 National Survey of Children, Waves 1, 2, & 3 (N. Zill, J.L. Peterson, K.A. Moore, & F.F. Furstenberg, Jr.);

National Child Care Survey, 1990: Parent and Low-Income Study (S.L. Hofferth, A. Brayfield, S. Deich, P. Holcomb, & F. Glantz);

A Profile of Child Care Settings: Home-Based and Center-Based Programs, 1989-1990 (E.E. Kisker, & V. Piper);

National Commission on Children: 1990 Survey of Parents & Children (K.A. Moore);

National Family Violence Surveys, 1975, 1985 (M.A. Straus, & R.J. Gelles);

National Health Interview Survey on Child Health, 1988 (National Center for Health Statistics);

Marital Instability Over the Life Course, 1986-1988 (A. Booth, D.R. Johnson, L.K. White, & J.N. Edwards);

Stanford Study of Child Custody: 1984-1990 (E.E. Maccoby, R.H. Mnookin, & C.E. Depner);

Treatment Process: A Problem at 3 Levels, 1988 (G.R. Patterson, & P. Chamberlain).

The above-listed data sets can be acquired either individually or as a set. The individual data sets are described in Chapters 28, 5, 1, 2, 4, 26, 13, 22, 6, and 16, respectively. The complete collection is described in Chapter 30.

Chapters 3, 7, 8, 9, 12, 14, 15, 21, 24, 25, 27, and 29 describe the following data sets available from various agencies of the federal government:

Current Population Survey (CPS) Child Support and Alimony Supplement, April 1979, 1982, 1984, 1986, 1988, and 1990 (U.S. Bureau of the Census);

1980, 1982, 1984, and 1986 High School and Beyond Sophomore and Senior Cohorts (National Center for Education Statistics);

National Education Longitudinal Study of 1988 (NELS:88) and First and Second Follow-Ups (1990, 1992) (National Center for Education Statistics);

National Longitudinal Study of the High School Class of 1972 (NLS-72) (National Center for Education Statistics);

National Health Interview Survey on Alcohol, 1988 (National Center for Health Statistics);

The 1981 Child Health Supplement to the National Health Interview Survey (National Center for Health Statistics);

The 1988 National Maternal and Infant Health Survey (National Center for Health Statistics);

Army Family Research Program: Family Factors in Retention, Readiness, and Sense of Community, 1986-1991 (Army Research Institute, Research Triangle Institute, Caliber Associates, & Human Resources Research Organization);

Current Population Survey (CPS) Marital and Fertility Supplements 1971-1988, 1990 (U.S. Bureau of the Census);

National Survey of Family Growth, Cycle IV, 1988 (NSFG) (National Center for Health Statistics);

Vital Statistics on Marriage and Divorce, 1968-1988 (National Center for Health Statistics).

Chapters 10, 11, 17, 18, 19, 20, and 25 describe data sets available from the Inter-university Consortium of Political and Social Research:

Youth-Parent Socialization Panel Study, 1965-1982 (M.K. Jennings, G.B. Markus, & R.G. Niemi);

Americans View Their Mental Health: 1957 & 1976 (G. Gurin, J. Veroff, S. Feld, E. Douvan, & R. Kulka);

General Social Surveys, 1972-1990 (GSS) (J.A. Davis, & T.W. Smith, National Opinion Research Center);

National Survey of Black Americans, 1979-1980 (J.S Jackson, M.B. Tucker, & G. Gurin);

Panel Study of Income Dynamics, 1968-1990 (PSID) (Survey Research Center, University of Michigan);

Time Use in Economic and Social Accounts, 1975-1976 and 1975-81 Time Use Longitudinal Panel Study (F.T. Juster).

Intergenerational Panel Study of Parents and Children: 1962-1985 (A. Thornton and D. Freedman).

Chapter 23 describes a data set available from the Center for Human Resource Research at Ohio State University:

National Longitudinal Surveys of Labor Force Behavior: Youth Survey and Child Supplement (The NLSY), 1979-1992 (The Center for Human Resource Research, The Ohio State University).

Products Available for Each Data Set

For the Sociometrics-processed data sets the following standard machine-readable files are available: a raw data file; a file of SPSS program statements; a file of SAS program statements; a dictionary of all variables; and a file of frequencies and descriptive statistics for all variables. Users may choose to get the files on floppy diskette, mainframe tape, or CD-ROM. Accompanying the machine-readable files is a printed and bound user's guide that:

(1) describes the study from which the data originate;
(2) displays all variable names and labels, organized by topic and type;
(3) displays a cross-tabulation of topics and types in the data set;
(4) provides frequencies for approximately 20 key variables that are included in most data sets (such as age, race, gender, etc.);
(5) provides the results of illustrative completeness and consistency checks;
(6) provides technical specifications for the machine-readable data and documentation files; and
(7) provides additional documentation as needed in appendices.

The original instruments used to collect the data are also available for optional purchase for the cost of reproduction.

The Family Research Toolkit

Most of the data sets described in this compendium are large and complex. In order to introduce students and researchers to these data sets, a learner's toolkit for the 1976-1987 National Survey of Children, consisting of a student's workbook, data diskette, and instructor's manual, is also available from Sociometrics. The toolkit describes the sampling, instrumentation, and data collection procedures that were used in assembling the National Survey of Children, and then presents a series of progressively more difficult problem sets dealing with the demographic, economic, psychological, and academic status and well-being of American children, and the relationships between children and their parents. All the problems require analysis of data from the National Survey of Children (provided on diskette as part of the research toolkit) for their solution.

The Teaching and Library Collection

For academic departments and libraries the data sets in the American Family Data Archive, along with their respective user's guides, are available on three CD-ROMs. Included in this teacher's and library collection is search and retrieval and data extracting software to locate variables of interest to a particular problem and to extract those variables within a single data set or across all data sets capable of speaking to such problem. The data extract files can be obtained in minutes, in user's choice of SPSS or SAS. Also included is the Family Research Toolkit to introduce the novice to secondary data analysis. Chapter 30 describes this data library collection in greater detail.

The Compendium of Data Sets in the Public Domain

Eleven of the 30 chapters in this book expand further on the studies and data sets included in the American Family Data Archive. The remaining 19 chapters describe other data sets—available from a variety of federal agencies, from the public archives at the Inter-university Consortium for Political and Social Research of the University of Michigan, and from the Center for Human Resource Research at Ohio State University—that speak to issues such as family health, violence, education, and labor force participation. While the latter group of 19 data sets do not have all the value-added, state-of-the-art documentation and software that accompany the data sets processed at Sociometrics, all are clean and well-documented, comprised of at least a machine-readable raw data file and an accompanying printed codebook.

Conclusion

We hope that family researchers, teachers, and students will take advantage of the quality data sets described in this compendium to further the state-of-the-art in family research and teaching. Secondary analysis of the data sets described herein should be a special boon to students writing masters theses and doctoral dissertations. For example, using the search and retrieval software included with the American Family Data Archive (chapter 30), such students can browse through the 22,000 variables in the collection at will, in no more than a weekend, to test whether their thesis and dissertation ideas can be studied with the data sets at hand. Once a topic is selected, analyses can be done and written up with considerable time and dollar savings compared with earlier eras. Professors and researchers can analyze data and write valuable scholarly papers without leaving the comfort of their office or home. Indeed, advances in technology and data base development have opened new opportunities for research and teaching on the American family. It is our hope that this book facilitates the seizing of such opportunities.

1

NATIONAL CHILD CARE SURVEY 1990: PARENT STUDY AND LOW-INCOME SUBSTUDY

Sandra L. Hofferth
April Brayfield
Sharon Deich
Pamela Holcomb
Frederic Glantz

PURPOSE OF THE STUDY

The National Child Care Survey (NCCS) was designed to collect nationally generalizable data on child care demand and supply, including the use and characteristics of child care arrangements, how child care affects parental employment patterns, how parents make decisions about child care, and the characteristics of the settings in which child care is provided. The survey focused on what kinds of child care arrangements were used, how those arrangements were chosen, and how they were paid for. This information will help inform policy makers, program planners, parents and others by providing a comprehensive picture of child care from the perspective of both child care consumers and providers.

This abstract focuses on the main study (the Parent Study) and one of the substudies, the Low-Income Substudy. The Parent Study surveyed parents in randomly selected households with children under age 13 between October 1989 and May 1990. Additional surveys and substudies that related to the Parent Study were: a survey of individuals who provide child care in their own homes, a survey of center-based child care providers, a survey of child care providers used by the respondents in the Parent Study, and a military substudy.

The Low-Income Substudy is a nationally representative survey of 972 households with total annual incomes below $15,000 and one or more children under age 13. It focused on what kinds of child care arrangements respondents used, how those arrangements were chosen, and how payments were made. Many of the questions in the survey focused primarily on the youngest child, including satisfaction with the primary and secondary arrangements used by that child, reasons for choosing those arrangements, alternative arrangements considered, and a detailed history of child care arrangements during the previous year for that child. Extensive data on employment history were gathered, including the relationship between work and child care in the past. Basic demographic information such as income, education, and ethnic group were also included.

METHODS

Sampling Design

The sample design was a three-stage clustered sample design. The first stage of the sampling frame consisted of all U.S. counties or county groups. A sample of 100 counties/county groups was drawn with probability-proportional-to-size sampling. The measure of size was the number of children under age five obtained from 1986 Census Bureau population estimates.

The second stage involved sampling telephone numbers within those counties/county groups. All possible banks of 100 contiguous telephone numbers were generated from the three-digit telephone exchanges used in those regions; 1,072 banks of 100 contiguous phone numbers were drawn from the 100 counties/county groups sampled in the first stage.

Finally, for each county or county group, a set number of telephone numbers was selected at random (without replacement) from the banks of 100 contiguous telephone numbers. The exact number drawn from each county or county group varied between 55 and 95 depending on the estimated probability of obtaining a residential phone number in that region.

The Parent Study

For the Parent Study, up to seven attempts were made for each telephone number in the sample. If an attempt resulted in a definite callback (i.e., a callback scheduled for a specific date and time), more than seven attempts could be made.

Each household contacted was screened for survey eligibility (a child under age 13 in the household). Within each eligible household, the interviewer asked to speak to the designated respondent. If the designated respondent (usually the mother of the youngest child living in the household) was not at home, interviewers probed for the best time to try to reach the designated respondent. Callbacks were handled automatically by Computer Assisted Telephone Interviewing (CATI) systems. Within the CATI system, definite callbacks always have priority over other samples available for calling, and if the original interviewer is not available, the call is sent to the first available interviewer.

The questionnaire was also translated into Spanish and programmed for administration by CATI. As interviewers encountered a Spanish-speaking respondent, they entered a special disposition code into the respondent's data base record, and then the respondents were re-contacted by Spanish-speaking interviewers.

Respondents who had questions about the survey were invited to call Abt Associates survey staff using their toll-free number. Most calls received were from parents very concerned that revealing their child care schedules might leave their children potentially vulnerable to kidnappers or child molesters. The Abt Project Director spoke with concerned parents about the purpose and legitimacy of the study and assured them of the confidentiality of all information gathered. Since this was a random-digit-dial telephone survey, in fact, their addresses were not known.

Attempts were made to screen and complete interviews with most persons who initially refused the interview. An additional 280 interviews were completed with persons who initially refused the survey. Over 2,000 households contacted during the refusal conversion effort were determined not to be eligible for the survey. In a final attempt to maximize response rates, respondents whose latest sample disposition was a callback or not available until after the scheduled close-out date for their sample block were contacted. Each eligible individual was offered a ten dollar incentive to complete the interview. This resulted in 71 additional persons completing interviews.

The Low-Income Substudy

Interviewers called 25,464 phone numbers generated according to the study design; 14,558 of these numbers turned out to be residential, and interviewers successfully screened 10,961 of these households (75.3% of the residential numbers). Of these, 555 turned out to be eligible for the survey, that is, had income under $15,000, and one or more children under age 13.

Every attempt was made to complete an interview with each eligible household, therefore a $10 incentive payment was offered to those who completed the interview. A total of 236 respondents were paid the incentive. Some respondents who were offered the incentive declined to give their names and addresses so the payments could not be mailed to them.

Periodicity

Interviews for the Parent Study were conducted between October 1989 and May 1990; for the Low-Income Substudy, between February and July 1990.

Unit of Analysis

The unit of analysis for the Parent Study was a household containing at least one child under 13 years of age. For the Low-Income Substudy the unit of analysis was a household with total annual family income under $15,000 having one or more children under age 13.

Response Rates: Parent Study

A total of 77,864 telephone numbers were included in the sample, yielding 6,328 eligible households, and 4,392 (69%) completed interviews with eligible households. This number is about 1,000 less than the target completed interview size of 5,386. The lower sample size was due to two factors: 1) a lower than expected eligibility rate, and 2) a lower than expected response rate among eligible households. The major reason for the low eligibility rate is thought to be hidden refusals—the denial by parents that they have children living in the household. The lower survey response rate reflects several factors, including the length of the interview and the well-documented increasing reluctance of the U.S. public to participate in telephone surveys.

Table 1. Response Rates: Parent Study

Status Number	Final Status Description	Classification of Final Status	Number of Sample Telephone Numbers	Percent of Original Sample
1.	Nonworking number	Nonresidential	22,968	29.5%
2.	Nonresidential number	Nonresidential	7,336	9.4%
3.	Residential number—answering machine, busy, no answer	Unknown Status	1,917	2.5%
4.	Refusal, it is not known whether the household contains any children under 13 years	Unknown Status	3,111	4.0%
5.	Refusal, the household has one or more children but it is not known whether any are under 13 years of age	Unknown Status	674	0.9%
6.	Spanish language, screening interview not completed	Unknown Status	25	0.03%
7.	Refusal to answer screening question on presence of any children under 13 yrs. of age	Unknown Status	625	0.8%

Table 1. Response Rates: Parent Study (continued)

Status Number	Final Status Description	Classification of Final Status	Number of Sample Telephone Numbers	Percent of Original Sample
8.	Other language, screening interview not completed	Unknown Status	286	0.4%
9.	Callback at opening screening interview not completed	Unknown Status	1,572	2.0%
10.	CATI malfunction	Unknown Status	19	0.02%
11.	Refusal, no children in the household	Ineligible	2,305	3.0%
12.	Completed screener, no children under 13 years of age in the household	Ineligible	30,698	39.4%
13.	Break-off during the interview	Eligible	893	1.2%
14.	Respondent unavailable during the field period	Eligible	80	0.1%
15.	Callback arranged, respondent did not complete interview	Eligible	963	1.3%
16.	Completed interview	Eligible	4,392	5.6%
TOTAL SAMPLE			77,864	100.0%

Response Rates: Low-Income Substudy

A total of 430 parent interviews were completed with eligible low-income households, resulting in a completion rate among eligible households of 78%. These 430 interviews were combined with the 672 low-income interviews from the main Parent Study, yielding a total of 1,102 low-income parent interviews. Of these, only 974 actually had family incomes under $15,000 and are included in the Low-Income Substudy.

Attrition

Not applicable.

CONTENT

Data Sources

The Parent Survey and its substudies were conducted using the CATI (Computer Aided Telephone Interview) system in its network mode. In the network mode, the sample telephone numbers are stored in the CATI system's database. The system's supervisor module stores the results of all attempts (disposition, date, time, and interview) and sends a sample of telephone numbers to each interviewing station based on the last disposition.

All interviewers on the NCCS had previously received general training on survey research interviewing. Project-specific training was conducted with special emphasis placed on key segments of the questionnaire, such as: the screening section, in which eligibility status is determined and the primary care giver is identified; Section A, which determines the living arrangement of the care giver and identifies the children in the household; Section B, on child care arrangements currently used; and Section F, on child care schedules for the previous week.

During the interviewing process, supervisors were present to evaluate interviewers and provide feedback concerning all aspects of the interview. Supervisors frequently completed reports covering the interviewer's performance concerning: expectation of confidentiality, verbatim reading of questions, probing nondirectly and appropriately, and feedback to the respondent.

Description of Questionnaire and Variables Covered: Parent Study

The following are the sections of the Parent Survey questionnaire and the types of questions asked in each section:

1. <u>Screener</u>. This section determined whether the household was eligible.

2. <u>Introduction</u>. Interviewers explained the study and established who in the household should be interviewed. The mother of the youngest child was the preferred respondent. If the youngest child's mother was deceased or did not live in the household, then the father or another adult familiar with the youngest child's schedule was interviewed. This section also established the age, sex, grade in school, and relationship to youngest child of any other children in the household under 13 as well as asking the health status of all children under 13.

3. <u>Child Care Arrangements for All Children in the Household</u>. This section asked the types of child care used, where they were provided, and, if appropriate, who sponsored the care.

4. <u>Household Expenditures for Child Care</u>. Detailed information was collected on the cost of the youngest child's care and aggregate information on the cost of care for other children in the household.

5. <u>Choice of Arrangements for Youngest Child</u>. Respondents were asked whether alternatives to the types of child care currently used were considered, how they learned of the current arrangements, and how much time elapsed between the decision to use care and commitment from care givers. Respondents were also asked about their satisfaction with the current care arrangements. The section concluded with questions concerning whether the respondents would prefer

some arrangement other than those currently used and why another arrangement would be preferred.

6. Perceptions of Alternatives for Youngest Child's Care. For the types of child care used, questions were asked about the number of children regularly cared for by the caregiver, how much time it took to travel to the arrangement, and what mode of transportation was used. For the types of care not used, respondents were asked about their perceptions of availability, cost, and travel time. Respondents were also asked how old their children would have to be to care for themselves and under what circumstances "self-care" should be allowed.

7. Child Care Schedule for Last Week. Interviewers recorded the number of hours each child care arrangement was used (a maximum of four arrangements per child). Child care schedules were recorded for up to five children under 13 years of age.

8. Employment Schedule for Respondent and Spouse. The number of hours worked during the previous week were recorded for up to two jobs. Information regarding the employer and occupation, the wage rate, and the place of employment was also collected for each job.

9. Substitute Child Care Arrangements. Interviewers probed for how respondents handled child care when a child was sick or the usual child care arrangements were not available.

10. Child Care History Over Last Twelve Months for Youngest Child. For school-age children, information regarding types of child care used during the summer was collected. For pre-school children, the begin dates for current child care arrangements were recorded. Information on the type, cost, and the duration of all child care arrangements used during the last year was collected. Respondents were also asked why they no longer used these arrangements.

11. Employment History—Last Twelve Months for Respondent, Spouse, or Partner. In this section begin dates for current jobs

were recorded. For jobs held during the 12 months previous to the interview, data regarding occupation, industry, number of hours worked weekly, number of weeks worked yearly, location, and their reasons for leaving these jobs. In addition, the mother of the youngest child was asked how many years she had worked for pay since 18, what effect having children had on her work schedule, and why she was or was not employed.

12. Employer Benefits. This section determined what child-related benefits (such as child care center, pre-tax deposit accounts, flex time, parental leave) were offered by the respondents' or spouses' employers.

13. Household Roster. For up to five household members 13 years of age or older, information was obtained about age, sex, relationship to the youngest child, highest level of education, and employment status. This section also asked whether the respondent, spouse, or partner had training or education specifically related to children, such as child development courses.

14. Basic Respondent Information. This section collected demographic information about the respondent, such as marital status, race, place of birth, religious preference, sources of income, total household income, etc. Questions eliciting respondent opinions about government policies on child care subsidies were also asked.

Description of Questionnaire and Variables Covered: Low-Income Substudy

The sections of the Low-Income Substudy questionnaire and the types of questions asked in each section are, in some cases, identical to those in the Parent Study. However, the sections are labeled differently and new sections have been added. Therefore, the entire list is included below.

Section S: Screener. This section determined whether the household was eligible.

Section A: Introduction. Interviewers explained the study and established who in the household should be interviewed. The mother of the youngest child was the preferred respondent. If the youngest child's mother was deceased or did not live in the household, then the father or another adult familiar with the youngest child's schedule was interviewed. This section also established the age, sex, grade in school, and relationship to youngest child of any other children in the household under 13 as well as asking the health status of all children under 13.

Section B: Child Care Arrangements for Up to Four Children in the Household. This section asked the types of child care used, where they were provided, and, if appropriate, who sponsored the care.

Section C: Household Expenditures for Child Care. Detailed information was collected on the cost of the youngest child's care and aggregate information on the cost of care for other children in the household.

Section D: Choice of Arrangements for Youngest Child. Respondents were asked whether alternatives to the types of child care currently used were considered, how they learned of the current arrangements, and how much time elapsed between the decision to use care and commitments from care givers. Respondents were also asked about their satisfaction with the current care arrangements. The section concluded with questions concerning whether the respondents would prefer some arrangement other than those currently used and why another arrangement would be preferred.

Section E: Perceptions of Alternatives for Youngest Child's Care. For the types of child care used, questions were asked about the number of children regularly cared for by the caregiver, how much time it took to travel to the arrangement, and what mode of transportation was used. For the types of care not used, respondents were asked about their perceptions of availability, cost, and travel time. Respondents were also asked how old their children would have to be to care for themselves and under what circumstances "self-care" should be allowed.

Section F: Child Care Schedule for Last Week. Interviewers recorded the number of hours each child care arrangement was used (a maximum of four arrangements per child). Child care schedules were recorded for up to four children under 13 years of age.

Section G: Employment Schedule for Respondent and Spouse. The number of hours worked during the previous week was recorded for up to three jobs. Information regarding the employer and occupation, the wage rate, and the place of employment was also collected for each job.

Section H: Substitute Child Care Arrangements. Interviewers probed for how respondents handled child care when a child was sick or the usual child care arrangements were not available.

Section I: Child Care History Over Last Twelve Months for Youngest Child. For school-age children, information regarding types of child care used during the summer was collected. For pre-school children, the begin dates for current child care arrangements were recorded. Information on the type, the cost, and the duration of all child care arrangements used during the last year was collected. Respondents were also asked why they no longer used these arrangements.

Section J: Employment History Over Last Twelve Months for Respondent, Spouse, or Partner. In this section, begin dates for current jobs were recorded. For jobs held during the 12 months previous to the interview, data regarding occupation, industry, number of hours worked weekly, number of weeks worked yearly, location, and wage rate were collected. Respondents were also asked their reasons for leaving these jobs. In addition, the mother of the youngest child was asked how many years she had worked for pay since age 18, what effect having children had on her work schedule, and why she was or was not employed.

Section K: Employer Benefits. This section determined what child-related benefits (such as child care center, pre-tax deposit accounts, flex time, parental leave) were offered by the respondents' or spouses' employers.

Section L: Household Roster. For up to five household members 13 years of age or older, information was obtained about age, sex, relationship to the youngest child, highest level of education, and employment status. The section also asked whether the respondent, spouse, or partner had training or education specifically related to children, such as child development courses.

Section M: Basic Respondent Information. This section collected demographic information about the respondent, such as marital status, race, place of birth, religious preference, sources of income, total household income, etc. Questions eliciting respondent opinions about government policies on child care subsidies were also asked.

Section N: Provider Locator. Interviewers requested the telephone number of the provider used by the youngest child for the greatest amount of time. This section was skipped if the provider cared for the child in the child's home or if the care was kindergarten, school, lessons, clubs, or sports. (These variables not archived by Sociometrics.)

Section O: Contact Information. Here the respondents were asked how willing they would be to participate in a similar survey in the future. (These variables not archived by Sociometrics.)

Number of Variables

The National Child Care Survey Parent Study contains 1,608 variables and 4,397 cases; the Low-Income Substudy, 1,419 variables and 974 cases.

Checklist of Topics Covered: Parent Study

X Gender / Gender Role
X Race / Ethnicity
X Age
X Education
X Occupation / Employment
X Physical Health / Disease
___ Nutrition
___ Clinical Activities
___ Biological Functioning / Development
___ Mental Health / Disease
___ Psychological Functioning / Development
___ Guidance / Counseling
___ Personality
___ Intellectual Functioning
___ Residential Mobility
X Dwelling
X Neighborhood / Community
X Region / State
X Marriage and Divorce
___ Cohabitation
X Family/Household Composition & Structure
___ Inter-Partner Relationships
___ Parent-Child Relationships
___ Inter-Sibling Relationships
___ Relationships with Other Kin

___ Relationships with Nonkin
___ Other Family/Household Characteristics
X Child Care
X Wealth / Finances / Material Things
X Receipt of Health, Mental Health, Social Services
___ Adoption / Foster Care
___ Childbearing / Pregnancy
___ Out-of-Wedlock Pregnancy & Parenthood
___ Abortion
___ Sexuality
___ Sex Education
___ Contraception
___ Sexually Transmitted Diseases
X Civic/Political Activities
X Friends / Social Activities
___ Social Support
___ Dating, Courtship
___ Recreation
X Religion
___ Crime / Delinquency / Behavior Problems
___ Substance Use
___ Agency Characteristics
___ Interview

Checklist of Topics Covered: Low-Income Substudy

X Gender / Gender Role
X Race / Ethnicity
X Age
X Education
X Occupation / Employment
X Physical Health / Disease
___ Nutrition
___ Clinical Activities
___ Biological Functioning / Development
___ Mental Health / Disease
___ Psychological Functioning / Development
___ Guidance / Counseling
___ Personality
___ Intellectual Functioning
X Residential Mobility
X Dwelling
X Neighborhood / Community
X Region / State
X Marriage and Divorce
___ Cohabitation
X Family/Household Composition & Structure
___ Inter-Partner Relationships
___ Parent-Child Relationships
___ Inter-Sibling Relationships
___ Relationships with Other Kin

___ Relationships with Nonkin
X Other Family/Household Characteristics
X Child Care
X Wealth / Finances / Material Things
X Receipt of Health, Mental Health, Social Services
___ Adoption / Foster Care
___ Childbearing / Pregnancy
___ Out-of-Wedlock Pregnancy & Parenthood
___ Abortion
___ Sexuality
___ Sex Education
___ Contraception
___ Sexually Transmitted Diseases
___ Civic/Political Activities
___ Friends / Social Activities Social Support
___ Dating, Courtship
___ Recreation
X Religion
___ Crime / Delinquency / Behavior Problems
___ Substance Use
___ Agency Characteristics
X Interview

Checklist of Key Variables: *Parent Study*

<u>X</u> Number of family members
<u>X</u> Identification of marital
    partners in family
____ Size of dwelling
<u>X</u> Type of dwelling
<u>X</u> Urban/rural residence
<u>X</u> Region/state of residence
<u>X</u> Family income
<u>X</u> Religious affiliation
<u>X</u> Relation of each family
    member to:
    <u>X</u> Reference person
    <u>X</u> All other members
<u>X</u> Age of family members
    <u>X</u> Respondent
    <u>X</u> Others
<u>X</u> Sex of family members

    <u>X</u> Respondent
    <u>X</u> Others
<u>X</u> Race of family members
    <u>X</u> Respondent
    ____ Others
<u>X</u> Marital status of family
    members
    <u>X</u> Respondent
    ____ Others
<u>X</u> Education of family
    members
    <u>X</u> Respondent
    <u>X</u> Others
<u>X</u> Occupation of family
    members
    <u>X</u> Respondent
    <u>X</u> Others

Checklist of Key Variables: *Low-Income Substudy*

<u>X</u> Number of family members
<u>X</u> Identification of marital
    partners in family
____ Size of dwelling
____ Type of dwelling
<u>X</u> Urban/rural residence
<u>X</u> Region/state of residence
<u>X</u> Family income
<u>X</u> Religious affiliation
<u>X</u> Relation of each family
    member to:
    <u>X</u> Reference person
    <u>X</u> All other members
<u>X</u> Age of family members
    <u>X</u> Respondent
    <u>X</u> Others
<u>X</u> Sex of family members

    <u>X</u> Respondent
    <u>X</u> Others
____ Race of family members
    <u>X</u> Respondent
    ____ Others
<u>X</u> Marital status of family
    members
    <u>X</u> Respondent
    ____ Others
<u>X</u> Education of family
    members
    <u>X</u> Respondent
    <u>X</u> Others
____ Occupation of family
    members
    <u>X</u> Respondent
    <u>X</u> Others

LIMITATIONS

Parent Study

The investigators point out certain problem areas during the data collection phase of the Parent Study:

1. Parents were reluctant to report the day by day whereabouts of their children. They felt doing so would expose their children to danger from kidnappers of child molesters. Even though interviewers were adept at providing assurances of confidentiality, some respondents refused to provide details concerning their childrens' schedules.

2. Detailed questions were asked concerning all "regular" child care arrangements used "once a week for the past two weeks." During interview training, special attention was paid to probing techniques which would make sure that the respondent understood what was meant by "regular" arrangements. Despite careful probing during the initial questions about use of child care arrangements, when the time came to complete the child's weekly schedule later in the interview, respondents also remembered arrangements they had previously reported as regular which were in fact intermittent. Interviewers noted these changes on the paper copies of the schedules and inserted flags into the schedule data file to explain discrepancies.

3. Response rates and eligibility rates were lower than anticipated (see section above on response rates), though this is a common problem in telephone surveys. In addition, disproportionately high number of households with children do not have telephones. Weights were constructed to adjust for differential response rates and for the omission of nontelephone households. The extent of bias due to the omission of nontelephone households appears small (see Hofferth, et al., 1991).

Low-Income Substudy

Response rates were lower than expected for the Low-Income Substudy, though this is a common problem in telephone surveys. Also, a disproportionately high number of households with children and low income do not have telephones. Weights were computed which adjusted for differential response rates as well as for differential sample coverage rates due to the existence of households without telephones.

SPONSORSHIP

The Parent Study and Low-Income Substudy were jointly sponsored by the Head Start Bureau of the Administration for Children, Youth, and Families of the U.S. Department of Health and Human Services and the National Association for the Education of Young Children.

GUIDE TO DATA AND DOCUMENTATION

File Structure

Machine-readable data and documentation files, along with a printed and bound User's Guide, are available in mainframe tape and microcomputer CD-ROM formats for both the main Parent Study and the Low-Income Substudy. Unless otherwise requested, files formatted for a mainframe computer are provided on a 9-track tape at a density of 6250 bpi, in EBCDIC recording mode with IBM Standard Labels. CD-ROM disks are in ISO 9660 format. A description of the contents of each machine-readable file is given below:

File 1 (Data): Raw data file. The format of this file is described in the "data list" section of the SPSS program file (file 2).

File 2 (SPSS Program): This file consists of SPSS program statements designed to read the raw data in file 1 and create an SPSS active file. The SPSS program file contains data list statements, variable names and labels, value labels, and missing value declarations.

File 3 (SAS Program): This file consists of SAS program statements designed to read the raw data in file 1 and create a SAS active file. The contents of this file are analogous to the contents of the previously described file 2. SPSS users should use file 2; SAS users, file 3. Users may need to add "job control language" (JCL) statements to the SAS program file to meet the requirements for their specific operating system. For some operating systems, e.g., Unix, running the SAS program statements may result in a "segmentation violation" message from SAS due to a limit on the number of independent sets of format labels (the current limit is about 300) that can be assigned to variables. The SAS Institute plans to release an updated version of SAS early in 1993 that will correct the problem. Until then, if a segmentation violation occurs, one solution is to edit the SAS program statements to remove format (value label) assignments for all variables unrelated to the analysis at hand.

File 4 (Dictionary; mainframe orders only): Sequential list of variable and value labels. This file consists of DISPLAY DICTIONARY output describing the SPSS-X active file created by the program in File 2. Variables are listed in sequential order. Variable names and labels, value labels, missing value designations, print formats, and write formats are clearly displayed.

File 5 (Statistics; mainframe orders only): Unweighted frequencies or other descriptive statistics for each variable. Descriptive statistics only are provided for variables with more than 50 value categories, such as respondent identification number, zip codes, etc.

List of Available Documentation

For each data set a User's Guide accompanies the machine-readable files and provides the following information: Summary; General study overview; Description of machine-readable files and supplementary documentation; Specifications for machine-readable files; Key characteristics report; Distribution of variables by topic and type; and Data completeness and consistency report.

Paper versions of the machine-readable SPSS or SAS program files and data documentation (files 2-5 above), and copies of the original instrument and codebook are available upon request (at 15 cents per page).

Contact

> Sociometrics Corporation
> American Family Data Archive
> 170 State Street, Suite 260
> Los Altos, CA 94022-2812
> (415) 949-3282

Cost

The cost for the machine-readable Parent Study data set (Data Set 13-14 of the American Family Data Archive) is $150; the Low-Income Substudy data set (Data Set 20-21), $100. This price includes the raw data, SPSS program statements, the SAS program statements, the Dictionary, and the Frequencies on mainframe tape, and the accompanying printed and bound User's Guide. The CD-ROM versions cost $175 each. Paper versions of the original NCCS Codebook and Instrument can be obtained for $43.50 and $12, respectively.

BIBLIOGRAPHY

Abt Associates Inc. (1990). *National child care survey: Main study and low-income substudy (final report on survey methods)*. Cambridge, MA: Author.

Brayfield, A. (1992, September). *Child care costs as a barrier to women's employment*. Final report to the Women's Bureau, U.S. Department of Labor, contract No. J-9-M-1-0072. Washington, DC: The Urban Institute.

Brayfield, A., Deich, S., & Hofferth, S. (1992). *Caring for children in low-income families: A substudy of the national child care survey 1990*. Washington, DC: National Association for the Education of Young Children.

Deich, S., Brayfield, A., & Hofferth, S. (1992). *National child care survey, 1990: Military substudy*. Washington, DC: National Association for the Education of Young Children.

Hofferth, S. (1992). The demand for and supply of child care in the 1990s. In A. Booth (Ed.), *Child care in the 1990s: Trends and consequences* (pp. 3-25). Hillsdale, NJ: Lawrence Erlbaum Associates.

Hofferth, S., Brayfield, A., Deich, S., & Holcomb, P. (1991). *National child care survey 1990*. Washington, DC: The Urban Institute.

Lang, E.L., Stone, V.E., Crutchfield, J.H., & Card, J.J. (1992). *National child care survey 1990, low-income substudy: A user's guide to the machine-readable files and documentation*. Los Altos, CA: Sociometrics Corporation, American Family Data Archive.

Stone, V.E., Lang, E.L., Crutchfield, J.H., & Card, J.J. (1991). *National child care survey 1990, parent study: A user's guide to the machine-readable files and documentation*. Los Altos, CA: Sociometrics Corporation, American Family Data Archive.

Willer, B., Hofferth, S., Kisker, E., Divine-Hawkins, P., Farquhar, E., & Glantz, F. (1991). *The demand and supply of child care in 1990: Joint findings from the national child care survey 1990 and the profile of child care settings*. Washington, DC: National Association for the Education of Young Children.

2

A PROFILE OF CHILD CARE SETTINGS: HOME-BASED AND CENTER-BASED PROGRAMS, 1989-1990

Ellen Eliason Kisker
Valarie Piper

PURPOSE OF THE STUDY

The primary objective of the Profile of Child Care Settings survey was to determine the levels and characteristics of early education and care that are available in the United States. It was also designed to address important social and economic changes in the nation regarding nonparental child care.

The surveys collected extensive data on a number of topics including hours of operation, child care fee amounts and frequencies, time spent on various child care activities, remuneration and functions of different staff members, program policies and links with other agencies, special services offered, contact with parents, as well as provider training and accreditation. Some of the variables provide demographic information about the counties where the home-based programs are located.

METHODS

Sampling Design

The study is based on interviews with nationally representative samples of regulated home-based family day care providers (n=583) and center-based formal early education and care programs (n=2,089).

The basic sample frame for the study consists of the home-based child care providers, child care centers, and early education programs that are licensed or registered by the state or county in which they are located. Because the coverage of licensing regulations varies among states, this basic sample frame was augmented with programs based in religious institutions, part-day preschool programs, and other programs that states may exempt from regulation. The basic sample frame was also augmented with public and private school-based programs, which rarely fall under the jurisdiction of child care licensing and are usually regulated by state education agencies. Two types of programs—unlicensed programs that serve only school-age children and unlicensed programs serving children exclusively on a drop-in basis—were excluded from the sample frame because they do not provide *regular* care for *preschool* children.

A two-stage clustered sample design was used to select a sample of early education and care providers. In the first stage a sample of counties were selected that were representative of counties in the United States. Counties were stratified according to region, metropolitan status, and poverty level, and sample counties were selected with probability proportional to the size of the population under age 5.

In the second stage of the sampling, a stratified random sample was selected of early education and care providers from the counties selected in the first stage. In order to draw the provider sample, a sample frame list of eligible providers was assembled; the providers were stratified according to whether they were regulated home-based programs, Head Start programs, public-school-based programs, or other center-based programs; and random samples were drawn from programs from each stratum. A total sample of 2,672 programs was interviewed.

Periodicity

The interviews took place between October 1989 and February 1990.

Unit of Analysis

Although the home-based programs are the basic unit of analysis for the home-based program survey, the instrument asked for individual information on up to 20 randomly selected children and up to 6 staff members in each child care program. Likewise, although the center-based programs are the basic unit of analysis for the center-based program survey, the instrument asked for specific information on up to 20 groups of children, up to 10 different fees, and a randomly selected teacher in each child care program.

Response Rates

The 583 cases in the home-based file represent an 87.1% completion rate among the sampled programs eligible for the study. Likewise, the 2,089 cases in the center-based file represent an 88.7% completion rate among the sampled programs eligible for the study.

Attrition

Not applicable.

CONTENT

Data Sources

The data were collected using computer-assisted telephone interviewing (CATI) methods, thus minimizing errors and ensuring that inconsistencies in responses were resolved prior to the conclusion of the interview. Separate survey instruments were used to interview regulated home-based child care providers and center-based program directors. Therefore, data from each of the two samples have been archived separately in the American Family Data Archive.

Survey respondents received advance materials, including a worksheet enabling them to prepare for the survey prior to the telephone interview.

Description of Variables Covered: Home-based Programs Survey

The survey of home-based family day care programs included questions on a number of topics such as: (a) **Care Provided**, e.g., child care goals, length of operation, racial breakdown of children, steps taken to fill vacancies, policies regarding handicapped and limited English proficiency children, as well as specific questions about the care of up to 20 individual children regarding each child's age, weekly attendance, fee amount and frequency, and relationship to the provider; (b) **Children's Activities**, e.g., percentage of time each day that children spend in various activities, allocation of time to plan children's activities, and frequency of parental meetings/home visits; (c) **Costs and Income**, e.g., criteria for different child care fees, funding from external agencies (federal, state, or local), and provision of snacks or meals; (d) **Help with Child Care**, e.g., number of helpers, parental status of helpers, as well as specific questions about assistance from up to six individual helpers regarding each person's age, type and amount of help provided, cash and noncash remuneration, and relationship to the principal provider; (e) **Health and Safety**, e.g., policy regarding sick children, administering medication, plans for medical and other emergencies, licensing, and liability insurance; (f) **Caregiver Characteristics and Experience**, e.g., education and training background, experience with conflicts between professional and family responsibilities, personal background (age, race, sex, marital status), and income from child care. In addition there were several "screener" questions that inquired about current licensure and child care status, and seven "contextual" variables with sociodemographic information about the counties in which the home-based programs are located.

With respect to the home-based study there are 633 variables, 7 of which provide demographic information about the counties where the programs are located. Four of these 7 demographic variables (Sociometrics NCY16001, NCY16003, NCY16006, NCY16009) contain factor scores from a factor analysis of 15 county-level variables.

The data file contains two types of "constructed" variables, (a) variables constructed from multiple questionnaire items, and (b) sets of dichotomous variables constructed from the response options to individual questionnaire items (i.e., each response option becomes a "yes/no" variable). Many of the constructed variables were derived from questionnaire items embedded in matrices of items in the original instrument. Although every attempt was made to label constructed variables appropriately, researchers are strongly encouraged to refer to the original instrument (see page 2-12 for ordering information).

Description of Variables Covered: Center-based Programs Survey

The survey of center-based early education and care programs included questions on a number of topics such as: (a) **General Characteristics**, e.g., child care goals, length of operation, days and hours of operation, and organizational sponsors; (b) **Admission Policies and Vacancies**, e.g., policies regarding handicapped and limited-English-proficiency children, as well as activities to find more children; (c) **Types of Children Served**, e.g., numbers of children broken down by age, race, and handicap status, specific information on up to 20 groups of children (labelled groups A-T) including group size, age of oldest and youngest group member, and group schedule and staffing requirements, as well as specific information on up to 10 different child care fees (labelled fees A-J) including fee amount and frequency, number and age range of children to which the fee is applied, and conditions under which different fees apply; (d) **Subsidies,** e.g., number of children for whom child care is subsidized by a federal, state, or local agency, and by what method of payment; (e) **Staff,** e.g., number of teachers, aides, specialists, and parents who comprise staff, educational background, race/ethnicity, fringe benefits, as well as details on a randomly selected individual staff member (age, training, work schedule, salary, benefits); (f) **Curriculum and Activities,** e.g., time that children spend in each of several types of activities (physical activity, watching educational TV, etc.), time spent in group activities, and parental involvement in children's activities and meetings; (g) **Meals,** e.g., preparation of meals/snacks, and participation in the Child Care Food Program; (h) **Health and Safety,** e.g., policies regarding sick children, administering medication, plans for medical and other emergencies, and physical and psychological testing; (i) **Operating Experiences,** e.g., licensing, accreditation, and inspection experiences, proportion of budget spent on salaries and benefits, and sources of income and in-kind donations.

In addition there were several "screener" questions that inquired about current child care focus (e.g., serving handicapped children primarily), and seven "contextual" variables with sociodemographic information about the counties in which the center-based programs are located.

With respect to the center-based study there are 887 variables, 7 of which provide demographic information about the counties where the programs are located. Four of these 7 demographic variables (Sociometrics NCY18002, NCY18003, NCY18006, NCY18009) contain factor scores from a factor analysis of 15 county-level variables.

The data file contains two types of "constructed" variables, (a) variables constructed from multiple questionnaire items, and (b) sets of dichotomous variables constructed from the response options to individual questionnaire items (i.e., each response option becomes a "yes/no" variable). Many of the constructed variables were derived from questionnaire items embedded in matrices of items in the original instrument. Although every attempt was made to label constructed variables appropriately, researchers are strongly encouraged to refer to the original instrument (see pages 2-11 and 2-12 for ordering information).

Linking Variables: Three Studies

Data in the study *A Profile of Child Care Settings: Home-Based Programs* (archived separately as AFDA # 15-16) can be linked to the companion study *A Profile of Child Care Settings: Center-Based Programs* (AFDA # 17-18) as well as to a study of child care by parents, *The National Child Care Survey 1990: Parent Study* (archived separately as AFDA # 13-14). Each of these three studies employs the same first stage primary sampling unit (PSU), which can be used as the linking variable. The variable in each study with PSU information is MEX16008 (in AFDA # 15-16), MEX18008 (in AFDA # 17-18), and RES13027 (in AFDA #13-14).

Number of Variables: Home-based and Center-based Programs Surveys

The Home-based Programs survey contains 633 variables and 583 cases. The Center-based Programs survey contains 887 variables and 2,089 cases.

Checklist of Topics Covered: Home-based Programs Survey

X Gender / Gender Role
X Race / Ethnicity
X Age
X Education
___ Occupation / Employment
___ Physical Health / Disease
X Nutrition
X Clinical Activities
___ Biological Functioning /
    Development
___ Mental Health / Disease
___ Psychological Functioning /
    Development
___ Guidance / Counseling
___ Personality
___ Intellectual Functioning
___ Residential Mobility
X Dwelling
X Neighborhood /
    Community
X Region / State
X Marriage and Divorce
___ Cohabitation
X Family/Household
    Composition & Structure
___ Inter-Partner Relationships
___ Parent-Child Relationships
___ Inter-Sibling Relationships
___ Relationships with Other Kin

___ Relationships with Nonkin
___ Other Family/Household
    Characteristics
X Child Care
X Wealth / Finances /
    Material Things
___ Receipt of Health, Mental
    Health, Social Services
___ Adoption / Foster Care
___ Childbearing / Pregnancy
___ Out-of-Wedlock Pregnancy
    & Parenthood
___ Abortion
___ Sexuality
___ Sex Education
___ Contraception
___ Sexually Transmitted
    Diseases
___ Civic/Political Activities
___ Friends / Social Activities
___ Social Support
___ Dating, Courtship
___ Recreation
___ Religion
___ Crime / Delinquency /
    Behavior Problems
___ Substance Use
X Agency Characteristics
X Interview

Checklist of Topics Covered: Center-based Programs Survey

X Gender / Gender Role
X Race / Ethnicity
X Age
X Education
___ Occupation / Employment
X Physical Health / Disease
X Nutrition
X Clinical Activities
X Biological Functioning /
   Development
___ Mental Health / Disease
___ Psychological Functioning /
   Development
___ Guidance / Counseling
___ Personality
___ Intellectual Functioning
___ Residential Mobility
___ Dwelling
X Neighborhood /
   Community
X Region / State
___ Marriage and Divorce
___ Cohabitation
___ Family/Household
   Composition & Structure
___ Inter-Partner Relationships
___ Parent-Child Relationships
___ Inter-Sibling Relationships
___ Relationships with Other Kin

___ Relationships with Nonkin
___ Other Family/Household
   Characteristics
X Child Care
X Wealth / Finances /
   Material Things
___ Receipt of Health, Mental
   Health, Social Services
___ Adoption / Foster Care
___ Childbearing / Pregnancy
___ Out-of-Wedlock Pregnancy
   & Parenthood
___ Abortion
___ Sexuality
___ Sex Education
___ Contraception
___ Sexually Transmitted
   Diseases
___ Civic/Political Activities
___ Friends / Social Activities
___ Social Support
___ Dating, Courtship
___ Recreation
___ Religion
___ Crime / Delinquency /
   Behavior Problems
___ Substance Use
X Agency Characteristics
X Interview

Checklist of Key Variables: Home-based Programs Survey

___ Number of family members
___ Identification of marital
    partners in family
___ Size of dwelling
_X_ Type of dwelling
___ Urban/rural residence
_X_ Region/state of residence
_X_ Family income
___ Religious affiliation
___ Relation of each family
    member to:
    ___ Reference person
    ___ All other members
___ Age of family members
    _X_ Respondent
    _X_ Others
___ Sex of family members

    _X_ Respondent
    _X_ Others
___ Race of family members
    _X_ Respondent
    _X_ Others
___ Marital status of family
    members
    _X_ Respondent
    ___ Others
___ Education of family
    members
    _X_ Respondent
    _X_ Others
___ Occupation of family
    members
    _X_ Respondent
    _X_ Others

Checklist of Key Variables: Center-based Programs Survey

___ Number of family members
___ Identification of marital
    partners in family
___ Size of dwelling
___ Type of dwelling
___ Urban/rural residence
_X_ Region/state of residence
___ Family income
___ Religious affiliation
___ Relation of each family
    member to:
    ___ Reference person
    ___ All other members
___ Age of family members
    _X_ Respondent
    _X_ Others
___ Sex of family members

    _X_ Respondent
    ___ Others
___ Race of family members
    _X_ Respondent
    _X_ Others
___ Marital status of family
    members
    ___ Respondent
    ___ Others
___ Education of family
    members
    _X_ Respondent
    _X_ Others
___ Occupation of family
    members
    ___ Respondent
    ___ Others

LIMITATIONS

None

SPONSORSHIP

The study was funded by the U.S. Department of Education, Office of Planning, Budget, and Evaluation.

GUIDE TO DATA AND DOCUMENTATION

File Structure

Machine-readable data and documentation files, along with printed and bound User's Guides, are available in both mainframe and microcomputer formats. Unless otherwise requested, files formatted for a mainframe computer are provided on a 9-track tape at a density of 6250 bpi, in EBCDIC recording mode with IBM Standard Labels. Files formatted for a microcomputer are provided in ASCII format on high-density 5¼" or 3½" diskettes; other microcomputer formats can be made available at the user's request, including CD-ROM. A description of the contents of each file is given below:

File 1 (Data): Raw data file. The format of this file is described in the "data list" section of the SPSS program file (File 2).

File 2 (SPSS Program): This file consists of SPSS program statements designed to read the raw data in File 1 and create an SPSS active file. For mainframe orders, the program statements conform to SPSS-X syntax; for microcomputer orders, the program statements conform to SPSS/PC and SPSS/PC+ syntax. The SPSS program file contains data list statements, variable names and labels, value labels, and missing value declarations.

File 3 (SAS Program): The file consists of SAS program statements designed to read the raw data in File 1 and create a SAS active file. The contents of this file are analogous to the contents of the previously described File 2. SPSS users should use File 2; SAS users, File 3. Mainframe SAS users may need to add Job Control Language (JCL) as appropriate for their system. PC-SAS users should be aware that PC-SAS may limit the size of the system file they can create to 200-300 variables. Thus PC-SAS users may need to edit the program statements accordingly.

File 4 (Dictionary; mainframe orders only): Sequential list of variable and value labels. This file consists of DISPLAY DICTIONARY output describing the SPSS-X active file created by the program in File 2. Variables are listed in sequential order. Variable names and labels, value labels, missing value designations, print formats, and write formats are clearly displayed.

File 5 (Statistics; mainframe orders only): Unweighted frequencies and other descriptive statistics for each variable. Descriptive statistics only are provided for variables with more than 50 value categories.

List of Available Documentation

Separate User's Guides for the Home-based and Center-based Programs surveys accompany the machine-readable files and provide the following information: Summary; General study overview; Description of machine-readable files and supplementary documentation; Specifications for machine-readable files; Key characteristics report; Distribution of variables by topic and type; and Data completeness and consistency report.

For each survey, paper versions of the machine-readable SPSS or SAS program files and data documentation, and copies of the original instrument, are available upon request (at 15 cents per page).

Contact

Sociometrics Corporation
American Family Data Archive
170 State Street, Suite 260
Los Altos, California 94022-2812
(415) 949-3282

Cost

The cost for the machine-readable data sets (Data Sets 15-16 and 17-18 of the American Family Data Archive) is $100 each. This price includes the raw data, SPSS program statements, the SAS program statements, the Dictionary, and the Frequencies in mainframe or microcomputer format, and the accompanying printed and bound User's Guide. The CD-ROM versions cost $175 each. A paper version of the original Instrument for Data Set 15-16 can be obtained for $6.45; for Data Set 17-18, $8.70.

BIBLIOGRAPHY

Hagy, A.P. (1992). *Child care quality: Hedonic prices, demand, and the effects of government subsidization*. Ph.D. dissertation, Duke University.

Kisker, E.E. (1992). *School readiness: The contribution of early education and care programs*. Princeton, NJ: Mathematics Policy Research.

Kisker, E.E., Hofferth, S.L., Phillips, D.A., Farquhar, E. (1991). *A profile of child care settings: Early education and care in 1990 (Volume I)*. U.S. Department of Education, Office of the Under Secretary.

Kisker, E.E., Hofferth, S.L., Phillips, D.A., Farquhar, E. (1991). *A profile of child care settings: Early education and care in 1990 (Volume II)*. U.S. Department of Education, Office of the Under Secretary.

Lang, E.L., & Card, J.J. (1992). *A profile of child care settings, home-based programs: A user's guide to the machine-readable files and documentation*. Los Altos, CA: Sociometrics Corporation, American Family Data Archive.

Lang, E.L., & Card, J.J. (1992). *A profile of child care settings, center-based programs: A user's guide to the machine-readable files and documentation*. Los Altos, CA: Sociometrics Corporation, American Family Data Archive.

Phillips, D., Voran, M., Kisker, E., Howes, C., & Whitebook, M. (1993). Child care for children in poverty: Opportunity or inequity? Submitted to *Child Development*.

Piper, V., & Kisker, E.E., (1991). *A profile of child care settings: Data documentation*. Princeton, NJ: Mathematica Policy Research.

Willer, B., Hofferth, S., Kisker, E.E., Hawkins, P., & Farquhar, E. (1991). *Child care demand and supply in 1990: Findings from the national child care survey 1990 and a profile of child care settings*. Washington, DC: National Association for the Education of Young Children.

3

CURRENT POPULATION SURVEY (CPS) CHILD SUPPORT AND ALIMONY SUPPLEMENT, APRIL 1979, 1982, 1984, 1986, 1988 AND 1990

U. S. Bureau of the Census

PURPOSE OF THE STUDY

The Current Population Survey (CPS) is the source of official U. S. Government statistics on employment and unemployment. The CPS has been conducted monthly for over 50 years. Currently, about 57,000 households (selected on the basis of area of residence to represent the entire nation as well as individual states and other specified areas) are interviewed for the CPS.

Although the main purpose of the survey is to collect information about employment, a very important secondary purpose is to collect information on the demographic status of the population, including information regarding age, sex, race, marital status, educational attainment, and family structure. From time to time, the survey includes additional questions on such important subjects as health, education, income, and previous work experience. The results obtained from these questions serve to update similar information collected once every ten years through the decennial census. This information is employed by government policy makers and legislators as important indicators of the nation's economic situation in addition to facilitating the planning and evaluation of many government programs.

The CPS provides current estimates of the economic status and activities of the population of the United States. Because it is not possible to develop one or two overall figures (such as the number of unemployed) that would adequately describe the whole complex of labor market phenomena, the CPS is designed to provide a large amount of detailed and supplementary data. Such data are made available to meet a wide variety of labor market information needs. Thus, the CPS is the sole source of monthly estimates of total employment and unemployment (both farm and nonfarm); nonfarm self-employed persons, domestics, and unpaid helpers in nonfarm family enterprises; and wage and salary employees.

The survey provides the only available distribution of workers by the number of hours worked (as distinguished from aggregate or average hours for an industry), permitting separate analyses of part-time workers, workers on overtime, etc. The CPS is also the only comprehensive source of current information on the occupation of workers and on the industries in which they work. Information is available from the survey not only for persons currently in the labor force but also for those who are outside the labor force. The characteristics of persons outside the labor force (whether married women with or without young children, disabled persons, students, older retired workers, etc.) can be determined from survey results. The survey also assesses current desire for work, past work experience, and intentions to seek employment among those persons outside the labor force.

The March CPS, also known as the Annual Demographic File, contains the basic monthly demographic and labor force data described above plus additional data on work experience, income, noncash benefits, and migration. The April CPS contains supplementary information on child support and alimony from a subset of March CPS respondents. Data from this portion of the survey are used to determine the size and distribution of the female population with children affected by divorce or separation. These data are used in order to better understand the characteristics of persons requiring child support and to help develop and maintain programs designed to assist them in obtaining this assistance.

METHODS

Sampling Design

The CPS sample is based on the civilian noninstitutional population of the United States. The sample is located in 729 sample areas comprising 1,973 counties and independent cities with coverage in every state and in the District of Columbia.

In all, some 71,000 housing units or other living quarters are assigned for interview each month; about 57,000 of them containing approximately 114,500 persons 15 years of age and over are interviewed. Also included are demographic data for approximately 33,500 children zero to fourteen years old and 650 Armed Forces members living with civilians either on or off base within these households. The remainder of the assigned housing units are found to be vacant, converted to nonresidential use, contain persons with residence elsewhere, or are not interviewed because the residents are not found at home after repeated calls, are temporarily absent, or are unavailable for other reasons. Approximately 14,000 noninterview households are present each month. In March of each year, supplemental data are collected for male Armed Forces members residing with their families in civilian housing units or on military bases. The Armed Forces members, however, are not asked the monthly labor force questions or the supplemental questions on work experience. The resulting file size is approximately 163,000 records.

In addition to the basic CPS questions, interviewers ask supplementary questions in March about the economic situation of persons and families for the previous year. About 39,000 of the housing units interviewed in March are interviewed again in April. In these housing units, all women 18 years of age and older, as well as women between the ages of 14 and 17 who have children, are asked supplemental questions. These questions concern child support and alimony payments. Of the 43,018 women found eligible in March of 1990, 39,474 were re-interviewed regarding child support and alimony in April. Child support and alimony information was imputed for the remaining 3,544 women. Table 1 presents the sample sizes and the imputation rates by marital status for the March and April 1990 CPS.

Table 1
Sample Sizes and Imputation Rates

Marital Status	Sample Size	Imputed Cases	Rates
Total	43,018	3,544	8.2
Married	24,773	1,411	5.7
Widowed	5,289	387	7.3
Divorced	3,927	710	18.1
Separated	1,175	205	17.4
Never married	7,854	831	10.6

Periodicity

The child support and alimony supplement has been conducted in April of 1979, 1982, 1984, 1986, 1988, 1989, and 1990.

Unit of Analyses

The unit of observation is individuals, families, and households.

Response Rates

The response rates are provided in Table 2 below:

Table 2
Description of Current Population Survey

Time Period	Number of sample areas	Housing units eligible [1]	
		Interviewed	Not interviewed
1990	729	57,400	2,600
April 1988-89	729	53,600	2,500
1985 to March 1988	729	57,000	2,500
1985	629/729 [2]	57,000	2,500
1982-1984	629	59,000	2,500
1980-1981	628	65,500	3,000
1978-1979	614	55,000	3,000

[1] Excludes about 2,500 Hispanic households added from the previous November sample.

[2] The CPS was redesigned following the 1980 Census of Population and Housing. During phase-in of the new design, housing units from the new and old designs were in the sample.

Attrition

Not applicable. The CPSs are a series of cross-sectional surveys.

CONTENT

Data Sources

Data are collected via in-person interviews in respondents' homes. Currently, the CPS interviews about 57,000 households monthly. Households are scientifically selected on the basis of area of residence to represent the nation as a whole, individual states, and other specified areas. Each household is interviewed once a month for four consecutive months one year, and again during the corresponding time period the following year. This technique enables the CPS to obtain month-to-month and year-to-year comparisons at a reasonable cost while minimizing the inconvenience to any one household. In addition to the basic CPS questions, interviewers ask supplementary questions in March about the economic situation of persons and families for the previous year. About 39,000 of the housing units interviewed in March 1990 were interviewed again in April 1990. In these housing units, all women 18 years of age and older, as well as women between the ages of 14 and 17 who had children, were asked supplemental questions concerning child support and alimony payments. Of the 43,018 women found eligible in March, 39,474 were interviewed in April. Child support and alimony information was imputed for the remaining 3,544 women. Table 1 (presented earlier) reported the sample sizes and the imputation rates by marital status for data collected in 1990.

Description of Variables Covered

We describe the 1990 CPS Alimony and Child Support file below and note changes from prior years' versions of this file.

The CPS March/April Match File: Alimony and Child Support comprises records for the six rotation groups common to the March and April 1990 Current Population Surveys. For females 15 years and over, data on alimony and child support collected from the April supplement are provided. These data highlight alimony and child support arrangements made at the time of separation or divorce, amount of payments actually received, and value and type of any property settlement.

This file also provides the usual monthly labor force data plus data on work experience, income, and migration. Comprehensive information is provided on the employment status, occupation, and type of industry for persons 15 years old and older. Additional data for persons 15 years old and older are available concerning the number of weeks and hours per week worked, reason for working full time, total income and income components, and residence on March 1, 1989.

Characteristics such as age, sex, race, household relationship, and Spanish origin are shown for each person in the household enumerated. The data on employment and income refer to the preceding year, although demographic data refer to the time during which the survey was conducted.

The file also contains data covering nine noncash income sources: food stamps; school lunch program; employer-provided group health insurance; employer-provided pension plan; personal health insurance; Medicaid; Medicare; CHAMPUS or military health care; and energy assistance. State of residence is uniquely identified, as are census geographic division and region. The 113 largest metropolitan statistical areas (CMSAs or MSAs), an additional 89 selected MSAs, 66 selected PMSAs, and 30 central cities in multi-central city MSAs or PMSAs are also uniquely identified.

Revisions to the April CPS survey. Several modifications, additions, and deletions were made to the April CPS questions in 1988. Three new questions were added to the 1988 survey concerning the absent father of the children from the most recent divorce or separation. These questions sought to establish the residence of the father; to ascertain the father's custody and visitation rights; and to determine the number of days in the previous year that the father either had custody of or visited his child(ren). Three questions on child support awards were also added to obtain information on the year of original child support award, changes in the award amount, and the year of most recent award change. In addition, questions were added to establish reasons why women who were awarded child support were not supposed to receive payments in the previous year and to determine if the child(ren)'s father provided health care benefits in the previous year. A follow-up question was added to determine what year a government agency had been contacted for the purpose of obtaining child support.

Due to space constraints and new data requirements, five questions were deleted from the survey: 1) receipt of AFDC payments; 2) amount of child support received as a result of seeking aid from a government agency; 3) frequency of receipt of alimony payments; 4) amount of alimony due; and 5) amount of alimony actually received. In addition, a question concerning the inclusion of health care benefits in child support awards was changed to inquire whether benefits were included in the *current* support agreement as opposed to the *original* support agreement.

Revisions to the March CPS Processing System.

Between 1988 and 1989, a new computer processing system was introduced for the March CPS in order to reflect the numerous questionnaire changes that had taken place since the introduction of the system in 1976. As part of this procedure, modifications were made to the basic strategy for imputing missing data. For further detail on these modifications and their subsequent effect on income and poverty rates, please refer to *Current Population Survey, March/April 1990 Match File: Child Support and Alimony Technical Documentation.*

Number of Variables

Approximately 200.

Checklist of Topics Covered

X Gender / Gender Role
X Race / Ethnicity
X Age
X Education
X Occupation / Employment
___ Physical Health / Disease
___ Nutrition
___ Clinical Activities
___ Biological Functioning / Development
___ Mental Health / Disease
___ Psychological Functioning / Development
___ Guidance / Counseling
___ Personality
___ Intellectual Functioning
X Residential Mobility
X Dwelling
___ Neighborhood / Community
X Region / State
X Marriage and Divorce
___ Cohabitation
X Family/Household Composition & Structure
___ Inter-Partner Relationships
___ Parent-Child Relationships
___ Inter-Sibling Relationships
___ Relationships with Other Kin

___ Relationships with Nonkin
___ Other Family/Household Characteristics
___ Child Care
X Wealth / Finances / Material Things
X Receipt of Health, Mental Health, Social Services
___ Adoption / Foster Care
X Childbearing / Pregnancy
___ Out-of-Wedlock Pregnancy & Parenthood
___ Abortion
___ Sexuality
___ Sex Education
___ Contraception
___ Sexually Transmitted Diseases
___ Civic/Political Activities
___ Friends / Social Activities
___ Social Support
___ Dating, Courtship
___ Recreation
___ Religion
___ Crime / Delinquency / Behavior Problems
___ Substance Use
___ Agency Characteristics
___ Interview

Checklist of Key Variables

X Number of family members
X Identification of marital
   partners in family
___ Size of dwelling
X Type of dwelling
X Urban/rural residence
X Region/state of residence
X Family income
___ Religious affiliation
___ Relation of each family
   member to:
   X Reference person
   ___ All other members
X Age of family members
   ___ Respondent
   ___ Others
X Sex of family members

X Respondent
___ Others
X Race of family members
   X Respondent
   ___ Others
___ Marital status of family
   members
   X Respondent
   ___ Others
___ Education of family
   members
   X Respondent
   ___ Others
___ Occupation of family
   members
   X Respondent
   ___ Others

LIMITATIONS

Information on child support payments is collected only from the most recent divorce or separation. Thus, data on women receiving support from previous marital disruptions are excluded.

In addition, the supplemental survey identifies women with children under 21 in the household, regardless of the relationship between the child(ren) and woman surveyed. Therefore, it is possible that the children present in the household are, in fact, not the woman's "own" children.

Furthermore, it is possible that the CPS may not accurately reflect child support income that is received by some women who receive AFDC income. The Child Support Enforcement amendments to the 1973 Social Security Act provided for AFDC child support payments contributed by the father to be paid directly to the welfare agency and not to the parent with whom the child lives. Thus, some women who receive AFDC income and who indirectly receive child support payments indirectly through AFDC may not be aware that those payments include child support and may not report the receipt of child support in the CPS supplement.

Finally, income may be underreported in the March/April supplements. As in most household surveys, estimates of money income derived from the March CPS are somewhat lower than are comparable estimates derived from independent sources, such as the Bureau of Economic Analysis. Moreover, this underreporting tends to be more pronounced for income sources such as public assistance and welfare, unemployment compensation, and property income.

SPONSORSHIP

The supplement was first conducted in April 1979 and was jointly sponsored by the Bureau of the Census and the Department of Health and Human Services (then Department of Health, Education, and Welfare). The April supplements of 1982, 1984, 1986, 1988, and 1990 were conducted by the Bureau of the Census and sponsored, in part, by the Office of Child Support Enforcement, Department of Health and Human Services.

File Structure

File Structure: Hierarchical.
File Size: 212,104 logical records; record size is 868 characters.
File Sort Sequence: Census state code (MSTSTATE), then
MSA/PMSA rank code.

List of Available Documentation

Bureau of the Census. (1991). *Current Population Survey, April 1988: Alimony and Child Support Technical Documentation* [machine-readable data file]. Washington, DC: Bureau of the Census [Producer & Distributor].

Bureau of the Census. (1990). *Current Population Survey, April 1988: Alimony and Child Support Technical Documentation* [machine-readable data file]. Washington, DC: Bureau of the Census [Producer & Distributor].

Data User Services Division, Data Access and Use Staff, U.S. Bureau of the Census. (1991). *Current population survey, March/April 1990 match file: Alimony and child support tape technical documentation.* Washington: Bureau of the Census.

Data User Services Division, Data Access and Use Staff, U.S. Bureau of the Census. (1990). *Current population survey, March/April 1988 match file: Alimony and child support tape technical documentation.* Washington: Bureau of the Census.

The technical documentation includes an abstract, pertinent information about the file, a glossary, code lists, and a data dictionary. One copy of the technical documentation accompanies each file order. When ordered separately, such documentation is available for $5 from Customer Services, Bureau of the Census, Washington, DC 20233.

Contact

For substantive questions:

Gordon Lester
Income Statistics Branch
Housing and Household Economic Statistics Division
U.S. Bureau of the Census
Washington, D.C. 20233
(301) 763-8576

For data tapes and documentation:

Customer Services
Bureau of the Census
Washington, D.C. 20233
(301) 763-4100

Cost

The 1990 file is available on 9-track tape reel or IBM 3480-compatible tape cartridge, 6250 or 1600 bpi, EBCDIC or ASCII, labeled or unlabeled. Tapes are priced at $1.25 per megabyte (MB) with a minimum cost of $175. All orders include a copy of technical documentation; additional copies are $10. To order the data file and documentation for this and other years (April 1979, 1982, 1984, 1986, and 1988), contact the Customer Services address provided above.

BIBLIOGRAPHY

Data User Services Division, Data Access and Use Staff, U.S. Bureau of the Census. (1991). *Current population survey, March/April 1990 match file: Alimony and child support tape technical documentation*. Washington, DC: Bureau of the Census.

Data User Services Division, Data Access and Use Staff, U.S. Bureau of the Census. (1990). *Current population survey, March/April 1988 match file: Alimony and child support tape technical documentation*. Washington, DC: Bureau of the Census.

U.S. Bureau of the Census. (1979). *Divorce, child custody, and child support* (Current Population Reports, Special Studies, Series P-23, No. 84). Washington, DC: U.S. Government Printing Office.

U.S. Bureau of the Census. (1981). *Child support and alimony: 1978* (Current Population Reports, Special Studies, Series P-23, No. 112). Washington, DC: U.S. Government Printing Office.

U.S. Bureau of the Census. (1985). *Child support and alimony: 1981* (Current Population Reports, Special Studies, Series P-23, No. 140). Washington, DC: U.S. Government Printing Office.

U.S. Bureau of the Census. (1986). *Child support and alimony: 1983* (Current Population Reports, Special Studies, Series P-23, No. 148). Washington, DC: U.S. Government Printing Office.

U.S. Bureau of the Census. (1989). *Child support and alimony: 1985* (Current Population Reports, Special Studies, Series P-23, No. 154). Washington, DC: U.S. Government Printing Office.

U.S. Bureau of the Census. (1990). *Child support and alimony: 1987* (Current Population Reports, Special Studies, Series P-23, No. 167). Washington, DC: U.S. Government Printing Office.

U.S. Bureau of the Census. (1991). *Child support and alimony: 1989* (Current Population Reports, Special Studies, Series P-60, No. 173). Washington, DC: U.S. Government Printing Office.

Zill, N., & Peterson, J.L. (1989). *Guide to federal data on children, youth, and families.* Washington, DC: Child Trends.

4

NATIONAL COMMISSION ON CHILDREN: 1990 SURVEY OF PARENTS AND CHILDREN

Kristin A. Moore

PURPOSE OF THE STUDY

The *National Commission on Children: 1990 Survey of Parents and Children* was a national telephone interview opinion survey conducted among 1,738 parents in the continental United States who live with their children. The purpose of the survey was to gather direct, up-to-date, and nationally representative data on the current state of family life; the quality of the relationship between parents and their children; and their interactions with the major institutions affecting the family, i.e., schools, the workplace, neighborhoods, and religious and civic organizations. The survey also obtained information on family demographic and socioeconomic background. The following issues were addressed:

1. What factors support a positive and stable parent-child relationship?

2. What is the role of educational, religious, social and cultural experiences in the lives of children?

3. To what degree do parents involve themselves in their children's educational and religious experiences?

4. To what degree do children talk with their parents about their life experiences such as dating, sex, drug and alcohol use, and their moral or religious concerns?

5. To what degree do parents and children worry about and plan for the child's future education and employment?

METHODS

Sampling Design

Subjects for this survey were identified from a national random sample of telephone numbers. The survey over-sampled households with children age ten and over. In addition, there was an over-sampling of families with black and Hispanic children. The distribution of parent interviews in the final sample consisted of 709 parents of nonblack, nonhispanic children, 483 parents of black children, and 546 parents of Hispanic children.

The sample of telephone numbers was selected by Survey Sampling, Inc. of Fairfield, Connecticut following Princeton Survey Research Associates' specifications. The sample was selected in three parts: a national sample of random-digit telephone numbers designed to produce a representative sample of the general population, a national sample of random-digit and listed telephone numbers designed to produce a representative sample of the black population living in areas with significant black population, and a national sample of random-digit and listed telephone numbers designed to produce a representative sample of the Hispanic population with Hispanic surnames.

Periodicity

The interviews were conducted between September 17 and November 23, 1990.

Unit of Analysis

The individual respondent (one parent and one child age 10 or over) was the unit of analysis.

Response Rates

The overall response rate was the product of three separate rates: the contact rate (proportion of working, residential telephone numbers where contact with a person was made), the cooperation rate (proportion of contacted households where screening information could be obtained), and the completion rate (proportion of eligible households where an interview was completed). Respondents who were unable to be interviewed due to illness, vacation, language problem (other than Spanish) or other such circumstances were considered ineligible.

On the basis of these considerations, the best estimate for the response rate for parents was 71%. The response rates for completing the child interviews were 82% for children reached as part of the general population sample, 81% for children reached as part of the black over-sample, and 84% for children reached as part of the Hispanic over-sample. The three response rates for children averaged 82% for an overall response rate for children.

Attrition

Not applicable.

CONTENT

Data Sources

Subjects for the survey were identified from a national random sample of telephone numbers and the data were collected in a national telephone interview opinion survey. The parent interview was conducted first. If the randomly selected child was age 10 or older, an interview was attempted with that child after the parent interview about that child was completed.

Description of Variables Covered

The survey collected information on sex and age of both parent and child; national origin and ethnicity, with questions about race and whether or not the respondent was of Spanish or Hispanic background; marital status and inter-partner relationships; religious preference; education, including questions about the highest school or college grade attained by the parent, and the type of school the child was attending; employment status, including information on full-time or part-time employment; family income; parent/child relationships and relationships with other relatives and nonrelatives; community of residence, including information on the Census region; household size, including the number of adults 18 or older living in the household and number of children 17 or younger living in the household; child care arrangements; crime, delinquency, and behavioral problems at school, at home, and in the neighborhood; friends and social activities, both for the parent and the child; guidance or counseling for parent/child problems; family/household characteristics and composition; and mental and physical health.

Number of Variables

The 1990 Survey of Parents and Children contains 495 variables and 1,738 cases.

Checklist of Topics Covered

X Gender / Gender Role
X Race / Ethnicity
X Age
X Education
X Occupation / Employment
X Physical Health / Disease
___ Nutrition
___ Clinical Activities
___ Biological Functioning / Development
X Mental Health / Disease
X Psychological Functioning / Development
X Guidance / Counseling
___ Personality
___ Intellectual Functioning
___ Residential Mobility
X Dwelling
X Neighborhood / Community
X Region / State
X Marriage and Divorce
___ Cohabitation
X Family/Household Composition & Structure
X Inter-Partner Relationships
X Parent-Child Relationships
X Inter-Sibling Relationships
X Relationships with Other Kin

X Relationships with Nonkin
X Other Family/Household Characteristics
X Child Care
X Wealth / Finances / Material Things
___ Receipt of Health, Mental Health, Social Services
___ Adoption / Foster Care
___ Childbearing / Pregnancy
___ Out-of-Wedlock Pregnancy & Parenthood
___ Abortion
___ Sexuality
___ Sex Education
___ Contraception
___ Sexually Transmitted Diseases
___ Civic/Political Activities
X Friends / Social Activities
___ Social Support
___ Dating, Courtship
___ Recreation
X Religion
X Crime / Delinquency / Behavior Problems
___ Substance Use
___ Agency Characteristics
X Interview

Checklist of Key Variables

X Number of family members
X Identification of marital
   partners in family
___ Size of dwelling
___ Type of dwelling
X Urban/rural residence
X Region/state of residence
X Family income
X Religious affiliation
X Relation of each family
   member to:
   X Reference person
   X All other members
X Age of family members
   X Respondent
   X Others
X Sex of family members

X Respondent
X Others
X Race of family members
   X Respondent
   X Others
X Marital status of family
   members
   X Respondent
   ___ Others
X Education of family
   members
   X Respondent
   X Others
X Occupation of family
   members
   X Respondent
   X Others

LIMITATIONS

By design, the sampling procedures for the supplemental samples underrepresented blacks living in geographic areas that did not contain concentrations of blacks, Hispanics who did not have Hispanic surnames, and members of both groups that lived in households with unlisted telephone numbers. The weighting procedures mitigate, to a large degree, these limitations of the sample design.

Also, nonresponse in telephone interview surveys produces some known biases in survey-derived estimates because participation tends to vary for different subgroups of the population, and these subgroups are likely to vary also on questions of substantive interest. For example, young men are more difficult than other adults to reach at home by telephone, and people with relatively low educational attainment are less likely than others to agree to participate in telephone surveys.

To avoid sampling bias in survey estimates for this survey, it is important to take into account the explicit over-sampling that was done to increase the representation of households with children age 10 to 17 and households with black and Hispanic children. In order to compensate for all of these known biases, the sample data for this survey should be weighted in analysis, using the appropriate weighting variable provided with the data.

SPONSORSHIP

The Survey was carried out under the sponsorship of the National Commission on Children.

GUIDE TO DATA AND DOCUMENTATION

File Structure

Machine-readable data and documentation files, along with a printed and bound User's Guide, are available in both mainframe and microcomputer formats. Unless otherwise requested, files formatted for a mainframe computer are provided on a 9-track tape at a density of

6250 bpi, in EBCDIC recording mode with IBM Standard Labels. Files formatted for a microcomputer are provided in ASCII format on high-density 5¼" or 3½" diskettes; other microcomputer formats can be made available at the user's request, including CD-ROM. A description of the contents of each file is given below:

File 1 (Data): Raw data file. The format of this file is described in the "data list" section of the SPSS program file (File 2).

File 2 (SPSS Program): This file consists of SPSS program statements designed to read the raw data in File 1 and create an SPSS active file. For mainframe orders, the program statements conform to SPSS-X syntax; for microcomputer orders, the program statements conform to SPSS/PC and SPSS/PC+ syntax. The SPSS program file contains data list statements, variable names and labels, value labels, and missing value declarations.

File 3 (SAS Program): The file consists of SAS program statements designed to read the raw data in File 1 and create a SAS active file. The contents of this file are analogous to the contents of the previously described File 2. SPSS users should use File 2; SAS users, File 3. Mainframe SAS users may need to add Job Control Language (JCL) as appropriate for their system. PC-SAS users should be aware that PC-SAS may limit the size of the system file they can create to 200-300 variables. Thus PC-SAS users may need to edit the program statements accordingly.

File 4 (Dictionary; mainframe orders only): Sequential list of variable and value labels. This file consists of DISPLAY DICTIONARY output describing the SPSS-X active file created by the program in File 2. Variables are listed in sequential order. Variable names and labels, value labels, missing value designations, print formats, and write formats are clearly displayed.

File 5 (Statistics; mainframe orders only): Unweighted frequencies and other descriptive statistics for each variable. Descriptive statistics only are provided for variables with more than 50 value categories.

List of Available Documentation

A User's Guide which accompanies the machine-readable files provides the following information: Summary; General study overview; Description of machine-readable files and supplementary documentation; Specifications for machine-readable files; Key characteristics report; Distribution of variables by topic and type; and Data completeness and consistency report.

Paper versions of the machine-readable SPSS or SAS program files and data documentation, and copies of the original instrument and codebook, are available upon request (at 15 cents per page).

Contact

> Sociometrics Corporation
> American Family Data Archive
> 170 State Street, Suite 260
> Los Altos, California 94022-2812
> (415) 949-3282

Cost

The cost for the machine-readable data set (Data Set 19 of the American Family Data Archive) is $100. This price includes the SPSS-X Program, the SPSS/PC Program, the SAS Program, the Dictionary, and the Statistics in mainframe or microcomputer format and the accompanying printed and bound User's Guide. The standard CD-ROM version costs $175. Paper versions of the original Codebook/Instrument can be obtained for $14.40.

BIBLIOGRAPHY

Daley, H.M., Peterson, E.C., Lang, E.L., & Card, J.J. (1992). *National commission on children 1990: survey of parents and children: A user's guide to the machine-readable files and documentation.* Los Altos, CA: Sociometrics Corporation, American Family Data Archive.

Moore, K.A. (1991). *National commission on children 1990 survey of parents and children: Methodological report*. Unpublished report, Washington, DC: Child Trends.

National Commission on Children (1991). *Beyond rhetoric: A new American agenda for children and families*. Washington, DC: U.S. Government Printing Office.

National Commission on Children (1991). *Speaking of kids: A national survey of children and parents*. Washington, DC: U.S. Government Printing Office.

5

1976-1987 NATIONAL SURVEY OF CHILDREN: WAVES I, II, AND III

Nicholas Zill
James L. Peterson
Kristin A. Moore
Frank F. Furstenberg, Jr.

PURPOSE OF THE STUDY

The purpose of the original 1976 (Wave I) National Survey of Children (NSC) was to assess the physical, social, and psychological well-being of different groups of American children; to develop a profile of the way children live and the care they receive; to permit analysis of the relationships between the condition of childrens' lives and measures of child development and well-being; and to replicate items from previous national studies of children and parents, permitting analysis of trends over time. The focus of the 1981 survey (Wave II) was on the effects that marital conflict and disruption had on children. The goals of this wave of the survey included: (1) developing a profile of the behavioral and mental health characteristics of children at various stages of the marital disruption process, and (2) examining the influence of child, parent, and family factors that are thought to influence the risk of childhood problems associated with marital disruption. The purpose of collecting data in 1987 (Wave III) was to examine the social, psychological, and economic well-being of sample members as they became young adults. In particular, their sexual and fertility behavior were a focus of interest. The existence of rich antecedent information on young people's aspirations, experiences and family background in the first two waves of the NSC provides an unusual opportunity to study the consequences of pregnancy and parenthood, over and above the influences of background differences.

METHODS

Sampling Design

The study population was defined as children living in households in the contiguous United States, age 7 to 11 years old. In 1976 (Wave I), interviews were conducted with the eligible child and the parent who would be most capable of providing information about the child (usually the mother). If a selected family had three or more eligible children, two were selected at random to be interviewed.

A multi-stage stratified probability sampling technique was used to generate a national sample of eligible households. Housing units within listing areas (usually blocks) of 160 people were then randomly selected for interviewers to call and screen for eligibility.

From these, 2,193 households were found to contain at least one eligible child. From these households, parent and child interviews were completed for 2,279 children in 1,747 households. An additional 22 parents provided information on children who were unable to be interviewed, making 2,301 children about whom some information was obtained. In 1,682 cases, school information was obtained from the child's main teacher.

Weights were developed to adjust for the oversampling of black children, and to correct for minor differentials between census and sample figures for age, sex, race, and residential location of the child.

For Wave II (1981), the same basic research design was followed as in 1976 with some variations in questionnaire content. As before, data were collected from the child, a parent, and a teacher. If the original parent was not available, the same criteria were used in selecting another adult respondent. Since the child was likely to have more than one teacher, the principal of the school designated whether the English, mathematics, or homeroom teacher knew most about the child. Interviews with parents and youth were conducted by telephone in most cases. Teachers filled out self-administered mailed questionnaires. A subset of interviews was conducted in person and the results were compared with the results from the telephone interviews. These comparisons revealed no important differences.

The Wave II sample was sub-sampled from Wave I respondents. Consistent with the focus on marital disruption as it affects children, all families who reported having a history of disruption, or who indicated having a high-conflict marriage were included in the 1981 sample. The remaining cases were divided into two groups: those for which school information was obtained in 1976 and those for which it was not. Both of these groups were subsampled, the latter at a much lower rate. A total of 1,423 children completed the second interview.

For the third and final wave, all children who participated in Wave II were eligible to be re-interviewed. A total of 1,147 interviews were completed with youth. In addition, four of the five parents whose child had died were interviewed about that child. Eight of the youth respondents were residents of penitentiaries; there would have been nine such respondents, but one escaped between the time the warden was contacted and the appointment date. Seventeen parents who had been interviewed in 1981 had died by 1987; in twelve cases a substitute parent was interviewed. When possible, the parent interview was completed even if a youth interview was not completed. Of the 28 youths who were away for the duration of the study, 25 were in the military and were stationed outside the United States.

Periodicity

There were three waves in which the panel was interviewed: Wave I (1976), Wave II (1981) and Wave III (1987).

Unit of Analysis

The unit of analysis was the individual child. Interviews conducted with parents were also included in the child's data file. Further, the interview with the child's school teacher was included in the child's data in the first two waves.

Response and Attrition Rates

Number of Respondents

Wave I   N=2,301[1] (79.7% of eligible households)
Wave II   N=1,423[2] (81.5% of eligible respondents)
Wave III   N=1,147[3] (80.6% of eligible respondents)

[1]Based on interviews with at least one child in 1,747 households, from an original sample base of 2,193 eligible households.
[2]Based on a subset of 1,794 respondents who completed the first wave interview and fit the Wave II subset specifications.
[3]Based on the 1,423 respondents who participated in both Waves I and II.

CONTENT

Data Sources

      Wave I questionnaires were administered in person to eligible children and the parent most familiar with the child. Later, questionnaires were administered to the teachers of the children. Wave II and III data were collected via telephone interviews (except for a small set of in-person interviews) with eligible children and their parents. Teacher interviews were conducted again in Wave II, but not in Wave III.

Description of Variables Covered

      Parent Questionnaire: Information in the Parent Survey focussed on the background family information, as well as information pertaining to the child.

Background Information:

      Marriage and family:
      marital history; household composition

      Residence:
      residential history; neighborhood quality; cost of housing

      Marital relationship:
      happiness; conflict; employment/welfare history

      Childrearing practices:
      self-evaluation; child care arrangements; religious training; discipline; quality of relationship; consistency; difficulties; information on pregnancy

      Health:
      mental; physical; emotional

      Demographics:
      age; sex; education; income; employment; religion

Patterns of socialization:
friendships; kin contact; dating

Relationship with former spouse:
conflict; nature of disruption; custody and visitation of children; financial arrangements

Attitudes:
stepchildren; marriage and family life; satisfaction with life

Parents:
received AFDC; lived away from home;

Information About Child:

Demographics:
age; sex; ordinal position

Health:
mental; physical; emotional; limiting conditions; psychological help; doctor visits; characteristics at birth

Parent-child relationship:
wantedness of child; quality of relationship; difficult periods; discipline; conflict; rules and responsibilities; decision making; babysitting; child care

Behavior:
delinquency; behavior problems; use of time; discussion of drugs/contraception; overall assessment of youth's life

Socialization:
friendships; social adjustment; social skills

Schooling:
grade; performance; behavior; aspirations and expectations; need for special resources; history

Relationship between child and parent living outside of home: communication; quality of relationship; childrearing; employment/education of outside parent

Child Questionnaire: Information on the Child Survey is similar to the Information About Child section of the Parent survey, except with more comprehensive information on the child's personal attitudes, beliefs, and behavior on various issues.

Schooling:
performance; behavior; aspirations and expectations; extracurricular activities; dropout history; characteristics of high school; courses taken outside of school

Health:
mental; physical; emotional; self-esteem

Socialization:
friendships; social adjustment; problems of neighborhood;

Behavior:
usual activities; delinquency; dating and sexual activities; television viewing; drug use history; time spent in activities in past twelve months; use of computer

Parent-Child relationship:
discipline; conflict; rules and responsibilities; decision making; quality of relationship; difficult periods; family activities, receipt of help; closeness to family members;

Relationship between child and parent living outside of home: interaction; quality of relationship; discipline

Attitudes:
marriage and family life; favorite activities; satisfaction with life; sex roles; welfare/child support; work; crime

Retrospection:
family experiences; parent and peer influences; peer behavior

Employment/finances:
current employment; wages; reasons for not working; job seeking; does youth have checking account, credit card, savings, transportation, medical insurance, or driver's license; receipt of gifts over $200 in past year

Health:
when last saw doctor/dentist; overall health rating

Psychological well being:
depression; life satisfaction; counselling received; psychoactive medication; what youth would change about himself/herself; with whom youth discusses problems; self-esteem; locus of control

Marriage history:
cohabitation history; characteristics of spouse/partner; dating behavior

Sexuality:
reasons for not having sex; ever raped; age, year, place, and contraception at first sexual intercourse; current sexual activity and contraception use; homosexual experience in past year

Pregnancy/childbearing:
first and most recent birth/pregnancy history; decision making in abortion, marriage, adoption, and welfare; prenatal care and participation in teen pregnancy programs; relationship of youth and partner at conception

Childrearing:
who cared for child; who lived with child; was parent in school, home, or work; satisfaction with child; social support for child; child support/custody/visitation agreements for parents of child

Religion:
have religious beliefs affected decisions about work, sex, or drugs

School Questionnaire: Topics covered in the school questionnaire include teacher assessment of the behavior and performance of the child.

Classroom characteristics

Behavior:
absences; need for discipline; social adjustment

Limiting conditions

Performance:
grade placement; academic performance; need for special measures; standardized test scores

Teacher characteristics

Number of Variables

There are a total of 4,118 variables across the three waves of data.

Checklist of Topics Covered

X Gender / Gender Role
X Race / Ethnicity
X Age
X Education
X Occupation / Employment
X Physical Health / Disease
___ Nutrition
X Clinical Activities
X Biological Functioning /
   Development
X Mental Health / Disease
X Psychological Functioning /
   Development
X Guidance / Counseling
X Personality
X Intellectual Functioning
X Residential Mobility
X Dwelling
X Neighborhood /
   Community
X Region / State
X Marriage and Divorce
X Cohabitation
X Family/Household
   Composition & Structure
X Inter-Partner Relationships
X Parent-Child Relationships
X Inter-Sibling Relationships
X Relationships with Other Kin

X Relationships with Nonkin
X Other Family/Household
   Characteristics
X Child Care
X Wealth / Finances / Material
   Things
X Receipt of Health, Mental
   Health, Social Services
X Adoption / Foster Care
X Childbearing / Pregnancy
X Out-of-Wedlock Pregnancy
   & Parenthood
X Abortion
X Sexuality
X Sex Education
X Contraception
X Sexually Transmitted
   Diseases
X Civic/Political Activities
X Friends / Social Activities
   Social Support
X Dating, Courtship
X Recreation
X Religion
X Crime / Delinquency /
   Behavior Problems
X Substance Use
___ Agency Characteristics
X Interview

Checklist of Key Variables

X Number of family members
X Identification of marital
   partners in family
X Size of dwelling
X Type of dwelling
X Urban/rural residence
X Region/state of residence
X Family income
X Religious affiliation
X Relation of each family
   member to:
   X Reference person
   X All other members
X Age of family members
   X Respondent
   X Others
X Sex of family members

   X Respondent
   X Others
X Race of family members
   X Respondent
   X Others
X Marital status of family
   members
   X Respondent
   X Others
X Education of family
   members
   X Respondent
   X Others
X Occupation of family
   members
   X Respondent
   X Others

LIMITATIONS

The initial response rate and the Wave II and III follow-up rates were all about 80 percent. While these response and follow-up rates are reasonably good, the cumulative effect across all three waves is that only 52 percent of those originally found to be eligible to be interviewed were included in the Wave III data. (This statistic adjusts for the subsampling done between Waves II and III.) To reduce biases introduced by selective attrition and response, the data have been re-weighted to match independent estimates on a set of factors which were found to be important predictors of attrition: age, sex, race, city size, family income, and residential location. Additionally, an adjustment was made for subsampling between Waves I and II. As a result, the weighted data are representative of the U.S. population of children born between September 1964 and December 1969 and living in the U.S. in 1976.

SPONSORSHIP

Wave I of the NSC was sponsored by the Foundation for Child Development (FCD) and the field work was conducted by the Institute for Survey Research. The 1981 Wave II research was jointly sponsored by the National Institute of Mental Health and FCD. The 1987 Wave III research was sponsored by the National Institute of Child Health and Human Development, the Office of the Assistant Secretary for Planning and Evaluation, the Robert Wood Johnson Foundation, and the Ford Foundation.

GUIDE TO DATA AND DOCUMENTATION

File Structure

Machine-readable files for Waves I, II, and III (merged) are available in both mainframe and microcomputer formats from the American Family Data Archive (AFDA data set 6-12). Unless otherwise requested, files formatted for a mainframe computer are provided on a 9-track tape at a density of 6250 bpi, in EBCDIC recording mode with IBM Standard Labels. Ordinarily, files formatted for a microcomputer are provided in ASCII format on high-density 5¼" diskettes. Other formats are available at the user's request. A description of the contents of each machine-readable file is given below:

File 1 (Data): Raw data file. The format of this file is described in the "data list" section of the SPSS program file (file 2).

File 2 (SPSS Program): This file consists of SPSS program statements designed to read the raw data in file 1 and create an SPSS active file. For mainframe orders, the program statements conform to SPSS-X syntax; for microcomputer orders, the program statements conform to SPSS/PC and SPSS/PC+ syntax. The SPSS program file contains data list statements, variable names and labels, value labels, and missing value declarations.

File 3 (SAS Program): This file consists of SAS program statements designed to read the raw data in file 1 and create a SAS active file. The contents of this file are analogous to the contents of the previously described file 2. SPSS users should use file 2; SAS users, file 3.

File 4 (Dictionary; mainframe orders only): Sequential list of variable and value labels. This file consists of DISPLAY DICTIONARY output describing the SPSS-X active file created by the program in File 2. Variables are listed in sequential order. Variable names and labels, value labels, missing value designations, print formats, and write formats are clearly displayed.

File 5 (Statistics; mainframe orders only): Unweighted frequencies or other descriptive statistics for each variable. Descriptive statistics only are provided for variables with more than 50 value categories, such as respondent identification number, zip codes, etc.

List of Available Documentation

A User's Guide which accompanies the machine-readable files provides the following information: Summary; General study overview; Description of machine-readable files and supplementary documentation; Specifications for machine-readable files; Key characteristics report; Distribution of variables by topic and type; and Data completeness and consistency report.

Paper versions of the machine-readable SPSS or SAS program files and data documentation, and copies of the original instrument and codebook are available upon request (at 15 cents per page).

Contact

American Family Data Archive
Sociometrics Corporation
170 State Street, Suite 260
Los Altos, CA 94022-2812
(415) 949-3282

Cost

The cost for the machine-readable data set (Data Set 06-12 of the American Family Data Archive) is $150. This price includes the raw data, SPSS program statements, the SAS program statements, the Dictionary, and the Frequencies in mainframe or microcomputer format, and the accompanying printed and bound User's Guide. The CD-ROM version costs $175. If you wish to obtain paper versions of the original NSC Codebooks, they are priced as follows: Wave I, $71.55, Wave II, $36.15, and Wave III, $45.15. Paper versions of the original NSC Instruments are priced as follows: Wave I, $20.25, Wave II, $18.30, and Wave III, $23.85.

BIBLIOGRAPHY

Furstenberg, F.F., Jr., Morgan, P.A., Moore, K.A., & Peterson, J.L. (1987). Race differences in the timing of adolescent intercourse. *American Sociological Review, 52*(4), 511-518.

Furstenberg, F.F., & Nord, C.W. (1985). Parenting apart: Patterns of childrearing after divorce. *Journal of Marriage and the Family, 47*: 893-904.

Furstenberg, Jr., F.F., Nord, C.W., & Zill, N. (1983) The life course of children of divorce: Marital disruption and parental contact. *American Sociological Review, 48*(5): 656-668.

Moore, K.A., Nord, C.W., & Peterson, J.L. (1989). Nonvoluntary sexual activity among adolescents. *Family Planning Perspectives, 21*(3), 110-114.

Moore, K.A., & Peterson, J.L. (1989). *Wave 3 of the national survey of children: Description of data (final report)*. Washington, DC.

Moore, K.A., Peterson, J.L., & Furstenberg, F.F., Jr. (1986). Parental attitudes and the occurrence of early sexual activity. *Journal of Marriage and the Family, 48*(4), 777-782.

Peterson, J.L., & Zill, N. (1981). Television viewing and children's intellectual, social, and emotional development. *Television & Children, 4*, 21-28.

Peterson, J.L., & Zill, N. (1986). Marital disruption, parent-child relationships, and behavioral problems in children. *Journal of Marriage and the Family, 48*(2), 295-307.

Zill, N., & Peterson, J.L. (1982, January). *Trends in the behavior and emotional well-being of U.S. children: Findings from a national survey*. Paper presented at the Annual Meeting of the American Association for the Advancement of Science, Washington, DC, Washington, DC: Child Trends.

Zill, N., & Peterson, J.L. (1982). Learning to do things without help. In L. M. Laosa & I. E. Sigel (Eds.), *Families as learning environments for children*. New York: Plenum.

Zill, N. (1983). *Divorce, marital conflict and children's mental health: Research findings and policy recommendations*. Testimony to the U.S. Senate Committee on Labor and Human Resources, Subcommittee on Family and Human Services.

Zill, N., & Peterson, J.L. (1983). *Marital disruption and children's needs for psychological help*. Working paper. Washington, DC: Child Trends.

Zill, N., Peterson, J.L., Moore, K.A., & Furstenberg, F.F. Jr. (1990). *1976-1987 national survey of children: waves 1, 2, and 3 (Child Trends, Inc.)* (Data Set 6-12, Crutchfield, J.H., Schwarz, S.M., and Card, J.J., Archivists) [machine-readable data file and documentation]. Washington, DC: Child Trends, Inc. (Producer). Los Altos, CA: Sociometrics Corporation, American Family Data Archive (Producer and Distributor).

Zill, N., & Rhoads, A. (1991). *Assessing family strengths in a national sample of families with adolescent children*. Washington, DC: Child Trends.

6

STANFORD CHILD CUSTODY STUDY, 1984-1990

Eleanor E. Maccoby
Robert H. Mnookin
Charlene E. Depner

PURPOSE OF THE STUDY

The Stanford Child Custody Project embodies two studies. The first, Study I, focuses on the evolution of child custody arrangements in divorcing families; Study II is a follow-up of adolescents from the Study I sample. The present report concerns Study I. Study II data are still being analyzed by the original investigators as of this writing and are not yet publicly available.

The Stanford Child Custody Study (Study I) is a three wave, longitudinal study of post-separation child custody arrangements in a sample of 1,124 families who filed for divorce in two California counties. All parents filed for divorce in either San Mateo or Santa Clara Counties between September 1984 and April 1985, and all had at least one child under the age of 16 at the outset of the study. Three separate telephone interviews were conducted with parents over a three-year period. Additional information was drawn from court records to determine the sequence of legal events and their relationship to the day-to-day lives of families. The study's longitudinal design serves to clarify several basic processes associated with divorce, including: 1) the evolution and maintenance of residence and visitation arrangements; 2) the legal process leading to settlement; 3) the degree of conflict and cooperation between divorced parents; 4) disengagement or continued involvement of the noncustodial parent; 5) compliance with legal and informal agreements; 6) family reorganization; and 7) remarriage.

American divorce law has undergone a number of recent reforms, and California has been at the vanguard of these reforms. One major change has been the shift away from the presumption in favor of maternal custody. At present, the law in nearly every state insists that no custody preference be given simply on the basis of gender. In fact, many states have gone beyond an insistence on gender neutrality in custody decisions to the promotion of joint custody arrangements and continued contact with both parents. In addition, the family legal system seems to be moving away from judicial regulation of post-divorce family life toward mediation and other methods of private dispute resolution. These reforms and their relationships to legal conflict, to co-parenting, and to stability and change in the post separation roles of mothers as compared with fathers provided the focus for this study of how divorcing parents make custodial arrangements for their children.

The Stanford Child Custody Study focuses on four central areas of inquiry:

1. *Gender role differentiation.* How are parental responsibilities, in fact, divided after divorce? By what processes are arrangements arrived at, and how similar are mothers and fathers in their post-separation parental roles?

2. *Legal conflict.* How much legal conflict is involved in the resolution of issues about custody, visitation, and financial support? Where there is conflict, how is it resolved?

3. *Contact: maintenance and change.* As time passes, how viable do the different arrangements for custody and visitation prove to be? Do arrangements that seemed to fit the family circumstances at the time of parental separation become obsolete as family circumstances change? How flexibly can families adapt their arrangements to such changes?; and

4. *Co-parenting relationships.* How commonly are divorced parents able to cooperate in regard to the daily lives of the children? When parents remain involved with the children, how frequently are the co-parental relationships instead characterized by conflict, in which the parents fight, or by disengagement, in which they avoid conflict by not communicating?

For Study I, investigators did not attempt to determine the adjustment of individual parents and children for the purposes of this study. Instead, the focus was on how custodial arrangements are set in place and how they work out over time.

METHODS

Four key features characterize the research design employed by this study. First, a longitudinal approach was employed in order to capture the dynamic process of family breakup and reorganization. A series of three interviews was conducted with divorcing parents to collect prospective data and to reduce bias introduced by intervening events and post hoc reconstruction of events by respondents. Retrospective questions were used to obtain information about events occurring between or before the measurement periods.

Second, investigators followed a cohort of families who all initiated the divorce process at roughly the same time. All participants began the study at an equivalent point in time (the onset of divorce) and engaged in successive interviews conducted according to the same timetable. The use of a cohort design permitted investigators to observe the status of families across a comparable set of marker points and ensured that differences between groups were not simply attributable to variation in time since the divorce.

Third, every effort was made to locate and recruit both parents for this study in order to achieve a balanced perspective on family interactions during and after divorce. However, limiting the sample to only those families in which both parents agreed to participate would have produced a severely biased sample; therefore, participation by both parents was sought but not required. Of the 1,124 families in the Time 1 data collection, 44% had both parents participating, 39% had only the mothers participating, and 17% had only the fathers involved. The most common reason for one-parent participation was the inability to locate the second parent. In the final year of the study, a concerted effort was made to locate non-resident parents who were not previously interviewed, and an additional 43 mothers and 110 father were included in the third wave of the study.

Fourth, investigators attempted to develop a sample with sufficient breadth and heterogeneity to permit comparisons of subgroups of families (for example, those with differing forms of custody, the full range of children's ages, varied economic circumstances, and diverse cultural backgrounds). Investigators were successful in recruiting subjects with a good dispersion of family characteristics, including the age, number, and sex of children and the sociodemographic status of parents. In addition, the ethnic composition of the sample is similar to that of the counties from which it was drawn. Blacks, Asians, native Americans are included in small proportions. Hispanics are the only minority group that is large enough (12%) to permit comparative analyses.

Sampling Design

The names of currently divorcing families were drawn from court records of divorce petitions in two California counties (Santa Clara County and San Mateo County). Eligible families were those initiating their divorces between September 1984 and March 1985 and who had children who would remain minors throughout the course of the study. Families who had been separated for a lengthy period prior to the formal initiation of divorce proceedings (more than fourteen months) were excluded from the study.

Of the 6,685 petitions for divorce that were screened for eligibility, 2,286 met the sampling criteria. Investigators attempted to locate potentially eligible families by using information contained in court records as well as telephone listings, reverse directories, calls to neighbors, or other referrals. Of those families that appeared eligible from the initial court records, 1,966 met the criteria for target families. Investigators located at least one parent in 1,395 of the eligible families and recruited 1,124 into the study.

Periodicity

The panel was interviewed at three points in time. The first (Time 1) occurred shortly after the petition for divorce was filed, typically about six months after separation. The second interview (Time 2) took place one year after the first (approximately one and a half years after separation), when many of the divorces had been completed. The third interview (Time 3) occurred after an additional two years had passed (about three and a half years after separation). At this time, protracted divorce proceedings were ending, and sufficient time had passed for families to establish new routines and relationships.

Unit of Analysis

Analysis can be done at the individual or family level. The data from the study have been split into two separate but linkable data sets: the first contains information about parents' feelings, attitudes, and general arrangements concerning the divorce; the second contains information about individual children. Family level analyses can be done by merging the two data sets on a special family ID variable.

Sample Size and Response Rates

Of the 6,685 petitions for divorce that were screened for eligibility, 2,286 appeared to be eligible for the study. Of those, an estimated 1,966 families fit the criteria for target families. By the conclusion of the initial data collection period (August 1985), investigators had located 61 percent of the families who appeared to be eligible according to the court dockets. Of the 1,395 eligible families who were located, the vast majority was willing to be interviewed, and 1,124 families were recruited into the study. There were 41 families in which both parents refused to participate, resulting in a refusal rate of 3 percent.

A comparison of families who were recruited into the study and eligible families who did not participate revealed that recruited and nonrecruited families were similar in family size and the gender of the children. The two groups did not differ significantly in the length of divorce proceedings, the likelihood of being awarded child support, or the amount of such awards, although an investigation of court records suggested that the proportion of unresolved divorces at the close of the study was higher among nonrecruited families. Recruited families appeared to show a "joint custody bias": They were less likely than nonrecruited families to leave legal custody requests unspecified and more likely to request both joint legal custody and joint physical custody. In addition, recruited families were more likely to be those whose children spent substantial time in both parental households rather than residing solely with one parent. Taken together, these findings suggest that the sample includes a somewhat higher proportion of families who prefer to share childrearing responsibilities than would be found among all divorcing families. Although attrition after initial recruitment was very low, sample loss served to accentuate this joint-custody bias.

Attrition

At Time 2, only those families who had participated at Time 1 were followed; no further attempts were made to locate or recruit other families eligible at Time 1. An estimated 4.6 percent of the families in the Time 1 sample were no longer eligible at Time 2 (primarily due to reconciliation). Of the 1, 072 families remaining eligible, approximately 5 percent could not be located, and an approximate 3 percent refused to participate. The remaining 978 families (91 percent) were interviewed. An estimated 1,002 families remained eligible to be interviewed at Time 3. Of these, about 7 percent could not be located, and an additional 1.5 percent refused to be interviewed. The remaining 91.5 percent were interviewed.

Sample Structure

	Wave I	*Wave II*	*Wave III*
Records Reviewed	6,685	—	—
Cases Pursued	2,286	1,124	1,075
Estimated Eligible	1,966	1,915	1,798
Wave I Families Eligible	—	1,072	1,002
Families Not Located	891	61	78
Family Located: Not Eligible	230	49	114
Family Located: Not Recruited	41	36	15
Families Recruited	**1,124**	**978**	**917**

Sample Structure (continued)

	Wave I	*Wave II*	*Wave III*
Parents Recruited	1,615	1,398	1,444
Mothers Recruited	936	799	783
Fathers Recruited	679	599	661
Both Parents Interviewed	491	420	527
Child Information	1,875	1,613	1,487
% of Pursued Cases Located	61.02	94.57	92.74
% of Estimated Eligible Families Recruited	57.16	51.08	51.00
% of Pursued Cases Recruited	54.67		
Loss Due to Location	43.34		
Loss Due to Refusal	1.99		
% of Pursued Cases Maintained		90.98	
Loss Due to Location		9.02	
Loss Due to Refusal		3.35	

The greatest loss to the sample resulted from a failure to locate eligible families at Time 1. Families remaining eligible at subsequent interviews were recruited at a rate of over 90 percent. Location difficulties remained the primary source of attrition among eligible families. Of the 1,124 families who started the study, data for all three waves of the study are available for 880, data for at least two waves are available for 135, and data for only one wave are available for 109 families.

Retention Rates

	% of Wave I Sample	% of Wave II Subset
Wave II	87.0	—
Wave III	81.6	93.8

CONTENT

Data Sources

Data were drawn from survey interviews. Each interview lasted approximately one hour, the duration varying with the number of children, the complexity of the dissolution process, and the verbal fluency of the respondent. Although telephone interviewing was the primary mode of data collection, face-to-face interviews and mail questionnaires were made available to respondents in order to maximize participation rates.

Questionnaires were administered to at least one parent in each target family. Whenever possible, both parents were interviewed; but, when one parent was not available, information on that parent was provided by the participating parent. Information on the children in the family was provided by the participating parent(s). In situations where the prospective subject was unable to be reached by telephone, a shorter, self-administered version of the questionnaire was mailed to the respondent.

During the first wave of data collection, 1,231 parents were interviewed by telephone or in person, and 384 completed a shorter version of the form by mail. Once investigators had established telephone information for a participant, subsequent interviews were able to be conducted by telephone or in person. At Time 2, only 28 interviews were conducted by mail, and no mail interviews were conducted at Time 3. For the initial two waves of data collection, the interview was translated into Spanish and administered by a bilingual interviewer to respondents who preferred to complete all or part of the interview in Spanish. At Time 1, this procedure added 31 families to the sample. These families were followed at Time 2, but funding constraints at Time 3 made it impossible to maintain the bilingual component of the study.

In addition to the interviews, further information was obtained from the court records themselves for the 933 divorces that were completed by September 1989. Investigators conducted a content analysis of the court records of the divorce proceedings and coded information about the duration of divorce proceedings, the involvement of third parties (e.g., attorneys and mediators), contested issues and their resolution, and the terms of the final judgment. At the conclusion of data collection in the summer of 1989, 170 families still had not completed legal divorce proceedings.

Description of Variables Covered

The first interview, which was conducted shortly after the divorce filing, obtained information on family background; number, age, and sex of children; financial resources; and education, occupation, and work schedule of the two parents. It also inquired extensively into the negotiation and dispute-resolution process the couple engaged in while attempting to arrive at an agreement on financial and custodial matters. Particular attention was given to the involvement of attorneys, mediators, and other professionals. In addition, interview questions explored the degree of conflict between the former spouses, any logistical problems associated with maintaining custodial and visitation arrangements, the children's reactions to the divorce, and the presence or absence of coordination between the parents with respect to the children's upbringing.

Waves II and III of the study retained many of the variables assessed in Wave I, while deleting some variables and adding others.

Number of Variables

There are a total of 2,459 variables across the three waves of data in the Family file. In the Child file, there are a total of 471 variables across the three waves.

Checklist of Topics Covered

- X Gender / Gender Role
- X Race / Ethnicity
- X Age
- X Education
- X Occupation / Employment
- X Physical Health / Disease
- ___ Nutrition
- X Clinical Activities
- X Biological Functioning / Development
- X Mental Health / Disease
- X Psychological Functioning / Development
- X Guidance / Counseling
- X Personality
- X Intellectual Functioning
- X Residential Mobility
- ___ Dwelling
- ___ Neighborhood / Community
- ___ Region / State
- X Marriage and Divorce
- X Cohabitation
- X Family/Household Composition & Structure
- X Inter-Partner Relationships
- X Parent-Child Relationships
- ___ Inter-Sibling Relationships
- X Relationships with Other Kin

- X Relationships with Nonkin
- X Other Family/Household Characteristics
- X Child Care
- X Wealth / Finances / Material Things
- X Receipt of Health, Mental Health, Social Services
- ___ Adoption / Foster Care
- ___ Childbearing / Pregnancy
- ___ Out-of-Wedlock Pregnancy & Parenthood
- ___ Abortion
- ___ Sexuality
- ___ Sex Education
- ___ Contraception
- ___ Sexually Transmitted Diseases
- ___ Civic/Political Activities
- ___ Friends / Social Activities
- ___ Social Support
- X Dating, Courtship
- X Recreation
- X Religion
- X Crime / Delinquency / Behavior Problems
- ___ Substance Use
- ___ Agency Characteristics
- X Interview

Checklist of Key Variables

___ Number of family members
X Identification of marital
    partners in family
___ Size of dwelling
X Type of dwelling
___ Urban/rural residence
___ Region/state of residence
X Family income
X Religious affiliation
X Relation of each family
    member to:
    X Reference person
    ___ All other members
X Age of family members
    X Respondent
    X Others
X Sex of family members

___ Respondent
X Others
X Race of family members
    X Respondent
    X Others
X Marital status of family
    members
    X Respondent
    X Others
X Education of family
    members
    X Respondent
    X Others
X Occupation of family
    members
    X Respondent
    X Others

LIMITATIONS

Since divorcing families were sampled from court records in only two California counties, the findings of this study may not be generalizable to divorcing families across the nation.

SPONSORSHIP

Funding for the research was provided by the National Institutes of Health (Contract 1R01 H019386) and the Stanford Center for Research on Families, Children and Youth (Contract 15165-01-00).

GUIDE TO DATA AND DOCUMENTATION

File Structure

Machine-readable data and documentation files are available in both mainframe and microcomputer formats from the American Family Data Archive (AFDA). The data from the study have been split into two separate data sets: the first contains information about parents' feelings, attitudes, and general arrangements concerning the divorce (AFDA data set 25-27); the second contains information about individual children (AFDA data set 28-30). Family level analyses can be done by merging the two data sets on a special family ID variable. Unless otherwise requested, files formatted for a mainframe computer are provided on a 9-track tape at a density of 6250 bpi, in EBCDIC recording mode with IBM Standard Labels. Ordinarily, files formatted for a microcomputer are provided in ASCII format on high-density 5¼" diskettes. Other formats, including CD-ROM, are available at the user's request. A description of the contents of each machine-readable file is given below:

File 1 (Data): Raw data file. The format of this file is described in the "data list" section of the SPSS program file (File 2).

File 2 (SPSS Program): This file consists of SPSS program statements designed to read the raw data in File 1 and create an SPSS active file. For mainframe orders, the program statements conform to SPSS-X syntax; for microcomputer orders, the program statements conform to SPSS/PC and SPSS/PC+ syntax. The SPSS program file contains data list statements, variable names and labels, value labels, and missing value declarations.

File 3 (SAS Program): This file consists of SAS program statements designed to read the raw data in File 1 and create an SAS active file. The contents of this file are analogous to the contents of the previously described File 2. SPSS users should use File 2; SAS users, File 3.

File 4 (Dictionary; mainframe orders only): Sequential list of variable and value labels. This file consists of DISPLAY DICTIONARY output describing the SPSS-X active file created by the program in File 2. Variables are listed in sequential order. Variable names and labels, value labels, missing value designations, print formats, and write formats are clearly displayed.

File 5 (Statistics; mainframe orders only): Unweighted frequencies or other descriptive statistics for each variable. Descriptive statistics only are provided for variables with more than 50 value categories, such as respondent identification number, zip codes, etc.

List of Available Documentation

Two User's Guides, one accompanying the machine-readable files for each of the two data sets (AFDA data set 25-27 and AFDA data set 28-30), provide the following information: Summary; General study overview; Description of machine-readable files and supplementary documentation; Specifications for machine-readable files; Key characteristics report; Distribution of variables by topic and type; and Data completeness and consistency report.

Paper versions of the machine-readable SPSS program files and data documentation, as well as copies of the original instrument and codebook are available upon request (at 15 cents per page).

Contact

Sociometrics Corporation
American Family Data Archive
170 State Street, Suite 260
Los Altos, CA 94022-2812
(415) 949-3282

Cost

The cost for the machine-readable data sets (Data Set 25-27 and Data Set 28-30 of the American Family Data Archive) is $100 each. This price includes the raw data, SPSS program statements, SAS program statements, Dictionary, Frequencies on mainframe tape or microcomputer diskette, and the accompanying printed and bound User's Guide. The CD-ROM versions of each data set are priced at $175 each. Paper versions of the original Instruments can be obtained for the following prices: Wave 1, $11.85; Wave 2, $13.35; and Wave 3, $16.95.

BIBLIOGRAPHY

Albiston, C.R., Maccoby, E.E., & Mnookin, R.H. (1990, Spring). Does joint legal custody matter? *Stanford Law and Policy Review*.

Buchanan, C., Maccoby, E.E., & Dornbusch, S.M. (1991). Caught between parents: Adolescents' experience in divorced homes. *Child Development, 62*, 1008-1029.

Kaplan, A.S., Lang, E.L., & Card, J.J. (1993). *Stanford child custody study, family 1984-1990: A user's guide to the machine-readable files and documentation*. Los Altos, CA: Sociometrics Corporation, American Family Data Archive.

Kaplan, A.S., Lang, E.L., & Card, J.J. (1993). *Stanford child custody study, child 1984-1990: A user's guide to the machine-readable files and documentation*. Los Altos, CA: Sociometrics Corporation, American Family Data Archive.

Maccoby, E.E., Buchanan, C.M., Mnookin, R.H., & Dornbusch, S.M. (in press). Post-divorce roles of mothers and fathers in the lives of their children. *Journal of Family Psychology*.

Maccoby, E.E., Depner, C.E., & Mnookin, R.H. (1988). Custody of children following divorce. In E. M. Hetherington and J. D. Arasteh (Eds.), *Impact of divorce single parenting and stepparenting on children*. Hillsdale, NJ: Lawrence Erlbaum.

Maccoby, E.E., Depner, C.E., & Mnookin, R.H. (1990). Coparenting in the second year after divorce. *Journal of Marriage and the Family, 52,* 141-155.

Maccoby, E.E., & Mnookin, R.H. (1992). *Dividing the child: Social and legal dilemmas of custody*. Cambridge, MA: Harvard University Press.

Mnookin, R.H., Maccoby, E.E., Albiston, C.R., & Depner, C.E. (1990). Private ordering revisited: What custodial arrangements are parents negotiating? In S. D. Sugarman and H. H. Kay (Eds.), *Divorce reform at the crossroads*. New Haven, CT: Yale University Press.

7

1980, 1982, 1984, AND 1986 HIGH SCHOOL AND BEYOND SOPHOMORE AND SENIOR COHORTS

The National Center for Education Statistics

PURPOSE OF THE STUDY

The High School and Beyond Longitudinal Study was conducted by the National Opinion Research Center (NORC) for the National Center for Education Statistics (NCES) as part of NCES' ongoing effort to gather policy-relevant data on education in the United States. This study followed cohorts of sophomore and senior high school students as they moved into adulthood. Base year data were collected in 1980 from administrators, teachers, parents, and students from 1,015 secondary schools. Sophomore and senior cohorts completed questionnaires and a battery of cognitive tests. Three follow-up surveys were administered in 1982, 1984, and 1986, focusing primarily on the student cohorts. A wide variety of data are available from this study, including transcript information, course offerings and enrollments, and teacher ratings for many student participants.

METHODS

Sampling Design

This study was conducted using a two-stage, stratified, clustered sampling design.

1980 Sampling Procedures: Sampling proceeded in two stages. A stratified, disproportionate probability sample produced 1,015 secondary schools as first stage units of selection. Schools were stratified by type, e.g., regular and alternative public, high-performance private, and Black, Cuban, or regular Catholic. The following strata were oversampled for the purposes of policy analysis: public schools with high percentages of Hispanic students; Catholic schools with high percentages of minority students; alternative public schools; and private schools with high-achieving students. Substitutions were made for schools refusing to participate in the study.

From the secondary school sample, 36 seniors and 36 sophomores were randomly selected from each participating school. Substitution was not used for sampled students refusing to participate. In schools with fewer than 36 students in these categories, all eligible students were included. Siblings, co-twins, and -triplets of 1,348 sampled students were identified as a nonprobability sample for inclusion into the study. School programs and attributes were assessed through a questionnaire distributed to principals or administrators from each school. A subsample of 14,103 teachers evaluated 18,291 students participating in the study. Parents of 3,367 sophomores and 3,197 seniors were selected for the parent questionnaire. A total of 28,240 seniors and 30,030 sophomores participated in the base year survey.

Sample Design for 1982, 1984, and 1986 Follow-Up Surveys: The sampling design employed in base year data collection was maintained in subsequent waves of data collection. In the 1982 follow-up, all sophomores sampled in 1980 were selected to participate in the 1982 follow-up, even if they had not actually participated in the base year survey. Seniors selected for the 1980 survey were subsampled for the 1982, 1984, and 1986 follow-ups. Students who were chosen for the study in 1980 but did not participate were approached again for participation in the 1982 follow-up survey.

Sampling Weights: The NCES has developed nine sample weights to compensate for oversampling of particular strata, unequal probabilities of participant selection, and different completion rates for follow-up surveys. Rationale and description of calculations for the weighting scheme are found in the Data File User's Manual compiled by the National Center for Education Statistics.

Periodicity

Data collection for High School and Beyond began in fall of 1980. Follow-up surveys were administered in 1982, 1984, and 1986. This study has been designed to augment the National Longitudinal Study of the High School Class of 1972 (NLS-72). Many items from the NLS-72 have been repeated in High School and Beyond, making direct comparisons between data sets possible.

Unit of Analysis

Primary units of analysis are the individual student and the student cohort.

Response Rates

Table 1 below shows 1980 base year response rates for senior and sophomore cohorts. The Data File User's Manual provides a complete breakdown of sample selection rates by school strata and sample allocation for student cohorts in subsequent waves of data collection.

Table 1

1980 Base Year Response Rates by Cohort

	Initial Selection	Questionnaire Completed N	%	Test Completed N	%
Sophomores	35,723	30,030	84	27,569	77
Seniors	35,981	28,240	81	25,069	72
Total	70,704	58,270	82	52,638	74

Attrition

Follow-up survey completion rates for the senior cohort were 94 percent in 1982, 91 percent in 1984, and 88 percent in 1986. Rates for the sophomore cohort are available in the Data File User's Manual for the 1980 Sophomore Cohort compiled by the National Center for Education Statistics.

CONTENT

Data Sources

Data were compiled from six primary sources: school administrators, teachers, students, parents of selected students, and transcript and financial aid records. Base year data were collected through on-campus administration of student surveys and tests. Students completed instruments as a group, and were permitted one hour to complete the questionnaire. Cognitive tests were administered immediately after questionnaires were collected. School, teacher, and parent questionnaires were distributed through the mail. Transcript and financial aid records were collected by principals or school administrators and released to the National Opinion Research Center (NORC). Follow-up data collection was accomplished primarily through mail-in questionnaire. Nonrespondents to mail surveys were interviewed by telephone or in person. All data collection was conducted by NORC.

Description of Variables Covered

Survey instruments administered in the base year included: student questionnaire and ID pages; cognitive test battery; school questionnaire; teacher comment checklist; and parent questionnaire. The cognitive test battery assessed verbal and quantitative abilities in both cohorts. The sophomore test included science and writing achievement measures, and the senior test measured abstract and nonverbal abilities. The student questionnaire included variables in the following topic areas:

> Education
>> coursework
>> performance
>> college plans
>> influence of peers, parents and teachers on goals
>> school-related activities
>> attitudes toward school
> Social and Demographic Characteristics
> Personality
> Personal Attitudes and Beliefs
> Family Background

Follow-up questionnaire included new topics relevant to the life experiences of each cohort, as well as items from previous questionnaire. For example, in 1982 former sophomores received the senior questionnaire, while former seniors updated demographic and family history information and answered questions related to work force participation, marital status, and post-high school education. Other follow-up survey topics included:

> Alcohol Use
> Computer Literacy
> Graduate Education Programs
> Military Experience

Unemployment History
Income and Financial Status
Voting and Television Habits
Personal Values

Data from school, administrator, teacher, and parent questionnaires have been organized into separate files by cohort. The following variables are included in each file:

School File: This file includes variables assessing institutional characteristics; faculty composition; enrollment; instructional programs; course offerings; participation in Federal programs or policy relevant groups; funding sources. The School questionnaire was completed by principals (or administrators) for all schools in the study (1980; 1982).

High School Offerings and Enrollments: Course offerings are identified by 6-digit code and can be linked to other data files. Data for 957 schools are included (1980; 1982)

Administrator and Teacher Survey: This questionnaire assessed school goals, work load, staff attitudes, guidance services. The instrument was distributed to a sample of 457 schools with responses from 10,370 teachers and 402 principals or other administrators (1984).

Local Labor Market Indicators: This file includes wage rates, employment, and personal income by state and is linked with school identification code (1980; 1982).

Language File: The language file contains 11,303 records for the combined sample of sophomores and seniors concerning experiences with non-English language usage (1980).

Parent File: This file contains questionnaire data from parents of 3,367 sophomores and 3197 seniors from student sample. Items include parents' education history, employment patterns, income, and plans for childrens' education (1980).

Twin and Sibling File: Responses from sampled twins, triplets, and sibs, and from twins and triplets of sample members make up this file. Included are 2,718 records. Twins or triplets are linked with family identification code (1980).

Teachers' Comments File: This file includes comments from teachers of students in both cohorts. Students were rated by an average of four different teachers (1980; 1984).

Friends' File: 58,270 records contain identification numbers of sampled students who reported having up to three friends within the sample. The file identifies first, second, and third choice friends (1980).

Transcripts File: This file contains grades, recorded absences, suspensions, and limited information about students who have dropped out of school. Standardized test scores are also included (1982).

Number of Variables

Cohort Files	1980	1982	1984	1986
Sophomore	638	1,885	2,500	3,300
Senior	638	1,713	2,400	3,200

Other Files : 1980 through 1986, for both cohorts

Administrators/Teachers/Counselors	1,143
School	269
Transcript	217
Course Offerings	480
Labor Market	56
Language	42
Parents	22
Friends	4

Checklist of Topics Covered

_X_ Gender / Gender Role
_X_ Race / Ethnicity
_X_ Age
_X_ Education
_X_ Occupation / Employment
_X_ Physical Health / Disease
___ Nutrition
___ Clinical Activities
___ Biological Functioning / Development
___ Mental Health / Disease
_X_ Psychological Functioning / Development
_X_ Guidance / Counseling
_X_ Personality
_X_ Intellectual Functioning
___ Residential Mobility
_X_ Dwelling
___ Neighborhood / Community
_X_ Region / State
_X_ Marriage and Divorce
___ Cohabitation
_X_ Family/Household Composition & Structure
___ Inter-Partner Relationships
___ Parent-Child Relationships
___ Inter-Sibling Relationships
___ Relationships with Other Kin

___ Relationships with Nonkin
___ Other Family/Household Characteristics
___ Child Care
_X_ Wealth / Finances / Material Things
_X_ Receipt of Health, Mental Health, Social Services
___ Adoption / Foster Care
_X_ Childbearing / Pregnancy
___ Out-of-Wedlock Pregnancy & Parenthood
___ Abortion
___ Sexuality
_X_ Sex Education
___ Contraception
___ Sexually Transmitted Diseases
_X_ Civic/Political Activities
_X_ Friends / Social Activities
___ Social Support
___ Dating, Courtship
_X_ Recreation
_X_ Religion
_X_ Crime / Delinquency / Behavior Problems
_X_ Substance Use
___ Agency Characteristics
_X_ Interview

Checklist of Key Variables

X Number of family members
___ Identification of marital
    partners in family
X Size of dwelling
___ Type of dwelling
X Urban/rural residence
X Region/state of residence
X Family income
X Religious affiliation
X Relation of each family
   member to:
   X Reference person
   ___ All other members
X Age of family members
   X Respondent
   ___ Others
X Sex of family members

 X Respondent
___ Others
X Race of family members
   X Respondent
   ___ Others
X Marital status of family
   members
   X Respondent
   ___ Others
X Education of family
   members
   X Respondent
   X Others
X Occupation of family
   members
   X Respondent
   X Others

LIMITATIONS

The complexity of the sampling design used in this study carries potential sources of bias. Therefore, the NCES recommends that sampling weights be used for all forms of statistical analysis. Several limitations to this study have also been noted by Zill and Peterson (1989). First, students provided almost 90 percent of the family background information available in this data set. However, some unreliability has been found in family background information provided by students when compared with the same information from their parents. Second, on 1980 questionnaires, many demographic variables were located at the end of the questionnaire. Slower students may have been unable to complete these items, and some descriptive data may be missing. For base year data collection, survey representatives reviewed all questionnaires at the survey site and gathered missing data whenever possible. The proportion of missing data was 29.1 percent for the senior cohort and 32.5 percent for the sophomore cohort. Finally, because the senior cohort was sampled from the in-school population, information on high school dropouts is available for the sophomore cohort only.

SPONSORSHIP

This study was sponsored by the National Center for Education Statistics, U.S. Department of Education, Contract number 300-84-0169. Oversampling of Hispanic strata was funded jointly by the Office of Bilingual Education and Minority Language Affairs and the Office for Civil Rights within the Department of Education. Data collection was conducted by the National Opinion Research Center under contract to the National Center for Education Statistics.

File Structure

Magnetic Tapes

Data tapes are available from the National Center for Education Statistics (NCES) and the Inter-university Consortium for Political and Social Research (ICPSR) at the University of Michigan.

NCES: A data tape containing all four waves of data is available for each cohort. Tapes are organized as follows:

1. Raw Data File
   Randomized ID number
   1982 follow-up flags and composites
   Base year questionnaire and test data
   1982 questionnaire data
   Selected base year school items
   1984 questionnaire data
   1984 flags, composites, and weights
   1986 questionnaire data
   1986 flags, composites, and weights
2. Record layout for raw data file
3. SAS control cards
4. SPSS-X control cards

ICPSR: Data files and machine-readable documentation (including SPSS and SAS control cards) are available for individual waves of data collection and are listed in Table 2 on the next two pages.

Table 2. ICPSR Data Files and Machine-Readable Documentation

Filename	Part(s)	Structure	Cases	Vars	Rec Length	Rec/ Case
1982						
Sophomore Cohort	1-3	Rectangular	29,737	1,744	3,115	1
Senior Cohort	4-5	Rectangular	11,995	1,233	2,627	1
Soph Transcripts	6-10	Hierarchical	15,941	141	320/40	
Course Offerings	11-14	Hierarchical	1,032	480	1,041/29	
Market Indicators	15-16	Rectangular	1,015	56	173	1
School Questionnaire	17-18	Rectangular	1,032	415	882	1
1984						
Soph Follow-up	1	Rectangular	14,825	2,500	4,548	1
Record Layout	2-4				80	
Senior Follow-up	5	Rectangular	11,995	2,400	3,762	1
Record Layout	6-8				80	
Student Transcript	9	Rectangular	7,776	25	415	1
Transcript Layout	10				80	
Transcript-Level	11	Rectangular	11,288	23	280	1
Term-Level Transcripts	12	Rectangular	51,730	18	62	1
Course-Level Transcripts	13	Rectangular	216,426	10	58	1
SAS Control Cards	14				80	
Principal Survey	15	Rectangular	402	280	80	10

Table 2. ICPSR Data Files and Machine-Readable Documentation (continued)

Filename	Part(s)	Structure	Cases	Vars	Rec Length	Rec/ Case
1984						
SAS Control Cards	16-28				80	
Counselors Survey	17	Rectangular	324	228	80	10
Guidance Survey	19	Rectangular	400	250	80	9
Teacher Survey	21	Rectangular	10,370	160	80	5
Teacher Survey Weights	23	Rectangular	537	225	80	2
School Survey, 1980	25	Rectangular	537	32	80	1
School Survey, 1982	27	Rectangular	537	25	80	1
1986						
Senior Follow-up	1	Rectangular	11,995	3,200	4,932	1
Record Layout	2				80	
SAS Control Cards	3				80	
SPSS Control Cards	4-9				80	
Sophomore Follow-up	10	Rectangular	14,825	3,300	5,637	1
SPSS Control Cards	11-20				80	
Record Layout	21				80	
SAS Control Cards	22				80	

7 - 12

CD-ROM

Data from the National Center for Education Statistics are available on CD-ROM. The disk includes information from the base year and the 1982, 1984, and 1986 follow-up surveys of high school sophomores and seniors as well as all questionnaire and testing data for both cohorts. In addition, the disk has school data from principals in 1980 and 1982, postsecondary spells of attendance, postsecondary institution characteristics, and student financial aid. Sophomore-only data include: parent responses, high school friends, language, high school transcripts, and postsecondary transcripts.

The disk has an electronic codebook with codes, labels, frequencies, and item wording. In addition, it contains software to create fully labeled SPSS-PC codes which allow the user to select desired variables using the electronic codebook. The ISO compact disk is structured to work within MS-DOS on an IBM-compatible computer with 20 megabytes or more of free hard-disk storage space.

The student data collection for the 4th follow-up (1992) has been completed and additional postsecondary transcripts are being collected now. Following that, a new CD-ROM will be released. The public use version will be in the form of an encrypted data set coupled with a table generator, which will be more user friendly than the current CD-ROM.

List of Available Documentation

Documentation and data tapes can be ordered from:

National Center for Education Statistics
U.S. Department of Education
555 New Jersey Avenue, NW
Washington, D.C. 20208-5652

Or:

Inter-university Consortium for Political and Social Research
P.O. Box 1248
Ann Arbor, Michigan 48106
(313) 763-5010

The NCES CD-ROM can be ordered from:

New Orders
Superintendent of Documents
P.O. Box 371954
Pittsburgh, PA 15250-7954

Contact

For further information about the study, contact the following people at NCES:

Aurora D'Amico (Mrs.)
Postsecondary Education Statistics Division
National Center for Education Statistics
555 New Jersey Avenue, NW
Washington, D.C. 20208-5652
(202) 219-1365
FAX (202) 219-1751

or

C. Dennis Carroll
Project Officer
National Center for Education Statistics
U.S. Department of Education
555 New Jersey Avenue, NW
Washington, D.C. 20208-5652
(202) 219-1774

or

Oliver Moles
Office of Educational Research and Improvement
U.S. Department of Education
555 New Jersey Avenue, NW
Washington, D.C. 20208-5652
(202) 219-1839

Cost

Magnetic tapes from the National Center for Education Statistics cost $175. If more than one tape is ordered at the same time, the price is $75 for the second and subsequent tapes. Please state tape specifications. Payment may be made by check, money order, or credit card.

Make check payable to U.S. Department of Education and mail to:

U.S. Department of Education
Information Technology Branch
555 New Jersey Avenue, NW
Washington, DC 20208-5725

Telephone orders for mainframe tapes may be placed by calling Jack Dusatko at (202) 219-1522.

The NCES CD-ROM data disk (stock #065-000-00470-4) is available for $23. Payment may be made by check (payable to the Superintendent of Documents), GPO Deposit Account, or credit card and mailed to:

New Orders
Superintendent of Documents
P.O. Box 371954
Pittsburgh, PA 15250-7954.

Members of the Inter-university Consortium for Political and Social Research can obtain these data sets from ICPSR at no cost. For nonmembers, the cost depends on the format requested. Contact ICPSR (313-763-5010) for a price quote.

BIBLIOGRAPHY

Carroll, C.D. (1989). *College persistence and degree attainment for 1980 high school graduates: Hazards for transfers, stopouts, and part-timers*. Washington, DC: U.S. Department of Education, Office of Educational Research and Improvement, National Center for Education Statistics.

Carroll, C.D. (1989). *Postsecondary enrollment, persistence, and attainment for 1972, 1980, and 1982 high school graduates*. Washington, DC: U.S. Department of Education, Office of Educational Research and Improvement, National Center for Education Statistics.

Eagle, E., Fitzgerald, R.A., Gifford, A., & Zuma, J. of MPR Associates, Inc. (1988). *High school and beyond—A Descriptive summary of 1980 high school seniors: Six years later*. Washington, DC: U.S. Department of Education, Office of Educational Research and Improvement, National Center for Education Statistics.

Gordon, H. (1990). *Who majors in science? College graduates in science, engineering, or mathematics from the high school class of 1980*. Washington, DC: U.S. Department of Education, Office of Educational Research and Improvement, National Center for Education Statistics.

Inter-university Consortium for Political and Social Research. (1992-1993). *Guide to resources and services*. Ann Arbor, MI: Author.

Kaufman, P. (1990). *The relationship between postsecondary and high school course-taking patterns: The preparation of 1980 high school sophomores who entered postsecondary institutions by 1984*. Washington, DC: U.S. Department of Education, Office of Educational Research and Improvement, National Center for Education Statistics.

Knepper, P.R. (1990). *Trends in postsecondary credit production, 1972 and 1980 high school graduates*. Washington, DC: U.S. Department of Education, Office of Educational Research and Improvement, National Center for Education Statistics.

Knight, S., Sebring, P., Glusberg, M., Hunt, E., & Spencer, B. of the National Opinion Research Center. (1988). *High school and beyond—Sophomore cohort postsecondary education transcript study. Data file users' manual.* Washington, DC: U.S. Department of Education, Office of Educational Research and Improvement, National Center for Education Statistics.

Knight, S., Sebring, P., Glusberg, M., Hunt, E., & Spencer, B. of the National Opinion Research Center. (1988). *High school and beyond—Sophomore cohort postsecondary education transcript study. Technical Report.* Washington, DC: U.S. Department of Education, Office of Educational Research and Improvement, National Center for Education Statistics.

National Center for Education Statistics. (1992). *NCES Data Available on CD-ROM for the First Time.* (Announcement NCES 92-001a). Washington, DC: U.S. Department of Education, Office of Educational Research and Improvement.

National Opinion Research Center. (1981). *High school and beyond school questionnaire.* University of Chicago: Author.

National Opinion Research Center. (1981) *High school and beyond parent questionnaire.* University of Chicago: Author.

National Opinion Research Center. (1980). *High school and beyond information for users.* University of Chicago: Author.

National Opinion Research Center. (1980). *High school and beyond language file code book.* University of Chicago: Author.

National Opinion Research Center. (1987). *High school and beyond, 1980 senior cohort, third follow-up (1986), data file user's manual, volume 2* (Contract No. 300-84-0169). Washington, DC: National Center for Education Statistics.

Spencer, B.D., Sebring, P., & Campbell, B. of the National Opinion Research Center. (1987). *High school and beyond third follow-up 1986. Sample design report*. Washington, DC: U.S. Department of Education, Office of Educational Research and Improvement, National Center for Education Statistics.

West, J. (1989). *The postsecondary vocational education of 1980 high school seniors: The two-year associate of arts degree*. Washington, DC: U.S. Department of Education, Office of Educational Research and Improvement, National Center for Education Statistics.

Zill, N., & Peterson, J.L. (Eds.). (1989). *Guide to federal data on children, youth, and families*. Washington, DC: Child Trends.

8

NATIONAL EDUCATION LONGITUDINAL STUDY OF 1988 (NELS:88) AND FIRST AND SECOND FOLLOW-UPS (1990, 1992)

The National Center for Education Statistics

PURPOSE OF THE STUDY

The National Education Longitudinal Study of 1988 (NELS:88) is a major longitudinal study sponsored by the National Center for Education Statistics of the U.S. Department of Education. It is designed to provide trend data about critical transitions experienced by young people as they develop, attend school, and embark on their careers. NELS:88 will furnish new information on how school policies, teacher practices, and family involvement affect student educational outcomes (i.e., academic achievement, persistence in school, and participation in postsecondary education).

NELS:88 is the third major longitudinal study sponsored by the National Center for Education Statistics of the U.S. Department of Education, the two predecessors being the National Longitudinal Study of the High School Class of 1972 (NLS-72) and High School and Beyond (HS&B). NLS-72 and HS&B surveyed high school seniors (and sophomores for HS&B) through high school, postsecondary education, and work and family formation experiences. Taken together, NELS:88, NLS-72, and HS&B, provide not only measures of educational attainment but also rich explanations of the reasons for and consequences of academic success and failure.

NELS:88 is one of the first national longitudinal education studies to begin surveying students as early as eighth grade. Some 25,000 eighth graders, their parents, their teachers, and their school principals were surveyed. The first and second follow-up surveys revisit the same sample of students in 1990 and again in 1992, when many are in tenth and twelfth grade, respectively.

Data from NELS:88 can be used to investigate the following:

o   students' academic growth over time, and the family, community, school, and classroom factors that promote or inhibit such growth;

o   the transition from middle/junior high school to secondary school;

o   the process of dropping out of school, as it occurs from eighth grade on;

o   the role of the school in helping the disadvantaged;

o   the school experiences and academic performance of language minority students;

o   attracting students to the study of mathematics and science; and

o   the features of effective schools.

METHODS

Sampling Design

Base Year Survey: The 1988 base year survey was conducted using a two-stage, stratified, probability design. A national sampling frame of 39,000 schools with eighth grade students was selected from a database provided by Quality Education Data, Inc. Sample schools were stratified by type (e.g., public, private, religious) and geographic location and then selected with probabilities proportional to their estimated eighth-grade enrollment. Private schools were oversampled. Substitution within superstrata was used for schools that refused to participate in the study. The following schools fell outside the scope of the study and were excluded from the sample: Bureau of Indian Affairs schools; schools for the handicapped; area vocational schools with no direct enrollment; and schools for dependents of U.S. personnel overseas. First-stage sampling resulted in 1,734 selections, of which 1,052 schools participated.

In second-stage sampling, 24 students were randomly selected from each school. In schools with less than 24 eighth-graders, all eligible students were selected. Students were excluded from the sample if: (a) primary enrollment was at another school, (b) a physical or mental disability precluded taking tests and filling out questionnaires, (c) they had dropped out from selected schools, (d) command of English was insufficient to complete tests or questionnaires, (e) they had transferred from selected schools, or (f) the student was deceased. A total of 26,435 students were selected, with 24,599 eighth graders participating in the study.

In addition to the core sample of students, Hispanic and Asian-Pacific Islander students were oversampled, adding approximately 2,200 students to the sample. Base year data collection also included a special oversampling of hearing-impaired students who were enrolled in Individualized Education Programs, but mainstreamed in English or mathematics classes.

Sampling Weights: Sample weights were derived from base year data to compensate for unequal probabilities of selection. Weights were based on the inverse of the probability of selection and on nonresponse adjustment factors. The NELS:88 Data File User's Manual provides a complete description of derivation and use of sample weights.

Periodicity

Base year data collection for the NELS:88 began in spring of 1988; the first follow-up survey was conducted during spring of 1990; the second follow-up survey was conducted during spring of 1992. A third follow-up study has been tentatively scheduled for 1994. Descriptions of the NELS:88 first (1990) and second follow-up (1992) studies are provided in Appendices A and B, respectively.

Unit of Analysis

The primary unit of analysis in this study is the individual student. Parent and teacher data sets may be analyzed separately, but are not based on probability samples.

Response Rates

Table 1 below shows weighted completion rates for NELS:88 base year surveys and tests. The NELS:88 Data File User's Manual also provides a breakdown of sample realization and completion rates by school type, urban/city classification, U.S. region, ethnicity, and minority school.

Table 1

NELS:88 Base Year Completion Rates

Instrument	Selected	Participated	Percent Complete
Student Survey	26,453	24,599	93.41
Student Test	24,599	23,701	96.53
Parent Survey	24,599	22,651	93.70
Teacher Ratings of Students	24,599	23,188	95.91
Teacher Surveys	5,680	5,193	91.40
School Survey	1,052	1,035	98.92

CONTENT

Data Sources

Data were collected from four sources: student survey and tests; and parent, teacher, and school administrator surveys. All instruments used in the NELS:88 were designed to maintain continuity and consistency with instruments used in the NLS-72, HS&B, and other current NCES studies.

Student Survey: Students completed a 45-minute self-administered questionnaire and an 85-minute cognitive test in group sessions. The cognitive test battery was developed by the Educational Testing Service. Field representatives from the National Opinion Research Center (NORC) reviewed questionnaires and tests for multiple-response or missing items; missing data were retrieved whenever possible.

Parent Survey: One parent of each student was asked to complete the parent questionnaire brought home by the student. Completed parent questionnaires were mailed or returned to the on-campus NORC representative by the student. Parents of Hispanic students were provided with a Spanish-language questionnaire or Spanish-speaking interviewer when necessary. Parents of Asian/Pacific Islander students were provided with a telephone interviewer who spoke their native language. Completion rates for Hispanic and Asian/Pacific Islander parents were 88.35 and 90.76 percent, respectively.

Teacher Survey: A self-administered teacher questionnaire was distributed to selected eighth grade teachers of sampled students. Prior to selecting teachers for the survey, schools were randomly assigned to one of four paired curriculum categories: mathematics/English; mathematics/social studies; science/English; and science/social studies. Teachers were selected for the survey based upon the school's curriculum assignment. Only teachers from the assigned categories were selected for the study. Questionnaires were distributed by mail.

School Administrator Survey: Principals or administrators from all participating schools received a questionnaire through the mail two weeks prior to on-campus survey administration.

Description of Variables Covered

Student Survey and Tests: The cognitive test battery was comprised of 116 items assessing reading comprehension, quantitative skills, scientific knowledge, and knowledge of U.S. history and government. The student questionnaire included variables in the following topic areas:

Family Background and Constitutional Factors
Gender; ethnicity; family composition; parents' occupation and education; jobs or chores done for pay.

Opinions and Values
Self-concept; locus of control; opinions about self.

School
Discipline; attitude towards drugs and alcohol; tardiness and absenteeism; homework; attitudes towards curriculum; performance; career or other counseling; participation in special programs; parental supervision.

Involvement with Community and Activities
> Cultural experiences; participation in neighborhood programs; extracurricular clubs or classes.

Life Goals
> Educational and occupational expectations; desired occupation.

Parent Survey: This instrument was designed to gather information on the factors that influence educational attainment and participation. Questions focused on:

Family Background and Constitutional Factors
> Gender; ethnicity; family composition; education; occupation; religion; income; employment status.

School
> Attitudes toward school policies; home educational support system; homework; performance expectations; homework and school guidance; physical or mental limitations of child; after school supervision; financial aid for future education.

Involvement with Community and Activities
> Family life; cultural and community activities

Life Goals
> Parental expectations of educational attainment for child.

Teacher Survey: The teacher questionnaire was designed to obtain student-level data in two areas: teachers' perceptions of classroom performance and personal characteristics, and curriculum content. Primary emphasis was placed in assessing factors that would explain NELS:88 students' future educational development and career outcomes, including equality, diversity, and quality of educational opportunity. Information on teachers' background and activities was also gathered.

School Administrator Survey: This questionnaire collected information on school, teacher, and student characteristics; policies and practices; grading and testing structure; programs and facilities; parental involvement in school; and school atmosphere.

Number of Variables

The number of variables for NELS:88 base-year questionnaires are listed below.

Student
    Cognitive Test Battery: 116 Items
    Survey: 408
Parent: 331
Teacher: 239
School: 211

Checklist of Topics Covered

- X Gender / Gender Role
- X Race / Ethnicity
- X Age
- X Education
- X Occupation / Employment
- X Physical Health / Disease
- ___ Nutrition
- ___ Clinical Activities
- ___ Biological Functioning / Development
- ___ Mental Health / Disease
- X Psychological Functioning / Development
- X Guidance / Counseling
- X Personality
- X Intellectual Functioning
- ___ Residential Mobility
- ___ Dwelling
- X Neighborhood / Community
- X Region / State
- X Marriage and Divorce
- ___ Cohabitation
- X Family/Household Composition & Structure
- ___ Inter-Partner Relationships
- X Parent-Child Relationships
- ___ Inter-Sibling Relationships
- X Relationships with Other Kin

- X Relationships with Nonkin
- X Other Family/Household Characteristics
- X Child Care
- X Wealth / Finances / Material Things
- X Receipt of Health, Mental Health, Social Services
- ___ Adoption / Foster Care
- X Childbearing / Pregnancy
- X Out-of-Wedlock Pregnancy & Parenthood
- ___ Abortion
- ___ Sexuality
- ___ Sex Education
- ___ Contraception
- ___ Sexually Transmitted Diseases
- X Civic/Political Activities
- X Friends / Social Activities
- ___ Social Support
- ___ Dating, Courtship
- X Recreation
- X Religion
- X Crime / Delinquency / Behavior Problems
- X Substance Use
- ___ Agency Characteristics
- X Interview

Checklist of Key Variables

X Number of family members
X Identification of marital
   partners in family
X Size of dwelling
___ Type of dwelling
X Urban/rural residence
X Region/state of residence
X Family income
X Religious affiliation
X Relation of each family
   member to:
   X Reference person
   X All other members
___ Age of family members
   X Respondent
   ___ Others
X Sex of family members

X Respondent
X Others
X Race of family members
   X Respondent
   X Others
X Marital status of family
   members
   ___ Respondent
   ___ Others
X Education of family
   members
   X Respondent
   X Others
X Occupation of family
   members
   X Respondent
   X Others

LIMITATIONS

Although the complexity of the sampling design used in this study carries potential sources of bias, an analysis of nonresponse at the school level, using an abbreviated form of the administrator questionnaire, suggests that bias introduced by school-level nonresponse was negligible. Assessment of student-level nonresponse bias was not undertaken. The quality of the NELS:88 base-year data was examined in the report "Quality of the Responses of Eighth-Grade Students in NELS:88." In this report, student responses are compared to their parents. The NCES recommends that sampling weights be used for all forms of statistical analysis.

Several small groups of schools and students were excluded from the study. Students were chosen to participate only if they had the mental and physical capacity to complete the questionnaire and test. Composition of the student sample may not match official enrollment statistics. School and student exclusion criteria also exclude various classes of parents from the study. Because the parent sample was determined by students selected, parents participating in the study may not constitute a statistical or representative sample of eighth grade parents.

SPONSORSHIP

This study was sponsored by the National Center for Education Statistics, U.S. Department of Education. Oversampling of the Hispanic and Asian/Pacific Islander student sample was funded by the U.S. Department of Education's Office of Bilingual Education and Minority Language Affairs (OBEMLA). Gallaudet University sponsored the oversampling of hearing-impaired students and audiological data about hearing impairments for sampled students. The National Science Foundation (NSF) co-sponsored the math and science teacher component of the study.

Instrument development was partially sponsored by the NSF, the National Endowment for the Humanities, OBEMLA, and the Office of Planning, Budget, and Evaluation. Data collection was conducted by the National Opinion Research Center under contract to the National Center for Education Statistics.

GUIDE TO DATA AND DOCUMENTATION

File Structure

Public release base-year data tapes have been produced for each component in the NELS:88: student, parent, teacher, and administrator. Each tape includes a data file based on the core sample: 1,052 schools, 24,599 students, 22,651 parents and 5,193 teachers. The student data tape includes data for 24,599 participants and OBEMLA student oversamples. The student data tape can be used alone or can be merged with the parent, teacher, or administrator data files. Tapes are organized with variables grouped into logical sets:

1. Raw Data File
   Randomized ID number
   Questionnaire and test data
   Base year weights, flags, and composites
2. SPSS-X control cards
3. SAS control cards
4. SAS system file

List of Available Documentation

Public release tapes and user's manuals may be obtained from the NCES. The following study supplements are not included on the NELS:88 public release tapes, but may be ordered through the NCES if a special license agreement (regarding confidentiality) is obtained: Christian Schools supplement; School Effects Supplement; and Survey of middle grades practices.

Contact

For general information about the study, contact:

Jeffrey A. Owings
National Center for Education Statistics
U.S. Department of Education
555 New Jersey Avenue, NW
Washington, D.C. 20208-5652
(202) 219-1777

For technical questions that are not answered by the user's manual contact:

Shi-Chang Wu
Longitudinal & Household Studies Branch
National Center for Education Statistics
U.S. Department of Education
555 New Jersey Avenue, NW
Washington, D.C. 20208-5652
(202) 219-1425

Cost

Magnetic tapes cost $175. Each additional file costs $75. The price to purchase all four files is $400. Please state tape specifications. Payment may be made by check, money order, or credit card. Base-year and first follow-up data are available on CD-ROMs in Eectronic Codebook (ECB) format. A single CD-ROM contains the following files:

o   Base-year student, parent, teacher, and school public release files in ASCII format;

o   First follow-up student, dropout, teacher, and school public release files in ASCII format;

o   Software for creating and operating the Electronic Codebook (ECB);

o   Base-year and first follow-up User's Manuals in ASCII and WordPerfect formats; and

o   ECB User Manual in ASCII and WordPerfect formats.

To operate this ECB, the user should have:

o   IBM-Compatible PC (necessary),

o   MS/DOS 3.3 or higher (necessary),

o   50 megabytes of available hard disk space (recommended),

o   80386 or higher processor (80286 runs slow),

o   PC-SAS or SPSS-PC software (ECB produces SAS & SPSS cards), and

o   CD-ROM reader (necessary).

To place an order by telephone with the Data Systems Branch call (202) 219-1547. To place an order by mail make checks payable to U.S. Department of Education and mail to:

U.S. Department of Education
Data Systems Branch
555 New Jersey Avenue, NW
Washington, DC 20208-5725

Credit card orders may be placed by calling (202) 219-1847/1522.

BIBLIOGRAPHY

Bradby, D., & Quinn, P. (1992). *Language characteristics and academic achievement: A look at Asian and Hispanic eighth graders in NELS:88 (NCES 92-479)*. Washington, DC: National Center for Education Statistics.

Hafner, A., Ingels, S.J., Schneider, B., & Stevenson, D. (1990). *A profile of the American eighth grader (NCES 90-458)*. Washington, DC: National Center for Education Statistics.

Hoachlander, E.G. (1991). *A profile of schools attended by eighth graders in NELS:1988 (NCES 91-129)*. Washington, DC: National Center for Education Statistics.

Horn, L., & Hafner, A. (1992). *A profile of American eighth grade math and science instruction (NCES 92-486)*. Washington, DC: National Center for Education Statistics.

Horn, L., & West, J. (1992). *A profile of parents of eighth graders (NCES 92-488)*. Washington, DC: National Center for Education Statistics.

Ingels, S.J., Abraham, S.Y., Karr, R., Spencer, B.D., & Frankel, M.R. (1990). *National education longitudinal study of 1988. Base year: Student component data file user's manual (NCES 90-464)*. Washington, DC: National Center for Education Statistics.

Ingels, S.J., Abraham, S.Y., Karr, R., Spencer, B.D., Frankel, M.R., & Owings, J.A. (1990). *National education longitudinal study of 1988. Base year: Teacher component data file user's manual (NCES 90-484)*. Washington, DC: National Center for Education Statistics.

Ingels, S.J., Abraham, S.Y., Karr, R., Spencer, B.D., Frankel, M.R., & Owings, J.A. (1990). *National education longitudinal study of 1988. Base year: Parent component data file user's manual (NCES 90-464)*. Washington, DC: National Center for Education Statistics.

Ingels, S.J., Abraham, S.Y., Karr, R., Spencer, B.D., Frankel, M.R., & Owings, J.A. (1990). *National education longitudinal study of 1988. Base year: School component data file user's manual (NCES 90-482)*. Washington, DC: National Center for Education Statistics.

Ingels, S.J., Scott, L.A., Lindmark, J.T., Frankel, M.R., Myers, S.L., & Wu, S.C. (1992). *National education longitudinal study of 1988 first follow-up: Student component data file user's manual, Volume I (NCES 92-030)*. Washington, DC: National Center for Education Statistics.

Ingels, S.J., Scott, L.A., Lindmark, J.T., Frankel, M.R., Myers, S.L., & Wu, S.C. (1992). *National education longitudinal study of 1988 first follow-up: student component data file user's manual, Volume II (NCES 92-088)*. Washington, DC: National Center for Education Statistics.

Ingels, S.J., Scott, L.A., Lindmark, J.T., Frankel, M.R., Myers, S.L., & Wu, S.C. (1992). *National education longitudinal study of 1988 first follow-up: School component data file user's manual (NCES 92-084)*. Washington, DC: National Center for Education Statistics.

Ingels, S.J., Scott, L.A., Lindmark, J.T., Frankel, M.R., Myers, S.L., & Wu, S.C. (1992). *National education longitudinal study of 1988 first follow-up: Dropout component data file user's manual (NCES 92-083)*. Washington, DC: National Center for Education Statistics.

Ingels, S.J., Scott, L.A., Lindmark, J.T., Frankel, M.R., Myers, S.L., & Wu, S.C. (1992). *National education longitudinal study of 1988 first follow-up: Teacher component data file user's manual (NCES 93-085)*. Washington, DC: National Center for Education Statistics.

Kaufman, P., & Bradby, D. (1992). *Characteristics of at-risk students in NELS:88 (NCES 92-042)*. Washington, DC: National Center for Education Statistics.

Kaufman, P., Rasinski, K.A., Lee, R., & West, J. (1991). *Quality of the responses of eighth-grade students in NELS:88 (NCES 91-487)*. Washington, DC: National Center for Education Statistics.

Spencer, B.D., Frankel, M.R., Ingels, S.J., Rasinski, K.A., & Tourangeau. R. (1990). *NELS:88 base year sample design report (NCES 90-463)*. Washington, DC: National Center for Education Statistics.

Rasinski, K.A., & West, J. (1990). *Eighth Graders' report of courses taken during the 1988 academic year by selected student characteristics (NCES 90-459)*. Washington, DC: National Center for Education Statistics.

Rock, D., & Pollack, J.M. (1991). *Psychometric report for the NELS:88 base year test battery (NCES 91-468)*. Washington, DC: National Center for Education Statistics.

Rock, D., Pollack, J.M., & Hafner, A. (1991). *The tested achievement of the national education longitudinal study of 1988 eighth grade class (NCES 91-460)*. Washington, DC: National Center for Education Statistics.

APPENDIX A:

NELS:88 FIRST FOLLOW-UP SURVEY, 1990

In the spring of 1990, the first follow-up survey gathered a second wave of data from the eighth grade cohort of 1988, the majority of whom were enrolled in tenth grade, and a first wave of data from "freshened" students (i.e., selected students who were enrolled in tenth grade in the spring term of 1990, but not enrolled in eighth grade in the base year).

Sampling Design

Self-administered questionnaires remained the principal mode of data collection for all respondents. Again, as in the base year, two teachers of each sampled student and students' current high school principal were asked to complete, respectively, a teacher and school administrator questionnaire. Sample members who had dropped out of school, and remained so at the time of data collection, were administered the dropout questionnaire and cognitive test battery.

In-school data collection methods adhered closely to those used in the base year of the survey. Although data collection procedures employed in the first follow-up were modeled after those of the base year, the design of the study necessitated several activities that had not been performed previously. First, in order to select the first follow-up sample, an extensive locating effort was undertaken. Second, the base year sample was "freshened" to generate a representative sample of the tenth grade class of 1990. Third, off-campus survey sessions, similar to those used in HS&B, were scheduled to administer the student or dropout questionnaire to sample members who were currently not enrolled in a first follow-up school at the time of data collection. And fourth, a subsample of first follow-up nonrespondents (and of base year ineligible students) was pursued in order to obtain a more precise estimate of the rate of dropping out for the eighth grade cohort of 1988.

Response Rate and Attrition

First year follow-up completion rates for base year retained sample members are presented below. In general, base year retained respondents participated at approximately the same rate in the first follow-up as they did in the base year (94%).

Table 1

Completion Rates for Base Year Sample Members

Retained in the First Year Follow-Up (1990)

Instrument	Selected	Participated	Percent Complete
Student Survey	19,363	18,221	94.10
Student Test	18,221	17,352	95.23
Teacher Ratings of Students	18,221	15,908	87.31
School Survey Data for Students	18,221	17,663	96.94

The NELS:88 first follow-up was sponsored by the National Center for Education Statistics, U.S. Department of Education; and by the National Science Foundation and Office of Bilingual Education and Minority Language Affairs.

The full survey for NELS:88 first follow-up was conducted between February and May 1990 by NORC, the Social Science Research Center at the University of Chicago. A first follow-up data file and user's manual for the student and the school data were made available in the spring of 1992. In January 1993, NCES announced the availability of dropout and teacher survey data collected as part of the 1990 first follow-up. With this release, all four components of the NELS:88 first follow-up are now available for public use.

APPENDIX B:

NELS:88 SECOND FOLLOW-UP STUDY, 1992

The NELS:88 second follow-up study is sponsored by the National Center for Education Statistics, U.S. Department of Education; and by the National Science Foundation and Office of Bilingual Education and Minority Language Affairs. NORC, a Social Science Research Center at the University of Chicago, is conducting the survey. The NELS:88 second follow-up places special emphasis on student planning activities related to transitions from high school to work, family formation, and/or postsecondary education.

Sampling Design

The design for the NELS:88 second follow-up study includes five questionnaires: student, school administrator, teacher, parent, and dropout. Students and dropouts completed cognitive tests in reading, science, social science, and math. The tests were designed to reflect twelfth grade coursework but also had enough overlapping items with the eighth and tenth grade tests to permit measurement of academic growth.

A new content domain for NELS:88 is offerings and enrollment and transcript data. Course offerings information will be especially useful for examining the learning environment of NELS:88 students. Course data provide information on the extent to which high school students have the opportunity to be exposed to various subjects. The student transcript information is useful for verifying student reported grades and courses. Moreover, being able to clearly identify what courses a student has taken in high school will produce more accurate data on high school program track than will student reports.

In 1992, the full survey for NELS:88 second follow-up was conducted between February and May by NORC, the Social Science Research Center at the University of Chicago. A second follow-up data file and user's manual will be available in late 1993.

9

THE NATIONAL LONGITUDINAL STUDY OF THE HIGH SCHOOL CLASS OF 1972 (NLS-72)

The National Center for Education Statistics
The National Opinion Research Center

PURPOSE OF THE STUDY

In 1972, in response to an expressed need from policymakers and researchers for data that would allow comparisons of student educational and vocational experiences with later outcomes, the National Center for Education Statistics implemented the first of a series of longitudinal studies which was called the National Longitudinal Study of the High School Class of 1972 (NLS-72). The NLS-72 data set is one of the four in the U.S. Department of Education's National Education Longitudinal Studies (NELS) program. NLS-72 represents a rich data source on a variety of life events experienced by a national sample of American students from the time they left high school until just after their 30th birthday. It supplies information on the educational, vocational, and personal development and examines the kinds of factors—personal, familial, social, institutional, and cultural—that may have affected that development. The collection provides a broad spectrum of information on each student and covers areas such as ability, socioeconomic status, home background, community environment, ethnicity, significant others, current activity at time of survey, educational attainment, school experiences, school performance, work status, work performance and satisfaction, goal orientations, marriage and the family, and military experience.

METHODS

Sampling Design

The Base Year

The base-year (1972) data were collected by Educational Testing Service (ETS) of Princeton, New Jersey. The sample design was a stratified two-stage probability sample. In the first stage of sample selection, schools were sampled without replacement from 600 strata. The strata were based on the following variables: type of control (public or private), geographic region, enrollment size, geographic proximity to institutions of higher education, proportion of minority group enrollment (for public schools), income level of the community, and degree of urbanization. For all but the smallest size stratum, schools were selected with equal probabilities; schools with fewer than

300 students were selected with probability proportional to enrollment. Also, schools in low-income areas and schools with high proportions of minority group enrollment were sampled at twice the rate used for the remaining schools. Two schools were selected from each of the final 600 strata. In the second state of sample selection, samples of 12th-grade students were selected from each of the sample schools. To the extent feasible, a simple random sample of the 18 students was selected at each school. Schools in low-income areas and schools with relatively high minority enrollment were oversampled to obtain an oversampling of low-income and minority students.

The First Through Fourth Follow-ups

The first through fourth follow-ups were conducted by the Research Triangle Institute (RTI) of Research Triangle Park, North Carolina. The first follow-up, 1973, added 4,450 students from additional schools to reduce the effects of a large base-year school noncooperation rate and of an incomplete frame of public schools. The additional schools were drawn from eight new strata. As before, 18 students per school were selected by simple random sampling. These students were retained in the sample for subsequent follow-up. No subsampling of the original base-year sample was done until the fourth follow-up, when a subsample of 1,016 respondents was selected for retesting with a battery of test items that had originally been administered during the base year. There was no subsampling for the collection of questionnaire data; all sample members received the fourth follow-up questionnaire.

The Fifth Follow-up

The fifth follow-up (1986) data was collected by the National Opinion Research Center (NORC), and was an unequal probability subsample of 14,489 members of the 22,652 respondents who participated in at least one of the five previous waves of NLS-72. A mail questionnaire was sent to the subsample. At the time of this survey, the sample members averaged 32 years of age and had been out of high school for 14 years. The fifth follow-up retained the essential features of the initial stratified multi-stage design and introduced no additional stratification or clustering. Various subgroups were retained in the fifth follow-up sample at different rates, but this disproportionate subsampling was achieved by modification of individual selection probabilities. With certain major exceptions, the fifth follow-up retention probabilities for sample members were inversely proportional to their base-year selection probabilities. The exceptions involved several groups of sample members: certain groups were oversampled or retained with very small initial selection probabilities were also retained with certainty; finally, sample members who failed to participate in the fourth follow-up were retained at a lower rate than others, because they were expected to be more expensive to locate and because they would be less useful for longitudinal analysis.

The subgroups of sample members who were retained with certainty because of their special policy relevance included:

1) Hispanics who participated in the fourth follow-up;
2) Teachers and "potential teachers" who participated in the fourth follow-up (a "potential teacher" was defined as a personal who majored in education in college, was certified to teach, expected to become a teacher, or who received a degree in the sciences);
3) Persons with a four-year or five-year college degree or a more advanced degree; and
4) Persons who were divorced, widowed, or separated from their spouses, or never-married parents.

These groups overlap and thus do not constitute distinct strata in the usual sense.

The remaining cases were cross-classified as either participants or nonparticipants in the fourth follow-up survey. Overall sampling rates for the participants and nonparticipants in the fourth follow-up were determined so as to optimize specific tradeoffs between cross-sectional analyses using fifth follow-up data and longitudinal analyses using fifth and fourth follow-up data. The fourth follow-up participants who were not subsampled with certainty were further partitioned into two groups—those who reported two years of college or less, and all others. The former group was subsampled for retention in the fifth follow-up at a rate 30 percent greater than the latter.

The fifth follow-up subsampling was carried out using systematic selection with unequal probabilities on a sorted file of students. Specifically, the list of the active population of students was sorted according to the stratum to which the student's school belonged; within these strata, the list of students was sorted according to the school from which the student was originally sampled. The structure of the list implies that the subsample is, for all practical purposes, a stratified two-staged sample from the original population. The design differs from the base-year design in that the student selection probabilities were equal in the base-year design but unequal in the fifth follow-up.

Periodicity

The base-year survey was conducted in the spring of 1972 on a deeply stratified national probability sample of 1,200 schools with 18 seniors per school. The first follow-up survey was conducted from October 1973 to April 1974. The second follow-up was conducted from October 1974 to April 1975, with forms mailed to 22,364 sample members. The third year follow-up survey was conducted from October 1976 to May 1977. The fourth follow-up survey was conducted from October 1979 to May 1980, with fourth follow-up questionnaires sent to 20,862 sample members. The fifth follow-up survey was conducted during the spring and summer of 1986.

Unit of Analysis

Sample members were seniors in high-school during the 1971-1972 academic year.

Response Rates

A total of 19,001 students from 1,061 high schools provided the base-year data. Student measures were completed by 16,683 seniors. The first follow-up survey added 4,450 1972 high school seniors from 257 additional schools to the base sample. The addition of this group was meant to compensate for school nonresponse in the base year.

Attrition

First follow-up forms were mailed to 22,654 students and obtained from 21,350, by mail, telephone interview, or personal interview. The second follow-up forms were mailed to 22,364 sample members and questionnaires were completed by 20,872 sample members by mail, telephone interview, or personal interview. Third follow-up forms were mailed to 21,807 sample members and 20,092 completed questionnaires were obtained by mail, telephone interview, or personal interview. The fourth follow-up questionnaire was sent to 20,862 sample members and obtained from 18,630 by mail, telephone interview, or personal interview. In addition, 5,548 respondents were also asked to complete a supplemental questionnaire. Additionally, a subsample of 1,016 persons were retested during the fourth follow-up on the subset of the base-year test battery. At the conclusion of the fourth year follow-up activities, a total of 12,980 individuals had provided information on all waves of questionnaires (base year and all four follow-up studies), representing 78 percent of the base-year respondents. The fifth follow-up survey was sent to a subsample of 14,489 members of the original sample of 22,652. A total of 12,841 persons returned the questionnaire, for a response rate of 89%.

The numbers of respondents participating in each of the five waves of NLS-72 are presented below. Also provided are the retention rates at each wave for those respondents who participated in the previous wave (i.e., 93.7% of the 16,683 seniors who completed the base-year survey were retained in the first follow-up).

Table 1
Response Rates

	Total Mailed	Number Obtained	% Previous Wave Retained
Base-year Survey	19,001	16,683	N/A
First Follow-up	22,654	21,350	93.7%
Second Follow-up	22,364	20,872	94.6%
Third Follow-up	21,807	20,092	93.9%
Fourth Follow-up	20,862	18,630	90.8%
Fifth Follow-up	14,489	12,841	88.6% *

* Response Rate

CONTENT

Data Sources

The Base Year

Base year data were collected in school.

The First Through Fourth Follow-ups

Data for the first through fourth follow-ups were collected by mail, telephone interview, or personal interview.

The Fifth Follow-up

In October 1985, locating packets were mailed to 14,489 members of the NLS-72 sample. The packet included a report about previous surveys, a letter of introduction, and an address form with space provided to update address information. Locating packets returned as undeliverable were routed to the in-house telephone locating shop. Of 2,252 undeliverable packets, telephone interviewers found updated addresses for 1,366 (61 percent) of them. The remainder was sent to field staff for intensive research. Of the cases assigned to field staff, 24%, (231 respondents) were updated. Locating activities continued for the remainder (645) into the main field period.

The field period began the second week of March and continued through mid-September. The packages mailed to the subsample contained questionnaires, a cover letter, a $5 respondent fee check, a pencil, and a return envelope. Survey materials were mailed first class with "address correction requested" specified on the envelopes.

Three weeks after the initial mailing, postcards were sent to participants to thank those who had responded and to encourage those who had not to do so. Telephone prompting of those who had not responded began approximately two weeks after postcards were mailed. Offers to remail questionnaires were made to those who reported not receiving the earlier mailings or had misplaced them. Administration of the questionnaire by telephone and in-person interviews began during the fourteenth week of the field period. At the end of 27 weeks, 12,841 completed questionnaires were obtained, accounting for a final response rate of 88.6%. The majority of questionnaires were completed without interviewer assistance: 72 percent of the sample (81 percent of the participants). Telephone interviews were conducted with 13 percent of the sample (15% of the participants), and in-person interviews accounted for 3.5 percent of the sample (4 percent of the participants).

Thirty-six items in the fifth follow-up questionnaire were designated as "critical questions" for editing purposes. Respondents who omitted one of these critical items, or who provided inconsistent or invalid responses to them, were contacted by telephone to provide the missing data (or to resolve the inconsistencies).

The fifth follow-up survey data were entered using a combination of keyed entry and optical scanning procedures. CADE (Computer Assisted Data Entry developed by NORC) enabled data entry operators to combine data entry with traditional editing procedures. The CADE system, an offshoot of CATI (Computer Assisted Telephone Interviewing), was designed to proceed question-by-question through critical numeric items. The program skipped over questions that were slated for scanning and questions that were legitimately skipped because of a filter question. Ranges were set for each question, thereby preventing illegitimate responses from being accidentally entered.

Validation procedures for the fifth follow-up centered on verification of data quality through item checks and verification of the method of administration for 10 percent of each interviewer's work. Each field manager was asked to validate cases from a random number assignment by telephoning the respondent to check several items of fact and to confirm the interview. No cases failed validation.

Description of Variables Covered

Three base-year data collection forms were sent to a total of 19,001 students from 1,061 high schools: a Test Battery, a School Record Information Form, and a Student Questionnaire. Data collected focused on factors relating to the student's personal/family background, education and work experience, plans, aspirations, attitudes, and opinions.

In the first follow-up survey, sample members were asked about their location in October 1973 and what they were doing with respect to work, education, and/or training. Similar information was requested for the same time period in 1972 to facilitate tracing of respondents' progress since they had left high school and to define the factors that might have affected that progress. Retrospective information on some base-year variables was requested from those added to the sample at this time.

The second follow-up survey requested similar information as the first but for the new time point; however, some new questions on work and education were included. Concurrently with the second follow-up, a special retrospective survey was conducted (using an Activity State Questionnaire) to obtain key activity status information about prior time points from those who had not provided this information previously.

The third follow-up survey included information on respondent status in October 1976, as well as for October of the intervening year (1975), and summaries of experiences and activities since the previous follow-up such as graduate school application and entry, job supervision, sex roles, sex and race biases, and a subjective rating of high school experiences.

The fourth follow-up survey requested summaries of educational and occupational activities and experiences since the previous follow-up, including status at the time points of October 1977, 1978, and 1979. Given the time since high school graduation for these respondents, some emphasis was placed on other activities (e.g., family formation, political participation) in the fourth follow-up instrument. Additionally, 5,548 individuals were asked to complete a supplemental questionnaire. Like the Activity State Questionnaire used in the second follow-up, this instrument was designed to collect key work and educational history data that had been requested but not obtained in prior follow-ups. A subsample of 1,016 persons were retested during the fourth follow-up on a subset of the base-year test battery as well.

The fifth follow-up survey offered the opportunity to gather information on experiences and attitudes of a sample for whom an extensive history already existed. As a result, many supplementary questionnaires were implemented during the fifth follow-up. In addition to requests for update on respondents' background information, new information was solicited regarding work experiences; employment histories; education and other training; family status; income; and opinions on a range of topics. The fifth follow-up expanded a number of topics covered in previous waves of data collection. The fifth follow-up survey utilized an event history format to obtain information about jobs held; schools attended; periods of unemployment; and marriage and divorce patterns. Additional question modules asked respondents about cohabitation episodes, including whether or not these episodes began as or became marriages; numbers of children resulting from the union; manner and method of parting (if relevant); and whether or not the respondent had more than three cohabitation episodes. Questions about first marriage solicited information on income; education; and activity status at the start and end of the marriage for both partners. Also included were variables specifically aimed at those respondents who had been divorced and dealt with property division; child custody and alimony arrangements; present living circumstances; and the tenor of the divorce process. An assortment of family status questions provided a detailed history of marriage(s); divorce; age and gender of children; and whether the children were born to them, adopted, step- or foster children. Respondents all provided information on the sharing of expenses within their households and economic transfers from one household to another. In addition, several items attempted to ascertain attitudes about the teaching professions; self-esteem; job satisfaction; satisfaction with school experience; and participation in community affairs. Also, there is a sequence of questions designed to understand the kinds of individuals who apply for and matriculate to graduate management programs. Finally, a small file contains details of divorce laws on a state by state basis.

Number of Variables

The entire study, waves 1 through 5, contains approximately 3,500 variables.

Checklist of Topics Covered

X Gender / Gender Role
X Race / Ethnicity
X Age
X Occupation / Employment
___ Physical Health / Disease
___ Nutrition
___ Clinical Activities
___ Biological Functioning /
   Development
___ Mental Health / Disease
X Psychological Functioning /
   Development
___ Guidance / Counseling
___ Personality
___ Intellectual Functioning
___ Residential Mobility
___ Dwelling
___ Neighborhood / Community
___ Region / State
X Marriage and Divorce
X Cohabitation
X Family/Household
   Composition & Structure
X Inter-Partner Relationships
X Parent-Child Relationships
X Inter-Sibling Relationships
___ Relationships with Other Kin
___ Relationships with Nonkin

___ Other Family/Household
   Characteristics
X Child Care
___ Wealth / Finances / Material
   Things
___ Receipt of Health, Mental
   Health, Social Services
X Adoption / Foster Care
X Childbearing / Pregnancy
X Out-of-Wedlock Pregnancy &
   Parenthood
___ Abortion
___ Sexuality
___ Sex Education
___ Contraception
___ Sexually Transmitted
   Diseases
X Civic/Political Activities
___ Friends / Social Activities
   Social Support
___ Dating, Courtship
___ Recreation
X Religion
___ Crime / Delinquency /
   Behavior Problems
___ Substance Use
___ Agency Characteristics
___ Interview

Checklist of Key Variables

<u>X</u> Number of family members
<u>X</u> Identification of marital
    partners in family
___ Size of dwelling
___ Type of dwelling
___ Urban/rural residence
___ Region/state of residence
___ Family income
___ Religious affiliation
___ Relation of each family
    member to:
    ___ Reference person
    ___ All other members
___ Age of family members
    ___ Respondent
    ___ Others
<u>X</u> Sex of family members

    <u>X</u> Respondent
    <u>X</u> Others
<u>X</u> Race of family members
    <u>X</u> Respondent
    <u>X</u> Others
<u>X</u> Marital status of family
    members
    <u>X</u> Respondent
    <u>X</u> Others
<u>X</u> Education of family
    members
    <u>X</u> Respondent
    <u>X</u> Others
<u>X</u> Occupation of family
    members
    <u>X</u> Respondent
    <u>X</u> Others

LIMITATIONS

Because the NLS-72 is based on a sample of high school seniors, it does not include persons who dropped out of school before their senior year—a substantial proportion. Thus, the data cannot be used to study the post-high school educational, economic, and social development of high school students in general, only of those who stay in school into their senior year.

The sampling frame for the base-year survey was incomplete among public schools, possibly adding some bias to the sample. Also, the noncooperative rate was relatively large. These deficiencies were corrected beginning with the second wave through the addition of a supplemental sample.

The cumulative attrition—from the base-year sample through the fourth follow-up—was 22%. While this is relatively good for panel studies of this size and type, it does introduce the possibility of bias in the resulting sample. Those not successfully followed are quite likely to be different from others in ways that are important for studying the school-to-work transition.

The sampling design is complex; both oversampling (initial sample), a supplemental sample (first follow-up) and subsampling (fifth follow-up) were used. Consequently, weights must be employed to generate descriptive statistics that represent the population universe.

SPONSORSHIP

The National Center for Education Statistics has been the primary sponsor of the NLS-72 surveys. However, as the sample has aged, other groups have taken interest in the surveys. The National Institute of Child Health and Human Development, the National Science Foundation, the Spencer Foundation, and the Graduate Management Admissions Council helped to fund supplementary survey questions to the fifth follow-up.

GUIDE TO DATA DOCUMENTATION

File Structure

Magnetic tapes are available from the National Opinion Research Center (NORC), the National Center for Education Statistics (NCES), and the Inter-university Consortium for Political and Social Research (ICPSR).

NORC: The NICHD edition of the NLS-72 data consists of three datasets. The first contains the base year through fourth follow-up reformatted file. This dataset includes virtually all the variables on the NCES edition of the base year-fourth follow-up file, and has been supplemented by 17 family history composites created by a Fortran program written at RAND by Gus Haggstrom and Tom Balschke. The second data set includes all the fifth follow-up questions, plus a number of composites created to facilitate use of the job history, education, unemployment, and family history sections. A number of composites were also created from Question 105, which deals with monetary and in-kind exchanges in which the respondent engages. The third data file is included as a useful supplement. This small file contains indicators of the adoption of no-fault divorce and marital property laws for all 50 states. The fifth follow-up data can be used alone or can be merged with the base year through fourth follow-up data.

NCES: A data tape is available and it is organized as follows:

1. Raw Data File
2. Record layout for raw data file
3. SAS control cards
4. SPSS control cards

ICPSR: Data files and machine-readable documentation are available in 11 data files (including SPSS and SAS control cards) and are listed in Table 2 on the next two pages.

Table 2. ICPSR Data Files and Machine-Readable Documentation

Filename	Part(s)	Structure	Cases	Vars	Rec Length	Rec/ Case
Student File	1	Rectangular	22,652	3,524	11,475	1
School File	2	Rectangular	1,318	504	1,284	1
School District Census File	3	Rectangular	3,493		4,999	1
FICE Code File	4	Rectangular	4,004		48	1
CEEB Instituitional Data Base File	5	Rectangular	4,139	84	452	1
Transcript Survey: Course-Level Record	6	Rectangular	490,906	10	58	1
Transcript Survey: Student-Level Record	7	Rectangular	14,759	18	62	1
Transcript Survey: Student-Level Record Layout	8				80	
Transcript Survey: Term-Level Record	9	Rectangular	122,584	18	62	1
Transcript Survey: Transcript-Level Record	10	Rectangular	24,431	23	280	1
Transcript Survey: SAS Control Cards	11				80	

Table 2. ICPSR Data Files and Machine-Readable Documentation (continued)

Filename	Part(s)	Structure	Cases	Vars	Rec Length	Rec/ Case
Fifth Follow-up, 1986: Student-Level Record	12	Rectangular	14,489	925	1,927	1
Fifth Follow-up, 1986: Student-Level Record Layout	13				80	
Fifth Follow-up, 1986: SAS Control Cards	14				80	
Fifth Follow-up, 1986: Teaching Supplement	15	Rectangular	1,147	290	80	8
Fifth Follow-up, 1986: Teaching Supplement Record Layout	16				80	
Fifth Follow-up, 1986: Teaching Supplement SAS Control Cards	17				80	

List of Available Documentation

NORC: The Data File User's Manual—NICHD Edition, codebooks, and machine-readable data for the fifth follow-up and a summary of the findings prior to the fifth follow-up are available.

NCES: The National Center for Education Statistics has machine-readable data and documentation on mainframe tape. The base-year through fifth follow-up data will be available on CD-ROM later in 1993.

ICPSR: The Inter-university Consortium for Political and Social Research has machine-readable data files and documentation. Supplementary documentation for this collection is available on microfiche.

Contact

At NORC contact:
Patrick Bova, Librarian
Paul B. Sheatsley Library
NORC
1155 East 60th Street
Chicago, IL 60637
(312) 753-7679

At NCES contact:
Aurora D'Amico (Mrs.)
National Center for Education Statistics
555 New Jersey Ave., NW
Washington DC 20208-5652
(202) 219-1365
FAX (202) 219-1751

At ICPSR:
ICPSR
P.O. Box 1248
Ann Arbor, MI 48106
(313) 763-5010

Cost

NORC (NICHD Edition):

Mainframe Tapes:

	6250 BPI		1600 BPI	
	# Tapes	Price	# Tapes	Price
EBCDIC FILE				
5th Follow-Up Only	1	$125	2	$150
Base to 4th and 5th Follow-Up	3	$200	10	$400
EBCDIC and SAS FILE				
5th Follow-Up Only	1	$125	3	$200
Base to 4th and 5th Follow-Up	5	$250	17	$600

Codebook:

Hard copy $100

NOTE: All tapes have codebook in machine-readable form as a file.

Send check, payable to NORC, to Mr. Patrick Bova at the address listed under "Contact" above.

NCES:

Magnetic tapes from the National Center for Education Statistics cost $175. If more than one tape is ordered at the same time, the price is $75 for the second and subsequent tapes. Please state tape specifications. Payment may be made by check, money order, or credit card.

Make check payable to U.S. Department of Education and mail to:

U.S. Department of Education
Information Technology Branch
555 New Jersey Avenue, NW
Washington, DC 20208-5725

Telephone orders for mainframe tapes may be placed by calling Jack Dusatko at (202) 219-1522.

ICPSR:

Members of the Inter-university Consortium for Political and Social Research can obtain NLS-72 from ICPSR at no cost. For non-members, the cost depends on the format requested. Contact ICPSR at (313) 763-5010 for a price quote. Please reference ICPSR #8085.

BIBLIOGRAPHY

Adelman, C. (1990). *Light and shadows on college athletes*. Washington, DC: U.S. Department of Education, Office of Educational Research and Improvement, Office of Research.

Adelman, C. (1992). *The way we are: The community college as American thermometer*. Washington, DC: U.S. Department of Education, Office of Educational Research and Improvement, Office of Research.

Adelman, C. (1992). *Tourists in our own land: Cultural literacies and the college curriculum*. Washington, DC: U.S. Department of Education, Office of Educational Research and Improvement, Office of Research.

Adelman, C. (1992). *Women at thirtysomething: Paradoxes of attainment*. Washington, DC: U.S. Department of Education, Office of Educational Research and Improvement, Office of Research.

Brandon, P.D. (1991, December). *The role of extended families, fathers, and economic constraints in mothers' child care choices.* Unpublished Ph.D. dissertation, Irving B. Harris Graduate School of Public Policy Studies, University of Chicago, Chicago, IL.

Brien, M.J. (1991, March). *Economic determinants of family structure: An examination of black and white differences.* Unpublished Ph.D. dissertation, Department of Economics, University of Chicago, Chicago, IL.

Brien, M.J., Lillard, L.A., & Waite, L.J. (1993). *Cohabitation, fertility, and marital dissolution.* Paper presented at March 31-April 3, 1993 meetings of the Population Association of America, Cincinnati, OH.

Carroll, C.D. (1989). *Postsecondary enrollment, persistence, and attainment for 1972, 1980, and 1982 high school graduates.* Washington, DC: U.S. Department of Education, Office of Educational Research and Improvement, National Center for Education Statistics.

Cooksey, E.C., & Rindfuss, R.R. (1992, September). *Using data from the national longitudinal study of the class of 1972 for research outside the education field.* (ICPSR Bulletin, 1-3). Ann Arbor, MI: Inter-university Consortium for Political and Social Research.

Eagle, E., Fitzgerald, R.A., Gifford, A., & Zuma, J. of MPR Associates, Inc. (1988). *National longitudinal study 1972—A descriptive summary of 1972 high school sophomores: Fourteen years later.* Washington, DC: U.S. Department of Education, Office of Educational Research and Improvement, National Center for Education Statistics.

Hafner, A., & Owings, J. (1991). *Careers in teaching: Following members of the high school class of 1972 in and out of teaching.* Washington, DC: U.S. Department of Education, Office of Educational Research and Improvement, National Center for Education Statistics.

Hyde, K.A. (1989). *Education, employment, marriage, and fertility: Factors in the life patterns and transitions of young women in the U.S.—1972-1986.* Unpublished doctoral dissertation, Department of Education, University of Chicago, Chicago, IL.

Inter-university Consortium for Political and Social Research. *Guide to Resources and Services, 1992-1993* (pp. 396-397). Ann Arbor, MI: Author.

Kane, J., & Spizman, L. (1988, Fall). Self-employment, self-selections, and income distribution. *St John's University Review of Business.*

Knepper, P.R. (1989). *Student progress in college: NLS-72 postsecondary education transcript study, 1984.* Washington, DC: U.S. Department of Education, Office of Educational Research and Improvement, National Center for Education Statistics.

Knepper, P.R. (1990). *Trends in postsecondary credit production, 1972 and 1980 high school graduates.* Washington, DC: U.S. Department of Education, Office of Educational Research and Improvement, National Center for Education Statistics.

Larsen, A.S., Watson, M.E., Duncan, D.P., Roccobono, J.A., & Burkheimer, G.J. of the Center for Educational Research and Evaluation, Research Triangle Institute. (1981). *Tabular summary of the fourth follow-up questionnaire data.* Washington, DC: U.S. Department of Education, National Center for Education Statistics.

National Opinion Research Center. (1986). *Annotated bibliography of NLS-72 references.* Research Triangle Park, NC: Research Triangle Institute.

National Opinion Research Center. (1987). *The national longitudinal study of the high school class of 1972 (NLS-72) fifth follow-up (1986) data file user's manual—NICHD edition.* Chicago, IL: Author.

Riccobono, J., Henderson, L.B., Burkheimer, G.J., Place, C., & Levinson, J.R. (1981). *National longitudinal study: Base year (1972) through fourth follow-up (1979) data file user's manual* (Vols. 1-3). Research Triangle Park, NC: Research Triangle Institute.

Sebring, P., et al. of the National Opinion Research Center. (1987). *The national longitudinal study of the high school class of 1972 (NLS-72), fifth follow-up (1986) teaching supplement: Data file user's manual (contractor report)*. Washington, DC: U.S. Department of Education, Office of Educational Research and Improvement, Center for Education Statistics.

Tourangeau, R., et al. (1987). *National longitudinal study of the high school class of 1972 (NLS-72) fifth follow-up (1986) data file user's manual (contractor report)*. Chicago, IL: National Opinion Research Center.

Weiss Y., & Willis, R.J. (forthcoming). Transfers among divorced couples: Evidence and interpretation. *Journal of Labor Economics*.

Willis, R.J., & Michael, R.T. (forthcoming). Innovation in family formation: Evidence of cohabitation in the U.S. In J. Ermisch (Ed.), *The family, the market and the state in aging societies*. Oxford University Press.

10

YOUTH-PARENT SOCIALIZATION PANEL STUDY, 1965-1982

M. Kent Jennings
Gregory B. Markus
Richard G. Niemi

PURPOSE OF THE STUDY

The Youth-Parent Socialization Panel Study was a three-wave, longitudinal panel study concerned with the evolution of political orientations and inter-generational influences upon that process. The study was designed to assess political continuity and change across time for two biologically related generations (parents and children). Major questions about life-cycle, generational, and period effects can be addressed with the data. At the core of the study are a number of standard political variables gathered during the three waves of interviews. A number of nonpolitical variables, such as demographics, are also available. Analysis can be done at the aggregate as well as the individual level since parent-child data can be linked through match-merging of cases by ID number.

METHODS

Sampling Design

The students interviewed in 1965 were chosen from a national probability sample of 97 secondary schools (including eleven nonpublic schools) selected with a probability proportionate to their size. Within each school, fifteen to twenty-one randomly selected seniors were interviewed. Since the sample was drawn from a universe of twelfth-graders, "drop-outs" (approximately 26 percent of the age cohort during this period) were eliminated from the school-age population.

Parents were selected randomly such that fathers were to be interviewed for one-third of the students, mothers were to be interviewed for another one-third, and both parents would be interviewed for the remaining one-third. Where the designated parent was permanently absent, the other parent or parent surrogate was interviewed.

In all three waves, interviews were conducted in person, except in special cases where the respondent was located in a remote area. In these cases, mail questionnaires were used. In 1973, 19.2% of the observations were conducted by mail; in 1982, 12.2% were.

Periodicity

Three waves of interviews were conducted for the Youth-Parent Socialization Panel Study: Wave I (1965), Wave II (1973), and Wave III (1982).

Unit of Analysis

The unit of analysis is the individual respondent. In this case, the respondent was either a high-school senior in 1965, or was the mother or father of a participating high-school senior. Separate cases are observed for parents and students, and parent and student cases can be linked together by merging ID numbers.

Sample Sizes

	Wave I 1965	Wave II 1973	Wave III 1982
Parents	1,562	1,179	898
Offspring	1,669	1,348	1,135

Attrition

The percentage values represent the proportion of Wave I respondents retained (i.e., re-interviewed) at subsequent waves:

	Wave I-II 1965-1973	Waves II-III 1973-1982	Waves I-III 1965-1982	Waves I-III adjusted[1]
Parents	75.5%	76.2%	57.5%	64%
Offspring	80.8%	84.2%	68.0%	70%

[1]Rate of attrition adjusted to exclude nonresponse due to death.

CONTENT

Data Sources

Information was gathered from children and their parents by questionnaire (interviewer-administered in most cases). The study was processed according to standard ICPSR processing procedures. The data were checked for illegal (wild) codes, which, whenever found, were corrected. In the codebook, additional comments, bracketed in < and > signs, were inserted by the study processor in order to facilitate nonsequential referencing and to provide further explanatory information.

Description of Variables Covered

The following list is a summary of topics and variables covered in the 1965 and 1973 studies. The 1982 study, which has recently been made publicly available by ICPSR, is similar to the first two waves, though its emphasis is on the maturing process, parental issues and family relationships. The variables assessed among parents and children vary only slightly in that, when appropriate, the question is reoriented to suit the particular respondent. For example, variables in the child survey which deal with "future goals" for the respondent child correspond to "future goals for children" in the parent survey.

> *Personal Background*: demographics (age, education, religion, etc.); marital status, and education/occupation of spouse; military experience.

> *School*: attitudes; activities and interpersonal relations; academic content.

> *Personal Attitudes/Affiliation*: attitudes toward various groups; religious beliefs; future plans (education and occupation); membership in organizations; activities outside school; personality variables.

> *Politics*: attitudes toward national pride and civil liberty; interest in public affairs; political involvement and political cynicism; political knowledge; government interest in public opinion; party identification; election voting behavior; measures of civil tolerance and political efficacy.

> *Family/Household Situation*: household composition; residential history; political background of parents; relationship with parents.

Scales on the following issues: government guaranteed job and living standard; rights of the accused; government aid to minorities; legalization of marijuana; school busing to achieve integration; equal rights for women; change in form of government; liberal/conservative views; U.S. foreign policy and Vietnam.

Number of Variables

Data from the first two waves of the study are included in ICPSR 7779. Waves I and II include 775 variables from the youth panel, and 720 variables from the parent panel. Data from the third wave are included in ICPSR 9143. For Wave III, there are 631 variables from the youth panel, and 629 variables from the parent panel.

Checklist of Topics Covered

X Gender / Gender Role	___ Relationships with Nonkin
X Race / Ethnicity	___ Other Family/Household
X Age	Characteristics
X Education	___ Child Care
X Occupation / Employment	X Wealth / Finances / Material
___ Physical Health / Disease	Things
___ Nutrition	___ Receipt of Health, Mental
___ Clinical Activities	Health, Social Services
___ Biological Functioning /	___ Adoption / Foster Care
Development	___ Childbearing / Pregnancy
___ Mental Health / Disease	___ Out-of-Wedlock Pregnancy
___ Psychological Functioning /	& Parenthood
Development	___ Abortion
___ Guidance / Counseling	___ Sexuality
X Personality	___ Sex Education
___ Intellectual Functioning	___ Contraception
X Residential Mobility	___ Sexually Transmitted
___ Dwelling	Diseases
___ Neighborhood /	X Civic/Political Activities
Community	X Friends / Social Activities
X Region / State	Social Support
X Marriage and Divorce	___ Dating, Courtship
___ Cohabitation	___ Recreation
X Family/Household	X Religion
Composition & Structure	___ Crime / Delinquency /
X Inter-Partner Relationships	Behavior Problems
X Parent-Child Relationships	___ Substance Use
___ Inter-Sibling Relationships	___ Agency Characteristics
___ Relationships with Other Kin	X Interview

Checklist of Key Variables

X Number of family members
X Identification of marital
   partners in family
___ Size of dwelling
___ Type of dwelling
X Urban/rural residence
X Region/state of residence
X Family income
X Religious affiliation
X Relation of each family
   member to:
   X Reference person
   ___ All other members
X Age of family members
   X Respondent
   X Others
X Sex of family members

X Respondent
X Others
X Race of family members
   X Respondent
   ___ Others
X Marital status of family
   members
   X Respondent
   ___ Others
X Education of family
   members
   X Respondent
   ___ Others
X Occupation of family
   members
   X Respondent
   X Others

LIMITATIONS

As is the case with any longitudinal panel study, one must be particularly concerned with contamination effects and respondent bias due to attrition. With respect to contamination effects, the investigators claim that, given the lengthy interval of time between the three waves and the nondramatic nature of the data collection, it is unlikely that a respondent's political character was significantly affected by participation in previous waves of data collection. Respondent bias is also a significant concern given the lengthy interval between waves. The investigators point out that even given the eight year delay between waves, the response rates of parents and children were extraordinarily high. In comparing the 1973 and 1965 samples, there were no significant political differences observed. There were few demographic differences between parents, except for a modestly lower representation of males, Northeasterners, and inhabitants of large metropolitan areas in the 1973 sample. Among youths in the 1973 sample, respondents were more often female, white, from smaller environs, academically more successful and more ambitious, from more privileged backgrounds, more interested in and knowledgeable about politics, more trusting of the government and of people in general, and more conservative in the partisan domain but equally or more liberal with respect to public policy issues.

Another problem in analyzing these data was in distinguishing between generational and nongenerational (i.e. life cycle or period) effects. In order to explore possible differences, the investigators compared data from a 1965 study of youth respondents who were not included in the panel sample with an additional set of data obtained from a study of high-school students in 1973. A detailed summary of this comparison can be found in Chapter 7 of *Generations and Politics*, authored by M. Kent Jennings and Richard G. Niemi.

SPONSORSHIP

The project was funded by the Danforth Foundation, the National Science Foundation, the Ford Foundation, and the National Institute on Aging.

File Structure

For the first two waves (ICPSR 7779), the OSIRIS data files contain one record per respondent, which includes data from both waves of the study. The data are formatted in a rectangular file so that the variables from the 1965 data collection appear first, followed by the 1973 variables. The third wave of data (ICPSR 9134) is available as a separate file, and the integrated three-wave data set is also available (ICPSR 9553).

List of Available Documentation

A comprehensive summary of the study, including the questionnaires and codebook, is available under the title *Youth-Parent Socialization Panel Study, 1965-1973* (1981), by M. Kent Jennings and Richard G. Niemi. The data sets are available from ICPSR (data set numbers 7779, 9134, and 9553).

Contact

Janet Vavra
Inter-university Consortium for Political and Social Research
P.O. Box 1248
Ann Arbor, MI 48106
(313) 763-5010

Cost

Members of the Inter-university Consortium for Political and Social Research (ICPSR) can obtain the data sets at no cost. Ask your ICPSR campus representative for assistance. If your institution is not a member of ICPSR, contact ICPSR for a price quote.

BIBLIOGRAPHY

Beck, P.A., & Jennings, M.K. (1969). Lowering the voting age. *Public Opinion Quarterly, 33,* 370-379.

Beck, P.A., & Jennings, M.K. (1991). Family traditions, political periods, and the development of partisan orientations. *Journal of Politics, 53,* 742-763.

Beck, P.A., & Jennings, M.K. (1982). Pathways to participation. *American Political Science Review, 76,* 94-108.

Beck, P.A., & Jennings, M.K. (1979). Political periods and political participation. *American Political Science Review, 73,* 737-750.

Beck, P.A., & Jennings, M.K. (1975). Parents as "middlepersons" in political socialization. *Journal of Politics, 37,* 83-107.

Jennings, M.K. (1967). Pre-adult orientations to multiple systems of government. *Midwest Journal of Political Science, 11,* 291-317.

Jennings, M.K. (1968). Parental grievances and school politics. *Public Opinion Quarterly, 32,* 363-378,

Jennings, M.K. (1975). Discontent with schools: Some implications for political socialization and behavior. *Youth and Society, 7,* 49-68.

Jennings, M.K. (1987). Residues of a movement: The aging of the American protest generation. *American Political Science Review, 81,* 367-382.

Jennings, M.K., & Langton, K.P. (1968). Political socialization and the high school civics curriculum in the United States. *American Political Science Review, 62,* 852-867.

Jennings, M.K., & Markus, G.B. (1988). Political involvement in the later years: A longitudinal survey. *American Journal of Political Science, 32,* 302-316.

Jennings, M.K., & Markus, G.B. (1976). Political participation and Vietnam-era war veterans: A longitudinal study. In N. Goldman and D. Segal (Eds.), *The social psychology of military research* (175-200). Beverly Hills, CA: Sage.

Jennings, M.K., & Markus, G.B. (1984). Partisan orientations over the long haul: Results from the three wave political socialization panel study. *American Political Science Review*, *78*, 1000-1018.

Jennings, M.K., & Markus, G.B. (1977). The effects of military service on political attitudes: A panel study. *American Political Science Review*, *71*, 11-147.

Jennings, M.K., & Niemi, R.G. (1968). Patterns of political learning. *Harvard Educational Review*, *38*, 443-467.

Jennings, M.K., & Niemi, R.G. (1968). The transmission of political values from parent to child. *American Political Science Review*, *62*, 169-184.

Jennings, M.K., & Niemi, R.G. (1971). The division of political labor between mothers and fathers. *American Political Science Review*, *65*, 69-82.

Jennings, M.K., & Niemi, R.G. (1974). *The political character of adolescence: The influence of families and schools*. Princeton, NJ: Princeton University.

Jennings, M.K., & Niemi, R.G. (1981). *Generations and politics: A panel study of young adults and their parents*. Princeton, NJ: Princeton University Press.

Jennings, M.K., & Niemi, R.G. (1981). *Codebook for the youth-parent socialization panel study, 1965-1973*. Ann Arbor, MI: Interuniversity Consortium for Political and Social Research.

Jennings, M.K., & Niemi, R.G. (1978). The persistence of political orientations: An overtime analysis of two generations. *British Journal of Political Science*, *8*, 333-363.

Jennings, M.K., & Niemi, R.G. (1975). Continuity and change in political orientations: A longitudinal study of two generations. *American Political Science Review, 64,* 1316-1335.

Markus, G.B. (1988). Stability and change in political attitudes: Observed, recalled, and "explained." *Political Behavior, 8,* 24-43.

Markus, G.B. (1979). The political environment and the dynamics of public attitudes: A panel study. *American Journal of Political Science, 23,* 338-359.

Niemi, R.G., & Jennings, M.K. (1991). Issues and inheritance in the formation of party identification. *American Journal of Political Science, 35,* 970-988.

11

AMERICANS VIEW THEIR MENTAL HEALTH: 1957 & 1976

Gerald Gurin
Joseph Veroff
Sheila Feld
Elizabeth Douvan
Richard Kulka

PURPOSE OF THE STUDY

The study, Americans View Their Mental Health, was an effort by the Joint Commission on Mental Illness and Health, under the direction of Congress, to evaluate the nation's resources for coping with mental illness. The survey was conducted by the University of Michigan Survey Research Center (SRC) and was designed to assess people's own evaluations of their mental health and the ways in which they handled emotional problems. Interviews were conducted first in 1957, and again with a new sample of respondents in 1976. The study provided an interesting opportunity to examine how changes in social stability and social structure over 20 years might affect people's own assessments of their quality of life in America.

METHODS

Sampling Design

The 2,460 respondents interviewed in 1957 constituted a representative sample of Americans, age 21 years or older, living in private households. Before the interviews were taken, seven regional special conferences were held in March 1957 to sensitize the interviewers to any problems that might arise because of the subject matter of the study. Interviews were conducted between March 28 and August 12, 1957.

The sample was drawn by using multi-stage area probability sampling techniques. In the first stage of sampling, 66 Primary Sampling Units (PSUs) were chosen as sample areas where interviewing would take place. Initially, all PSUs were sorted into 66 relatively homogeneous strata before specific ones were chosen as sampling points: one PSU was randomly chosen from each of the 66 strata. A PSU consisted of a county or collection of counties that fell into a Standard Metropolitan Statistical Area (SMSA). Since each of the 12 largest SMSAs constituted a single stratum by itself, all 12 automatically fell into the sample. A PSU was randomly selected from each of the remaining 54 strata.

Each selected PSU was then subdivided into smaller "secondary" areas, some of which were selected as the areas where dwelling units would be sampled. Within most urban secondary areas, the dwelling units sampled were selected from a city directory or by virtue of their location in a randomly selected block. In other areas, dwelling units were sampled in small geographic regions which were randomly selected.

Within each selected dwelling unit, one adult was randomly chosen to be interviewed. Three to ten callbacks were made by the interviewer in an attempt to reach individuals who were not at home.

The sampling procedure for the 1976 survey was similar to that employed in 1957. However, there were differences between the two samples in both the number of sample areas and in the number of designated respondents. The metropolitan areas and counties sampled, exclusive of the 12 major areas, were increased to 62 strata in 1976. Thus, a total of 74 sample areas were used. Sample size also differed between the two surveys; the 1957 survey was designed to yield about 2,500 interviews, while 1976 survey was designed to obtain about 2,300.

Three questionnaire forms (designated A, B, and C) were randomly assigned to respondents in the 1957 survey. Most of the questions, especially those dealing directly with the central objectives of the study, were asked on all three forms. Other questions were asked on only one or two of the three forms. The placement of some questions on only one or two of the questionnaires allowed for the inclusion of exploratory items while keeping the length of the interview reasonable. For the Thematic Apperception Test (TAT) portion of the survey, two-thirds of the sample (715 males and 904 females) were selected. Males and females were shown different sets of TAT pictures.

The survey structure was similar in both studies, although there were some differences. See *Description of Variables Covered* below for more information.

Periodicity

The study was conducted first in 1957, and then again with different respondents in 1976 (i.e., no attempt was made to re-interview respondents of the 1957 study).

Unit of Analysis

The unit of analysis is an individual respondent, 21 years of age or older, living in a private household in America.

Response Rates

In 1957, a total of 2,460 respondents (out of a potential sample of approximately 2,925) were interviewed. Five percent of the prospective respondents were not reached at home, even after up to ten callbacks. Of those eligible respondents found at home, eight percent refused to participate in the survey; 84% of the designated respondents were successfully interviewed.

In 1976, a total of 2,264 respondents (out of a potential sample of approximately 3,189) were interviewed. This yield constituted 71% of all designated respondents.

Attrition

Not applicable.

CONTENT

Data Sources

Three different questionnaires were randomly assigned to the respondents. While the three questionnaires were very similar, there were some slight variations to allow for the inclusion of exploratory items.

The original data were re-coded to eliminate inappropriate characters (ampersands and dashes). The data were also checked for inconsistent and illegal codes. These were corrected by referring to the original interview schedules. However, in a few instances it was impossible to be certain that the use of inappropriate code categories was completely consistent.

The codebook follows the order of the questionnaires, with the exception of the TAT section, which is located at the end of the data set. Information in the codebook appearing in carets (<>) was inserted by the processor to clarify the meaning of the text or to provide further explanatory information.

Description of Variables Covered

The questionnaire focused on several areas of life in which persons might experience problems—including marriage and parenthood, work, and general social relationships. Open- and closed-ended questions were used to explore how respondents felt about these areas, the problems respondents had in connection with them, and the way in which the problems were handled.

Information was sought regarding the respondent's use of leisure time, including group memberships and time spent with friends and relatives. Respondents were asked what things worried them and how they dealt with these worries. They were asked also to assess present happiness, the happiest time of their lives, and how they faced periods of unhappiness. Additional questions probed reactions to normal conflict situations, such as failing to do well or experiencing anger at someone close. Respondents' self perceptions were also explored.

Views about marriage in general were sought, as were specific opinions about the respondent's own marriage and spouse, and the respondent's self-evaluation as a spouse. The problems experienced by divorced and separated respondents were also addressed. A similar series of questions concerned respondents' general attitudes toward parenthood, as well as specific information about their children, their conceptions of the parental role, and their evaluations of themselves as parents. In addition, respondents were asked how they had handled problems which arose in their marriages and with their children.

Next, questionnaire items addressed respondents' occupations and work experiences. Respondents were asked whether they were satisfied with their jobs, whether they would prefer other jobs, and whether they would continue working if it were not financially necessary. Problems on the job were explored, and information was sought about methods of handling these problems. Most of the job-related questions were asked of men only. Full-time housewives were asked for their assessments of their roles and whether they had ever wanted careers. Appropriate work-related questions were addressed to retired persons and to the unemployed. And, respondents were asked about sources from which they sought job-related assistance or advice.

Finally, respondents were questioned about their past and present physical and mental health. Respondents' experiences with professional help as well as their knowledge of and attitudes toward sources of assistance with emotional and personal problems were explored. Personal data assessed included the respondent's age, sex, race, education, birthplace, religious preference and frequency of church attendance, parents' birthplace, father's occupation, and family income. Variables assessed in the TAT section included affiliation, achievement, and power.

Some items from the first study were not repeated in the second study because they were deemed irrelevant. Some questions (e.g., "Do you ever drink more than you should?"), though they lacked clarity, were repeated because they were considered to be important to the evaluation of change. New items were devised for the 1976 study in order to assess the topics of subjective well-being and styles of coping with problems. Other questionnaire items concerned help-seeking for situational crises and an assessment of feelings of depression.

Number of Variables

In the 1957 study, there were 426 variables in the original data set, although only 321 of these variables are included in the ICPSR data set. In the 1976 study, there are 850 variables.

Checklist of Topics Covered

X   Gender / Gender Role
X   Race / Ethnicity
X   Age
X   Education
X   Occupation / Employment
X   Physical Health / Disease
___ Nutrition
X   Clinical Activities
___ Biological Functioning / Development
X   Mental Health / Disease
X   Psychological Functioning / Development
X   Guidance / Counseling
X   Personality
___ Intellectual Functioning
___ Residential Mobility
X   Dwelling
X   Neighborhood / Community
X   Region / State
X   Marriage and Divorce
___ Cohabitation
X   Family/Household Composition & Structure
___ Inter-Partner Relationships
X   Parent-Child Relationships
___ Inter-Sibling Relationships
___ Relationships with Other Kin

X   Relationships with Nonkin
___ Other Family/Household Characteristics
X   Child Care
X   Wealth / Finances / Material Things
X   Receipt of Health, Mental Health, Social Services
___ Adoption / Foster Care
___ Childbearing / Pregnancy
___ Out-of-Wedlock Pregnancy & Parenthood
___ Abortion
___ Sexuality
___ Sex Education
___ Contraception
___ Sexually Transmitted Diseases
___ Civic/Political Activities
X   Friends / Social Activities
___ Social Support
___ Dating, Courtship
X   Recreation
X   Religion
___ Crime / Delinquency / Behavior Problems
X   Substance Use
___ Agency Characteristics
X   Interview

Checklist of Key Variables

X Number of family members
___ Identification of marital
    partners in family
___ Size of dwelling
___ Type of dwelling
X Urban/rural residence
X Region/state of residence
X Family income
X Religious affiliation
X Relation of each family
    member to:
    X Reference person
    ___ All other members
X Age of family members
    X Respondent
    X Others
X Sex of family members

    X Respondent
    X Others
X Race of family members
    X Respondent
    ___ Others
X Marital status of family
    members
    X Respondent
    X Others
X Education of family
    members
    X Respondent
    X Others
X Occupation of family
    members
    X Respondent
    X Others

LIMITATIONS

Since the sampling procedure restricted the survey to private households, it excluded residents of: military establishments; hospitals; educational, penal, and religious institutions; hotels; larger rooming houses; logging and lumber camps; etc. Thus, a great many people who were transient, as well as a good many who might have indicated considerable distress on questionnaire items, may have been omitted from the sample.

The principal investigators also point out that there was an unusually low response rate in the 1976 survey, especially when compared with the 1957 survey. As a potential explanation for this, they claim that the world has changed in many ways which may have limited the household survey's success. For one, the investigators assert that Americans have become less trusting and open with strangers. In addition, and perhaps even more important, most American households are deserted during the daytime hours in which persons were ordinarily interviewed or contacted in order to schedule interview appointments. With wives and mothers at work, there is no one at home to be contacted. Finally, the principal investigators note that nonresponse rates in densely populated metropolitan areas are especially high.

SPONSORSHIP

The project was sponsored by The Joint Commission on Mental Illness and Health, which had been directed by Congress to evaluate the nation's resources for coping with mental illness. Funding for the 1976 study was provided in part by the National Institutes of Mental Health.

GUIDE TO DATA AND DOCUMENTATION

File Structure

There are two components of the Osiris data set. The Osiris dictionary gives the format and other information for each variable in the Osiris data file. The dictionary or dictionary-codebook file is used in conjunction with the Osiris software package. The Osiris data file is constructed with a single logical record length of 903 bytes for each respondent.

The 1957 data set is available from ICPSR (#3503) and includes 321 variables and 2,460 cases. The 1976 data set, also available from ICPSR (#7948), contains 2,264 cases and approximately 850 variables. ICPSR has also released a third data set (#7949), which includes the 262 variables that overlap in the 1957 and 1976 studies. The total number of cases for the third data set is 4,724 (the number of 1957 and 1965 cases combined).

List of Available Documentation

A comprehensive summary of the 1957 study, including the questionnaires and codebook, is available under the title *Americans View Their Mental Health* (1975), by Gerald Gurin, Joseph Veroff, and Sheila Feld. The 1976 study, including the codebook, is summarized in *The Inner American* (1981), by Joseph Veroff, Elizabeth Douvan, and Richard Kulka. This book also provides detailed comparison and analysis between the two studies.

Contact

Janet Vavra
Inter-university Consortium for Political and Social Research
P.O. Box 1248
Ann Arbor, MI 48106
(313) 763-5010

Cost

Members of the Inter-university Consortium for Political and Social Research can obtain the data sets at no cost. Ask your ICPSR campus representative for assistance. If your institution is not a member of ICPSR, contact ICPSR for a price quote.

BIBLIOGRAPHY

Bryant, F.B., & Veroff, J. (1982, Oct.). The structure of psychological well-being: A sociohistorical analysis. *Journal of Personality & Social Psychology, 43*(4), 653-673.

Bryant, F.B., & Veroff, J. (1984, June). Dimensions of subjective mental health in American men and women. *Journal of Health & Social Behavior, 25*(2), 116-135.

Crohan, S.W., & Veroff, J. (1989, May). Dimensions of marital well-being among white and black newlyweds. *Journal of Marriage and the Family, 51*(2), 373-383.

Depner, C.E., & Veroff, J. (1979, April). Varieties of achievement motivation. *Journal of Social Psychology, 107*(2), 283-286.

Gurin, G., Veroff, J., & Feld, S. (1980). *Americans view their mental health.* New York: Arno.

Kulka, R.A., Veroff, J., & Douvan, E. (1979, March). Social class and the use of professional help for personal problems: 1957 and 1976. *Journal of Health & Social Behavior, 20*(1), 2-17.

Veroff, J. (1961). Thematic apperception in a nationwide sample survey. In J. Hagen (Ed.), *Contemporary issues in thematic apperceptive methods*, Springfield: Charles C. Thomas.

Veroff, J. (1983, September). Contextual determinants of personality. *Personality & Social Psychology Bulletin, 9*(3), 331-343.

Veroff, J., et al. (1981). *Mental health in America.* New York: Basic Books.

Veroff, J., Atkinson, J.W., Feld, S.C., & Gurin, G. (1960). The use of thematic apperception to assess motivation in a nationwide interview study. *Psychological Monographs: General and Applied, 74*, 1-32.

Veroff, J., Depner, C., Kulka, R., & Douvan, E. (1980, December). A comparison of American motives: 1957 versus 1976. *Journal of Personality and Social Psychology, 39*(1-6), 1249-1262.

Veroff, J., Douvan, E., & Kulka, R. (1981). *The inner American: A self-portrait from 1957 to 1976.* New York: Basic Books.

Veroff, J., & Feld, S. (1970). *Marriage and work in America.* New York: Van Nostrand Reinhold.

Veroff, J., Feld, S., & Crockett, H. (1966). Explorations into the effects of picture cues on thematic apperceptive expression of achievement motivation. *Journal of Personality and Social Psychology, 3,* 171-181.

Veroff, J., Feld, S., & Gurin, G. (1962, April). Achievement motivation and religious background. *American Sociological Review, 27,* 205-217.

Veroff, J., Gurin, G., & Feld, S. (1962). Dimensions of subjective adjustment. *Journal of Abnormal and Social Psychology, 64, 3,* 192-205.

Veroff, J., Reuman, D., & Feld, S. (1984, Nov.). Motives in American men and women across the adult life span. *Developmental Psychology, 20*(6), 1142-1158.

12

THE NATIONAL HEALTH INTERVIEW SURVEY ON ALCOHOL, 1988

National Center for Health Statistics

PURPOSE OF THE STUDY

Each year, the National Center for Health Statistics (NCHS) conducts the National Health Interview Survey (NHIS). The purpose of the NHIS is to provide national and regional information on major health issues, including incidence of acute illness and accidental injuries, prevalence of chronic conditions and impairments, the extent of disability, and utilization of health care services. The annual survey is regularly supplemented by additional questions that address health issues of current interest. In 1988, the NHIS was supplemented by the National Health Interview Survey on Alcohol (NHIS-A). This questionnaire assessed alcohol consumption patterns and related subjects, and was co-sponsored by the National Institute on Alcohol Abuse and Alcoholism.

METHODS

Sampling Design

Sampling procedures for the survey included a multistage area probability design, permitting continuous sampling and interviewing of representative households across the United States. Households were chosen from a probability sample of the civilian, noninstitutionalized population.

General sampling procedures for the NHIS: Primary sampling units are drawn from a larger set of geographically defined sampling units. A sampling unit is defined as a county, a small group of contiguous counties, or a Metropolitan Statistical Area. Sampling units are divided into four panels, each a representative sample of the United States population. Within a sampling unit, segments of approximately 40 households are further defined. Eight households from each segment are then selected for the NHIS sample. In order to increase the precision of estimates for black members of the population, oversampling of black households has been part of the sampling procedure since 1985. Overall, this design increases flexibility in sample size manipulations and implementing follow-up studies. Both national and regional estimates may be obtained from sample data.

In 1988, the NHIS collected health information from a sample of approximately 122,000 family members in 47,000 families. The Alcohol Survey was administered to one randomly selected participant, 18 years of age or older, in each selected household. In order to obtain national estimates, it is recommended that all person-level variables be analyzed using the annual basic weight provided in the NHIS-A data tape. Variables measured by reports of events in a two-week period should be multiplied by the two-week weight to obtain the annual national estimate.

Periodicity

The NHIS has conducted two surveys focussing on alcohol consumption and related issues: 1983 and 1988.

Unit of Analysis

The primary unit of analysis is the individual.

Response Rates

Annual response rate for the NHIS is greater than 95 percent of eligible households in the sample. Overall response rate for the NHIS-A was approximately 87 percent, yielding 43,809 interviews.

Attrition

Not applicable.

CONTENT

Data Sources

Alcohol survey data were collected through face-to-face interviews. Participants were randomly chosen from those household members over the age of 18 that had already agreed to participate in the NHIS. Because of the sensitive nature of some of the questions, participants were given the option of using a self-administered questionnaire format on the second half of the survey. Thirty-five percent or approximately 15,333 of the NHIS-A sample chose this option. Interviews were conducted by trained personnel from the U.S. Bureau of the Census. The average time per interview was 50 minutes.

Description of Variables Covered

The NHIS-A questionnaire was designed with three main sections. Demographic and basic health variables from the NHIS comprised the first part of the questionnaire. Questions covering alcohol consumption patterns were divided into two sections, A and B. Section A was administered to all participants and began with a set of questions that categorized participants in one of the following "drinking status" categories: abstainer, lifetime infrequent drinker, current drinker, and former drinker. In addition, participants were asked to report on the drinking habits of family members; perceptions of what constitutes light, moderate, and heavy drinking; and selected chronic health conditions such as diabetes and heart disease. Different sets of questions from Section B were administered to participants depending on the particular drinking status assigned by the interviewer. Section B asked for specific information on drinking behavior, reasons for drinking or not drinking, and existence of alcohol-related problems.

Number of Variables

NHIS Demographic and Basic Health Variables:	68
Alcohol Variables Sections A and B:	269
Other (Weights, Region, Sampling Unit, etc.):	19
Total Variables in Alcohol Supplement	356

Total Number of Respondent Records: 43,809

Checklist of Topics Covered

X Gender / Gender Role
X Race / Ethnicity
X Age
X Education
X Occupation / Employment
X Physical Health / Disease
___ Nutrition
X Clinical Activities
___ Biological Functioning / Development
___ Mental Health / Disease
___ Psychological Functioning / Development
___ Guidance / Counseling
___ Personality
___ Intellectual Functioning
___ Residential Mobility
X Dwelling
X Neighborhood / Community
X Region / State
X Marriage and Divorce
___ Cohabitation
X Family/Household Composition & Structure
___ Inter-Partner Relationships
___ Parent-Child Relationships
___ Inter-Sibling Relationships
___ Relationships with Other Kin

___ Relationships with Nonkin
X Other Family/Household Characteristics
___ Child Care
X Wealth / Finances / Material Things
X Receipt of Health, Mental Health, Social Services
___ Adoption / Foster Care
X Childbearing / Pregnancy
___ Out-of-Wedlock Pregnancy & Parenthood
___ Abortion
___ Sexuality
___ Sex Education
___ Contraception
___ Sexually Transmitted Diseases
___ Civic/Political Activities
___ Friends / Social Activities
___ Social Support
___ Dating, Courtship
___ Recreation
___ Religion
___ Crime / Delinquency / Behavior Problems
X Substance Use
___ Agency Characteristics
X Interview

Checklist of Key Variables

X Number of family members
X Identification of marital
    partners in family
X Size of dwelling
X Type of dwelling
X Urban/rural residence
X Region/state of residence
X Family income
____ Religious affiliation
X Relation of each family
    member to:
    X Reference person
    X All other members
X Age of family members
    X Respondent
    X Others
X Sex of family members

    X Respondent
    X Others
X Race of family members
    X Respondent
    X Others
X Marital status of family
    members
    X Respondent
    X Others
X Education of family
    members
    X Respondent
    ____ Others
X Occupation of family
    members
    X Respondent
    ____ Others

LIMITATIONS

Because the NHIS-A surveyed individuals 18 years of age and older, direct information on pre-teen or adolescent drinking patterns within the family is not available.

Self-reports of individual drinking patterns and behavior may be inconsistent. Minor inconsistencies in these data were allowed if, for example, they occurred on nonadjacent questions. Obvious inconsistencies in self-estimates of drinking patterns were adjusted to reflect the highest reported value. Out of range values were retained in the data set, and may be eliminated or recoded at the discretion of the analyst.

SPONSORSHIP

The National Health Interview Survey on alcohol was co-sponsored by the National Center for Health Statistics and the National Institute on Alcohol Abuse and Alcoholism. National Health Interview Surveys conducted by the National Center for Health Statistics are funded through the provisions made by the National Health Survey Act of 1956.

GUIDE TO DATA AND DOCUMENTATION

File Structure

An IBM standard-label, 6250 bpi Public Use Data Tape is available from the National Technical Information Service. The tape contains data from the NHIS basic health and demographic questionnaire in the first section, and data from the alcohol questionnaire beginning in location 336. The location and arrangement of specific alcohol data fields is different from the order in which the corresponding questions appear on the questionnaire.

Although Section B of the questionnaire asked different sets of questions to different types of drinkers, many of the questions were identical or similar. Fields originally allocated for similar questions asked of different drinkers have been condensed.

Respondents were asked to assess the drinking status of each other adult in the family. These individuals were identified by person number. The data tape includes the following NHIS basic health and demographic information for these family members: sex, age, education, and relationship to the household reference person (the only relationship code available). These data, for up to six persons, are found in locations 447 to 494.

List of Available Documentation

The Public Use Data Tape contains microdata from the alcohol questionnaire and summary data from the NHIS basic health and demographic questionnaire for each sample person. It is possible to link records from this file to records of the same person in other files from the 1988 NHIS.

Contact

> Division of Health Interview Statistics
> National Center for Health Statistics
> Presidential Building, Room 850
> 6525 Belcrest Road
> Hyattsville, MD 20782
> (301) 436-7085

For more information:

> Gerry E. Hendershot, Ph.D.
> Chief, Illness and Disability Statistics Branch
> Division of Health Interview Statistics
> National Center for Health Statistics
> 6525 Belcrest Road, Room 860
> Hyattsville, MD 20782
> (301) 436-7089

Cost

> $200

Dawson, D.A. (1992). The effect of parental alcohol dependence on perceived children's behavior. *Journal of Substance Abuse, 4,* 329-340.

Dawson, D.A. (1993). Relative frequency of heavy drinking and the risk of DSM-III-R alcohol dependence. *British Journal of Addiction* (in press).

Dawson, D.A. (1993). Patterns of alcohol consumption: Beverage effects on gender differences. *British Journal of Addiction, 88,* 133-138.

Dawson, D.A., & Archer, L. (1992). Gender differences in alcohol consumption: Effects of measurement. *British Journal of Addiction, 87,* 119-123.

Dawson, D.A., Grant, B.F., & Harford, T.C. (1992). Parental history of alcoholism and probability of marriage. *Journal of Substance Abuse, 4,* 117-129.

Dawson, D.A., & Grant, B.F. (in press). Gender effects in diagnosing alcohol abuse and dependence. *Journal of Clinical Psychology.*

Dawson, D.A., Harford, T.C., & Grant, B.F. (1992). Family history as a predictor of alcohol dependence. *Alcoholism: Clinical and Experimental Research, 16,* 572-575.

Grant, B.F. (1992). Prevalence of the proposed DSM-IV alcohol use disorders: United States, 1988. *Journal of Substance Abuse, 87,* 309-316.

Grant, B.F., Chou, S.P., Pickering, R.P., & Hasin, D.S. (1992). Empirical subtypes of DSM-III-R alcohol dependence: United States, 1988. *Drug and Alcohol Dependence, 30,* 75-84.

Grant, B.F., Harford, T.C., Hasin, D.S., Chow, P., & Pickering, R. (1992). DSM-III-R and the proposed DSM-IV alcohol use disorders, United States, 1988: A nosological comparison. *Alcoholism: Clinical and Experimental Research, 16*, 215-221.

Harford, T.C., Parker, D.A., Grant, B.F., & Dawson, D.A. (1992). Alcohol use and dependence among employed men and women in the United States in 1988. *Alcoholism: Clinical and Experimental Research, 16*, 146-148.

National Center for Health Statistics (1987). *Health interview statistics.* U.S. Public Health Service: U.S. Government Printing Office.

National Center for Health Statistics. *1988 National health interview survey on alcohol.* Hyattsville, MD: Author.

Schoenborn, C.A. (1991) *Exposure to alcoholism in the family: United States, 1988.* (Advance Data from Vital and Health Statistics, No. 205). Hyattsville, MD: National Center for Health Statistics.

Stinson, F.S., DeBakey, S.F., & Steffens, R.A. (1992). Prevalence of DSM-III-R alcohol abuse and/or dependence among selected occupations, United States, 1988. *Alcohol Health and Research World, 16*, 165-172.

13

NATIONAL HEALTH INTERVIEW SURVEY ON CHILD HEALTH, 1988

National Center for Health Statistics

NATIONAL HEALTH PLAN EXPENDITURE SURVEY OVER THE HEALTH, 1996

PURPOSE OF THE STUDY

Since 1957, the National Health Interview Survey (NHIS) has asked a standard set of health and demographic questions about each member of sample families. In addition, one or more questionnaires on special health topics has been administered to one or more selected family members. For 1988, the NHIS special topic focussed on the health of one randomly selected child zero to seventeen years of age in each sample household, thus creating the Child Health Supplement (NHIS-CH). In addition to the Child Health Supplement the standard core questionnaire contained the usual items on demographic and health information for other individuals within the sample child's household: child care, marital history of the child's parents, geographic mobility, circumstances of the pregnancy and birth, injuries, impairments, acute conditions, chronic conditions, passive smoking, sleep habits, school problems, developmental problems, and use of health care services.

METHODS

Sampling Design

The sample design of the survey has undergone changes following each decennial census. This periodic redesign of the NHIS sample allows the incorporation of the latest population information and statistical methodology into the survey design. The data presented in this report are from an NHIS sample design first used in 1985. It is anticipated that this design will be used until 1995.

The sample design plan of the NHIS follows a multistage probability design that permits a continuous sampling of the civilian noninstitutionalized population residing in the United States. The sample does not include persons residing in nursing homes, members of the armed forces, or U. S. nationals living abroad. The survey is designed in such a way that the sample scheduled for each week is representative of the selected population, and the weekly samples are additive over time. This design permits estimates for high-frequency measures or for large population groups to be produced from a short period of data collection. The annual sample is designed so that tabulations can be provided for each of the four major geographical regions. Because interviewing is done throughout the year, there is no seasonal bias for annual estimates. The continuous data collection also has administrative and operational advantages because fieldwork can be handled on a continuous basis with an experienced, stable staff.

For the first stage of the sample design, the United States is considered to be a universe composed of approximately 1,900 geographically defined primary sampling units (PSUs). A PSU consists of a county, a small group of contiguous counties, or a metropolitan statistical area. The PSUs collectively cover the 50 states and the District of Columbia. The 52 largest PSUs are selected into the sample with certainty and are referred to as self-representing PSUs. The other PSUs in the universe are referred to as non-self-representing PSUs. These PSUs are clustered into 73 strata, and 2 sample PSUs are chosen from each stratum with probability proportional to population size. This gives a total of 198 PSUs selected in the first stage.

Within a PSU, two types of second stage units are used: area segments and permit area segments. Area segments are defined geographically and contain an expected eight households. Permit area segments cover geographical areas containing housing units built after the 1980 census. The permit area segments are defined using updated lists of building permits issued in the PSU since 1980 and contain an expected four households.

Within each segment all occupied households are selected for interview. On occasion, a sample segment may contain a large number of households. In this situation the households are subsampled to provide a manageable interviewer workload.

The sample was designed so that a typical NHIS sample for the data collection years 1985 to 1995 will consist of approximately 7,500 segments containing about 59,000 assigned households. Of these households, an expected 10,000 will be vacant, demolished, or occupied by persons not in the selected population of the survey. The expected sample of 49,000 occupied households will yield a probability sample of about 127,000 persons.

13 - 2

Features of the NHIS Sample Redesign

Starting in 1985, the NHIS design incorporated several new design features. The major changes include the following:

1. *The use of an all-area frame.* The NHIS is now designed so that it can serve as a sample frame for other NCHS population-based surveys. In previous NHIS designs about two-thirds of the sample was obtained from lists of addresses compiled at the time of the decennial census; that is, a list frame. Due to U.S. Bureau of the Census confidentiality restrictions, these sample addresses could be used for only those surveys being conducted by the U.S. Bureau of the Census. The methodology used to obtain addresses in the 1985 NHIS area frame does not use the census address lists. The sample addresses thus obtained can be used as a sampling frame for other NCHS surveys.

2. *The NHIS as four panels.* Four national subdesigns, or panels, constitute the full NHIS. Each panel contains a representative sample of the U.S. civilian noninstitutionalized population. Each of the four panels has the same sampling properties, and any combination of panels defines a national design. Panels were constructed to facilitate the linkage of NHIS to other surveys, and also to efficiently make large reductions in the size of the sample by eliminating panels from the survey.

3. *The oversampling of black persons.* One of the goals in designing the current NHIS was to improve the precision of estimates for black persons. This was accomplished by the use of differential sampling rates in PSUs with between about 5- and 50-percent black population. Sampling rates for selection of segments were increased in areas known to have the highest concentrations of black persons. Segment sampling rates were decreased in other areas within the PSU to ensure that the total sample in each PSU was the same size as it would have been without oversampling black persons.

4. *The reduction of the number of sampled PSUs.* Interviewer travel to sample PSUs constitutes a large component of the total field costs for the NHIS. The previous NHIS design included 376 PSUs. Research showed that reducing the number of sample PSUs while increasing the sample size within PSUs would reduce travel costs and

also maintain the reliability of health estimates. The design now contains 198 PSUs.

5. *The selection of two PSUs per non-self-representing stratum.* In the previous design, one PSU was selected from each non-self-representing stratum. This feature necessitated the use of less efficient variance estimation procedures; the selection of two PSUs allows more efficient variance estimation methodology.

Periodicity

The National Health Interview Survey is a continuous survey.

Unit of Analysis

The individual respondent (one adult and one child age zero to seventeen) is the unit of analysis.

Response Rates

The overall response rate for the NHIS-CH is about 91 percent.

Attrition

Not applicable.

CONTENT

Data Sources

The National Health Interview Survey (NHIS) is a continuous, cross-sectional survey representing the household population of the United States. Typically, different households are sampled every year by face-to-face interview with a sample of about 122,000 family members in about 47,000 families. For the 1988 NHIS-CH, additional information was collected for one randomly selected child zero to seventeen years of age in each NHIS sample household, resulting in a sample of 17,110 children. When possible (in 80 percent of cases), the respondent for the NHIS-CH was the mother of the sample child. If the mother was not available, the respondent was another adult member of the family who was well-informed about the sample child's health.

Careful procedures are followed to assure the quality of data collected in the interview. Most households in the sample are contacted by mail before the interviewers arrive. Potential respondents are informed of the importance of the survey and assured that all information obtained in the interview will be held in strict confidence. Interviewers make repeated trips to a household when a respondent is not immediately found. The success of these procedures is indicated by the response rate for the survey, which has been between 95 and 98 percent over the years.

When contact is made, the interviewer attempts to have all family members of the household 19 years of age and over present during the interview. When this is not possible, proxy responses for absent adult family members are accepted. In most situations, proxy respondents are used for persons under 19 years of age. Persons 17 and 18 years of age may respond for themselves, however.

Interviewers undergo extensive training and retraining. The quality of their work is checked by means of periodic observation and by reinterview. Their work is also evaluated by statistical studies of the data they obtain in their interviews. A field edit is performed on all completed interviews so that if there are any problems with the information on the questionnaire, respondents may by recontacted to solve the problem.

Completed questionnaires are sent from the U.S. Bureau of the Census field offices to NCHS for coding and editing. To ensure the accuracy of coding, a 5-percent sample of all questionnaires is recoded and keyed by other coders. A 100-percent verification procedure is used if certain error tolerances are exceeded. Staff of the Division of Health Interview Statistics then edit the files to remove impossible and inconsistent codes.

Description of Variables Covered

Key demographic variables covered in this survey are: the sex and current age of the sample child, the child's reported main racial background, the marital status of the child, the highest school year completed and whether or not the child is currently going to school or is on vacation, the child's employment status in the past two weeks, the annual family income of the child, the region where the child resides, and the total number of persons in the sample child's household.

There are a wide range of variables that cover the child's health. A partial list follows: the child's current height and weight; prenatal care and child's birthweight; visits to doctors, dentists, and hospitals; whether or not household members smoke; health status of the child; age of child when s(he) had an accident, injury, or poisoning; whether or not the child's activity is restricted or if child has a permanent impairment; whether or not the child missed school due to his/her health; the child's bedtime schedule; the mental health of the child; whether or not the child has growth or developmental delays; and whether or not the child receives Medicaid.

Number of Variables

The data file for the 1988 study includes 1,347 variables and 17,110 cases.

Checklist of Topics Covered

- X Gender / Gender Role
- X Race / Ethnicity
- X Age
- X Education
- X Occupation / Employment
- X Physical Health / Disease
- ___ Nutrition
- X Clinical Activities
- X Biological Functioning / Development
- X Mental Health / Disease
- X Psychological Functioning / Development
- ___ Guidance / Counseling
- ___ Personality
- ___ Intellectual Functioning
- X Residential Mobility
- X Dwelling
- X Neighborhood / Community
- X Region / State
- X Marriage and Divorce
- ___ Cohabitation
- X Family/Household Composition & Structure
- ___ Inter-Partner Relationships
- X Parent-Child Relationships
- ___ Inter-Sibling Relationships
- ___ Relationships with Other Kin
- ___ Relationships with Nonkin
- ___ Other Family/Household Characteristics
- X Child Care
- X Wealth / Finances / Material Things
- X Receipt of Health, Mental Health, Social Services
- ___ Adoption / Foster Care
- X Childbearing / Pregnancy
- ___ Out-of-Wedlock Pregnancy & Parenthood
- ___ Abortion
- ___ Sexuality
- ___ Sex Education
- ___ Contraception
- ___ Sexually Transmitted Diseases
- ___ Civic/Political Activities
- ___ Friends / Social Activities
- ___ Social Support
- ___ Dating, Courtship
- ___ Recreation
- ___ Religion
- ___ Crime / Delinquency / Behavior Problems
- ___ Substance Use
- ___ Agency Characteristics
- X Interview

Checklist of Key Variables

X Number of family members
X Identification of marital
  partners in family
___ Size of dwelling
X Type of dwelling
___ Urban/rural residence
X Region/state of residence
X Family income
___ Religious affiliation
X Relation of each family
  member to:
   X Reference person
   X All other members
X Age of family members
  X Respondent
  X Others
X Sex of family members

  X Respondent
  X Others
X Race of family members
  X Respondent
  X Others
X Marital status of family
  members
  X Respondent
  X Others
X Education of family
  members
  X Respondent
  X Others
X Occupation of family
  members
  X Respondent
  X Others

LIMITATIONS

It should be noted that the health characteristics described by NHIS estimates pertain only to the resident, civilian noninstitutionalized population of the United States living at the time of the interview. Therefore, the exclusion of persons residing in nursing homes, members of the armed forces, institutionalized persons, and U.S. nationals living abroad could be considered a limitation (albeit a minor one for a study of child health!).

SPONSORSHIP

The 1988 National Health Interview Survey on Child Health (NHIS-CH) was cosponsored by the National Institute for Child Health and Human Development and the Health Resources and Services Administration.

GUIDE TO DATA AND DOCUMENTATION

File Structure

Machine-readable data and documentation files are available in mainframe tape format or on CD-ROM for microcomputers. A description of the contents of each file is given below.

File 1 (Data): Raw data file. The format of this file is described in the "data list" section of the SPSS program file (file 2).

File 2 (SPSS Program): This file consists of SPSS-X program statements designed to read the raw data in file 1 and create an SPSS-X active file. The SPSS-X program file contains data list statements, variable names and labels, value labels, and missing value declarations.

File 3 (SAS Program): This file consists of SAS program statements designed to read the raw data in file 1 and create a SAS active file. The contents of this file are analogous to the contents of the previously described file 2. SPSS Users should use file 2; SAS users, file 3. Users may need to add "job control language" (JCL) statements to the SAS program file to meet the requirements for their specific operating system. For some operating systems, e.g., Unix, running the SAS program statements may result in a "segmentation violation" message from SAS due to a limit on the number of independent sets of format labels (the current limit is about 300) that can be assigned to variables. The SAS Institute plans to release an updated version of SAS early in 1993 that will correct the problem. Until then, if a segmentation violation occurs, one solution is to edit the SAS program statements to remove format (value label) assignments for all variables unrelated to the analysis at hand.

File 4 (Dictionary): Sequential list of variable and value labels. This file consists of DISPLAY DICTIONARY output describing the SPSS-X active file created by the program in File 2. Variables are listed in sequential order. Variable names and labels, value labels, missing value designations, print formats, and write formats are clearly displayed.

File 5 (Statistics): Unweighted frequencies or other descriptive statistics for each variable. Descriptive statistics only are provided for variables with more than 50 value categories, such as respondent identification number, zip codes, etc.

List of Available Documentation

A User's Guide which accompanies the machine-readable files provides the following information: Summary; General study overview; Description of machine-readable files and supplementary documentation; Specifications for machine-readable files; Key characteristics report; Distribution of variables by topic and type; and Data completeness and consistency report.

Paper versions of the machine-readable SPSS and SAS program files and data documentation (files 2-5 above), and copies of the original instrument and codebook, are available upon request (at 15 cents per page).

Contact

Sociometrics Corporation
American Family Data Archive
170 State Street, Suite 260
Los Altos, California 94022-2812
(415) 949-3282

Cost

The cost for the machine-readable data set (Data Set 33-34 of the American Family Data Archive) is $150. This price includes the raw data, SPSS program statements, the SAS program statements, the Dictionary, and the Frequencies in mainframe tape, and the accompanying printed and bound User's Guide. The CD-ROM version costs $175. Paper versions of the Original NHIS-CH Codebook and Instrument cost $27.15 and $14.40, respectively.

BIBLIOGRAPHY

Aday, L. (1992). *Health insurance and utilization of medical care for chronically ill children with special needs* (Advance Data from Vital and Health Statistics, No. 215). Hyattsville, MD: National Center for Health Statistics.

Bloom, B. (1990). *Health insurance and medical care: Health of our nation's children, United States, 1988* (Advance Data from Vital and Health Statistics, No. 188). Hyattsville, MD: National Center for Health Statistics.

Corman, H., & Kaestner, R. (1992). The effects of child health on marital status and family Structure. *Demography 29*(3), 389-408.

Dawson, D.A. (1991). Family structure and children's health: United States, 1988. National Center for Health Statistics. *Vital Health Statistics, 10*(178).

Dawson, D.A., & Cain, V.S. (1990). *Child care arrangements: health of our nation's children, United States, 1988* (Advance Data from Vital and Health Statistics, No. 187). Hyattsville, MD: National Center for Health Statistics.

Hardy, A.M. (1991). Incidence and impact of selected infectious diseases in childhood. Center for Health Statistics. *Vital Health Statistics, 10*(180).

Holmes, B.C., Kaplan, A.S., Lang, E.L., & Card, J.J. (1991). *National health interview survey on children, 1988: A user's guide to the machine-readable files and documentation.* Los Altos, CA: Sociometrics Corporation, American Family Data Archive.

Newacheck, P.W. (1992). Characteristics of children with high and low usage of physician services. *Medical Care, 30*(1), 30-42.

Overpect, M.D., & Moss, A.J. (1991). *Children's exposure to environmental cigarette smoke before and after birth: Health of our nation's children, United States, 1988* (Advance Data from Vital and Health Statistics, No. 202). Hyattsville, MD: National Center for Health Statistics.

U.S. Department of Health and Human Services, Public Health Service, Centers for Disease Control, National Center for Health Statistics (1988). *NHIS Public Use Tape Records: Outline of Items and Codes.*

U.S. Department of Health and Human Services, Public Health Service, Centers for Disease Control, National Center for Health Statistics (1991). *Vital and Health Statistics: Current Estimates From the National Health Interview Survey, 1990 (Series 10, No.181).*

Zill, N., & Schoenborn, C.A. (1990). *Developmental, learning, and emotional problems: Health of our nation's children, United States, 1988* (Advance Data from Vital and Health Statistics, No. 190). Hyattsville, MD: National Center for Health Statistics.

14

THE 1981 CHILD HEALTH SUPPLEMENT TO THE NATIONAL HEALTH INTERVIEW SURVEY

National Center for Health Statistics

PURPOSE OF THE STUDY

Since 1957, the National Health Interview Survey (NHIS) has conducted household interviews using representative samples of the noninstitutional U.S. civilian population. The purpose of the NHIS is to provide national data on the incidence of acute illness and accidental injuries, the prevalence of chronic conditions and impairments, the extent of disability, the utilization of health care services, and other health-related topics. The annual survey is regularly supplemented by additional questions that address health issues of current interest. In 1981, the supplemental topics were devoted entirely to children.

Development of the Child Health Supplement began in the spring of 1978 when a panel of child health experts was formed by the National Institute of Child Health and Human Development to advise the NHIS staff. The panel met several times in 1978 and 1979 and was instrumental in selecting specific child health topics. In addition, input was received from federal agencies and programs concerned with child health. The supplement went through many revisions as it was informally pretested, and a formal pretest in 1980 resulted in further refinements.

METHODS

Sampling Design

The sampling plan for the NHIS follows a multistage probability design which permits continuous sampling of households. The survey is designed to yield national estimates, although estimates can also be obtained for the four geographic regions of the U.S. The households selected for interview are a probability sample representative of the target population. Excluded from the sample are institutionalized patients, persons on active duty with the Armed Forces, United States nationals living in foreign countries, and persons who have died during the year preceding the interview.

General NHIS Sampling Procedures: A sample of 376 primary sampling units (PSUs) are selected from the approximately 1,900 geographically-defined PSUs in the United States. Within the target PSUs, about 12,000 segments are randomly selected. Data are then collected from each eligible household within the segments. Data collection is spread evenly throughout the year with roughly 800 households interviewed each week. Each calendar year, data are collected from approximately 40,000 households containing about 110,000 persons.

The 1981 Child Health Supplement gathered data on 15,416 children. For each NHIS family having one or more children under 18 years of age, one child was selected at random for the Child Health Supplement.

Periodicity

Child health supplements were part of the NHIS in 1981 and 1988.

Unit of Analysis

The primary unit of analysis is the individual child.

Response Rates

Annual response rate for the NHIS is usually between 96 and 98 percent of the eligible households sampled. Response rate for the 1981 NHIS core questionnaire was 97.1 percent and interviews were completed for 97.9 percent of the children in this group of respondents for an effective response rate of 95.1 percent.

Attrition

Not applicable to this study because the 1988 sample was independent of the 1981 sample, i.e., no attempt was made in 1988 to reinterview respondents from the 1981 study.

CONTENT

Data Sources

Survey data were collected through personal interviews. The biological mother was the preferred respondent for the children, and in

82 percent of the cases, she was interviewed. Ten percent of the respondents were biological fathers with the remainder consisting of other caretakers. The U.S. Bureau of the Census conducted field interviewing as an agent of the National Center for Health Statistics (NCHS).

Description of Variables Covered

The 1981 Child Care Supplement included variables in the following topic areas:

> Family Structure
> Child Care Arrangements
> Breastfeeding
> Motor and Social Development
> Medications
> Birth and Prenatal Events
> Lifetime Hospitalizations and Surgery
> Chronic Conditions
> Weight
> Eyes and Teeth
> School Attendance and Performance
> Behavior Problems
> Social Effects of Ill Health
> Sleep Habits

Additionally, in the core of the NHIS questionnaire, data were collected for the same children on health-related restrictions on activities, accidents and injuries, illness or impairment, doctor visits, dental visits, and basic socioeconomic information such as race and family income. This data set should prove useful as a baseline national sample for comparisons with smaller or more specific data sets.

Number of Variables

Total Number of Variables: 1,462

Checklist of Topics Covered

X Gender / Gender Role	___ Relationships with Nonkin
X Race / Ethnicity	X Other Family/Household
X Age	Characteristics
X Education	X Child Care
X Occupation / Employment	X Wealth / Finances / Material
X Physical Health / Disease	Things
X Nutrition	X Receipt of Health, Mental
X Clinical Activities	Health, Social Services
X Biological Functioning /	X Adoption / Foster Care
Development	X Childbearing / Pregnancy
___ Mental Health / Disease	___ Out-of-Wedlock Pregnancy
___ Psychological Functioning /	& Parenthood
Development	___ Abortion
___ Guidance / Counseling	___ Sexuality
___ Personality	___ Sex Education
___ Intellectual Functioning	___ Contraception
X Residential Mobility	___ Sexually Transmitted
X Dwelling	Diseases
X Neighborhood /	___ Civic/Political Activities
Community	___ Friends / Social Activities
X Region / State	___ Social Support
X Marriage and Divorce	___ Dating, Courtship
___ Cohabitation	___ Recreation
X Family/Household	___ Religion
Composition & Structure	X Crime / Delinquency /
___ Inter-Partner Relationships	Behavior Problems
___ Parent-Child Relationships	___ Substance Use
___ Inter-Sibling Relationships	___ Agency Characteristics
___ Relationships with Other Kin	X Interview

Checklist of Key Variables

X Number of family members
X Identification of marital
  partners in family
X Size of dwelling
X Type of dwelling
X Urban/rural residence
X Region/state of residence
X Family income
___ Religious affiliation
X Relation of each family
  member to:
  X Reference person
  X All other members
X Age of family members
  X Respondent
  X Others
X Sex of family members

X Respondent
X Others
X Race of family members
  X Respondent
  X Others
X Marital status of family
  members
  X Respondent
  X Others
X Education of family
  members
  X Respondent
  X Others
X Occupation of family
  members
  X Respondent
  X Others

LIMITATIONS

In accordance with the design of this study, only the biological parent or other caregiver reported on the health of the selected child. Older children, who may have been better able to answer certain health questions, were not included as respondents. Because a single child was randomly selected from the families interviewed, comparisons between children within a family are not possible. Although the sample itself was large, many questions within the survey focused on specific health issues, such as early development. This limits the range of information available on adolescent and teenage health care.

SPONSORSHIP

The 1981 Child Health Supplement was co-sponsored by the National Center for Health Statistics, the National Institute for Child Health and Human Development and the Health Resources and Services Administration.

GUIDE TO DATA AND DOCUMENTATION

File Structure

A 6250 bpi density Public Use Tape containing 15,416 records is available from the Division of Health Interview Statistics.

List of Available Documentation

The following documentation can be ordered from the Division of Health Interview Statistics of the National Center for Health Statistics:

National Center for Health Statistics. *1981 Child Health Supplement to the National Health Interview Survey*. [Public Use Tape Documentation]. Hyattsville, MD: National Center for Health Statistics.

Alternate Source for Data and Documentation

This data set is also available from the Data Archive on Adolescent Pregnancy and Pregnancy Prevention, Sociometrics Corporation. The data set (DAAPPP Data Set No. 86-87) is available on mainframe tape for $150, microcomputer floppy diskettes for $100, or CD-ROM for $175. The files consist of:

1) Raw Data File (LRECL=2400 BLKSIZE=24000)

2) SPSS Program Statements—SPSS-X for mainframe or SPSS/PC and SPSS/PC+ for microcomputer designed to read and document the raw data file (SAS program statements are available for an additional charge of $50)

3) A User's Guide

Contact

National Center for Health Statistics
Scientific and Technical Information Branch
3700 East-West Highway, Room 2-44
Hyattsville, MD 20782
(301) 436-8500

or

Sociometrics Corporation
170 State Street, Suite 260
Los Altos, CA 94022-2812
(415) 949-3282

Cost

The cost is $160 from National Center for Health Statistics.

or

The cost for the Sociometrics Corporation machine-readable data set (DAAPPP Data Set 86-87) is $150 for mainframe computer tape or $100 for hi-density diskettes. This price includes the raw data, SPSS program statements, and the accompanying printed and bound

User's Guide. SAS program statements are an additional $50. The CD-ROM version costs $175. Paper versions of the original Codebook and Instrument can be obtained for $37.05 and $10.65, respectively.

BIBLIOGRAPHY

Kovar, M.G. (1985). Use of medications and vitamin-mineral supplements by children and youths. *Public Health Reports, 100*(5), 470-473.

Moss, A.J., Overpeck, M.D., Hendershot, G.E., Hoffman, H.J., & Berendes, H.W. (1985). Prenatal smoking and childhood morbidity. In *Proceedings from the International Conference on Smoking and Reproductive Health,* San Francisco, CA, October 15-17.

Poe, G. (no date). *Design and procedures for the 1981 child health supplement to the National Health Interview Survey.* Hyattsville, MD: The National Center for Health Statistics.

Ritter, P.L., & Card, J.J. (1986). *1981 child health supplement to the National Health Interview Survey, A user's guide to the machine readable files and documentation* (Data Set 86-87). Los Altos, CA: Sociometrics Corporation, Data Archive on Adolescent Pregnancy and Pregnancy Prevention.

Zill, N., & Peterson, J.L. (Eds.). (1989). *Guide to federal data on children, youth, and families.* Washington, DC: Child Trends.

15

THE 1988 NATIONAL MATERNAL AND INFANT HEALTH SURVEY

National Center for Health Statistics

PURPOSE OF THE STUDY

The 1988 National Maternal and Infant Health Survey (NMIHS) was conducted by the National Center for Health Statistics (NCHS) to study factors relating to poor pregnancy outcome such as: inadequate prenatal care; inadequate and excessive weight gain during pregnancy; pregnancy and delivery complications; and maternal smoking, drinking, and drug use. Data were obtained from mothers and the hospital and prenatal care provider they used.

METHODS

Sampling Design

Before a four-state pretest and the main survey were conducted, small-scale pilot tests were done in the NCHS questionnaire laboratory. Participants in the U.S. Department of Agriculture's Women, Infants, and Children (WIC) program and mothers who had lost an infant were recruited for pilot tests which were conducted by NCHS's National Laboratory for Cognition and Survey Methodology Measurement, which is overseen by NCHS's Office of Research and Methodology. Special attention was given to the wording of questions for mothers who had suffered a fetal or infant loss; and, prior to the pretest, support groups of mothers who had miscarriages, still-births, or infant deaths provided insight about the sensitivity of the questionnaire and its accompanying brochure.

The Bureau of the Census, under contract from NCHS, collected NMIHS pretest and main survey data. The NMIHS pretest was conducted between October 1987 and January 1988, and was based on 247 live births, 127 late fetal deaths, and 201 infant deaths that occurred during 1987 in Arkansas, Michigan, Tennessee, and Wisconsin. It was designed to test data-collection methods in general, and two methods of contacting unmarried mothers in particular.

The Bureau of the Census collected NMIHS main survey data for NCHS between January 1989 and June 1991. The survey drew stratified random samples from calendar year 1988 vital records from 48 states, the District of Columbia, and New York City. The samples included 9,953 certificates of live birth, 1,000 urban Indian certificates of live birth, 3,309 reports of fetal death at 28 weeks' gestation or more, and 5,332 certificates of death for infants under 1 year of age. Because black infants have rates of low birthweight and infant mortality about twice those of white infants, low- and very low-birthweight black and white infants were oversampled in the natality component of the study. In addition, black infants were oversampled in the fetal death and infant death components to obtain a sufficient number of high-risk births for special studies. Hispanics were oversampled in Texas, since 33.7 percent of 1988 Texas births were to Hispanics.

Mothers were mailed a 35-page questionnaire, a brochure, and a prepaid return envelope. To follow up on nonresponses, the following was done: a second mailing of the questionnaire, a postcard reminder, and then contact by a Census interviewer for a telephone or personal interview. The Census interviewers worked for and were trained by Census field supervisors who had received sensitivity training from a social worker specializing in grief counseling. Each mother was asked to provide names and addresses for all prenatal care providers, the hospital of delivery, and all hospitals where she or the baby were admitted before and after delivery. The mothers were also asked to sign a request statement allowing prenatal care providers and hospitals to release medical information to NCHS. If an interview was taken by telephone, the request statement was read to the mothers, and the interviewer signed it attesting to the agreement. If agreement was not obtained, questionnaires were not mailed to the hospitals or prenatal care providers. Request statements were routinely included with questionnaires that were sent to prenatal care providers and hospitals which helped increase their response rate.

The brochure that was included with the questionnaire was designed to encourage maternal participation, and emphasized the importance of the survey, described its voluntary and confidential nature, and stressed that the mother's participation could provide information that might help other women. A "call collect" telephone number was provided to allow mothers to call the NCHS and complete the questionnaire by telephone in English or Spanish. Mothers were offered up to 12 free self-help brochures on a variety of topics, including prenatal care, breast-feeding, and dealing with grief. Over 20,000 of these self-help brochures were mailed to mothers.

Using the names and addresses supplied by the mother, the Bureau of the Census staff sent prenatal care providers a 16-page questionnaire and hospitals a 32-page questionnaires. Medical providers received a questionnaire, the mother's request statement, a prepaid return envelope, and a brochure that emphasized the survey's importance, its confidentiality, and its endorsement by professional associations. Prenatal care providers and hospitals who did not respond received a second mailing of the questionnaire and up to two telephone reminders from the Bureau of the Census. If hospitals did not respond after the telephone reminders they were contacted a third time by the American Medical Record Association (AMRA) and were remailed a questionnaire if necessary.

Periodicity

Although this was the first NMIHS conducted, there have been previous studies which resemble the NMIHS, including the National Natality Surveys (1963, 1964-1966, 1967-1969, 1972, and 1980); a National Infant Mortality Survey (1964-1966); and a National Fetal Mortality Survey (1980). The NMIHS is equivalent to a combination of these three studies.

There was also a 1991 Longitudinal Follow-up (LF) of NMIHS mothers conducted by the National Opinion Research Center (NORC) with about 9,400 mothers whose infants were born alive and still living in 1991. The children of the NMIHS mothers were then 3 years old. Mothers were asked to provide addresses for the child's hospital(s) and health care provider(s) to obtain data from them as well. This follow-up permitted research on health and development of low- and very-low birthweight babies, maternal health, and child care and safety. Random samples of 1,000 NMIHS mothers who experienced infant deaths and 1,000 mothers who had stillbirths were also recontacted to collect information on subsequent pregnancies, consideration of adoption and foster care, and depression after the loss of an infant.

Unit of Analysis

The unit of analysis is the birth, infant death, or late fetal death; but the respondent is the mother who had a baby or experienced a fetal or infant death during pregnancy. Cases in the

NMIHS data file contain merged data from the vital record, the mother, the prenatal care provider, and the hospital questionnaires about the mother and infant.

Response Rates

A total of 18,594 mothers participated in the 1988 NMIHS, 9,953 mothers who had live births, 3,309 women who had late fetal deaths, and 5,332 women who had infant deaths. These final samples weight up to national estimates of 3,898,922 live births, 15,259 late fetal deaths, and 38,917 infant deaths to U.S. residents age 15 and over. The overall response rate for the national file of 18,594 mothers was 71%; it was 74% for live birth mothers, 69% for fetal death mothers, and 65% for infant death mothers. The response rate for hospitals was 68%, and for prenatal care providers was 47%. The response rate for mothers in the LF portion was 88%, but data collection from child health care providers in the LF has not yet been completed.

Attrition

Not applicable.

CONTENT

Data Sources

Data on the mother and her pregnancy, including prenatal and postnatal care, were obtained from three sources: (1) the 35-page questionnaire completed by the mother, (2) the 32-page questionnaire completed by the hospital which cared for the mother during birth, and (3) the 16-page questionnaire completed by the prenatal care provider.

Questionnaires were edited manually and keyed, and computer consistency and range checks were done. Vague, inappropriate, and uninterpretable responses as well as unanswered questions were imputed on mothers' questionnaires as necessary and are so indicated on the data tape.

Description of Variables Covered

Mothers' Questionnaire: Topics covered in the Mothers' Questionnaire include prenatal and infant information, as well as some demographic information.

Prenatal care and health habits: Number of weeks pregnant at first prenatal visit; total number of prenatal visits; access and/or barriers to prenatal care; source of payment for prenatal care; smoking, drinking, and drug use; and WIC participation.

Delivery: Length of hospital stay and source of payment for delivery.

Hospitalization before/after delivery: Number of admissions; number of outpatient visits; use of Center for Epidemiologic Studies Depression (CES-D) scale.

Previous and subsequent pregnancies: Gestational age and birthweight; smoking; and WIC participation.

Mother's and father's characteristics: Marital status; mother's height and weight; age; education; race; and occupation-work patterns.

Family income: Income 1 year before delivery.

Baby's health: Infant feeding practices; source of payment for infant care; child care; WIC participation; history of illness; vaccinations; and hospitalizations.

Prenatal Care Provider and Hospital Questionnaire: Topics covered in the Prenatal Care Provider and Hospital Questionnaire include information on the biological functions and behavior at the prenatal stage.

Prenatal care provider and hospital: Date of mother's last menstrual period; timing and results of amniocentesis, chorionic villus sampling, sonogram/fetal doptone device, and tests for sexually transmitted diseases; values at each prenatal visit for weight, blood pressure, hematocrit/hemoglobin, urine glucose/protein; medications/vitamins; patient education and referral; postpartum visits; and source of payment for care.

Hospital Questionnaire: Topics covered in the Hospital Questionnaire includes some information on prenatal biological functions, as well as clinical behavior and infant measures after birth.

Hospitalization for delivery: Delivery diagnosis and procedures using the International Classification of Diseases, 9th revision, Clinical Modification; maternal values at delivery for weight, blood pressure, hematocrit/hemoglobin. urine glucose/protein; induction of labor; anesthesia; electronic and other types of fetal monitoring; and type of delivery/trial of labor.

Maternal hospitalizations before/after delivery: Diagnoses and procedures.

Health status and care of infant: Diagnoses and procedures; infant resuscitation; infant values at delivery for head circumference, length, weight, APGAR scores at one and five minutes; gestational age; infant feeding methods; and admission to a neonatal intensive care unit.

Infant rehospitalization after delivery: Diagnoses and procedures; and weight at admission and discharge.

Number of Variables

There are a total of 18,594 cases, including live births, fetal deaths, and infant deaths. There are over 2,000 variables in the NMIHS, and an additional 1,000 in the 1991 LF.

Checklist of Topics Covered

X Gender / Gender Role
X Race / Ethnicity
X Age
X Education
X Occupation / Employment
X Physical Health / Disease
X Nutrition
X Clinical Activities
X Biological Functioning / Development
X Mental Health / Disease
___ Psychological Functioning / Development
X Guidance / Counseling
___ Personality
___ Intellectual Functioning
___ Residential Mobility
___ Dwelling
___ Neighborhood / Community
X Region / State
X Marriage and Divorce
___ Cohabitation
___ Family/Household Composition & Structure
___ Inter-Partner Relationships
___ Parent-Child Relationships
___ Inter-Sibling Relationships
___ Relationships with Other Kin

___ Relationships with Nonkin
___ Other Family/Household Characteristics
X Child Care
X Wealth / Finances / Material Things
X Receipt of Health, Mental Health, Social Services
X Adoption / Foster Care
X Childbearing / Pregnancy
X Out-of-Wedlock Pregnancy & Parenthood
X Abortion
___ Sexuality
___ Sex Education
X Contraception
X Sexually Transmitted Diseases
___ Civic/Political Activities
___ Friends / Social Activities
___ Social Support
___ Dating, Courtship
X Recreation
___ Religion
___ Crime / Delinquency / Behavior Problems
X Substance Use
___ Agency Characteristics
X Interview

Checklist of Key Variables

___ Number of family members
 X Identification of marital
    partners in family
___ Size of dwelling
___ Type of dwelling
 X Urban/rural residence
 X Region/state of residence
 X Family income
___ Religious affiliation
___ Relation of each family
    member to:
    ___ Reference person
    ___ All other members
 X Age of family members
    X Respondent
    X Others
 X Sex of family members

    X Respondent
    X Others
 X Race of family members
    X Respondent
    X Others
 X Marital status of family
    members
    X Respondent
    ___ Others
 X Education of family
    members
    X Respondent
    X Others
 X Occupation of family
    members
    X Respondent
    X Others

LIMITATIONS

The NMIHS provides excellent information on prenatal care, health habits, the delivery episode, and postnatal care. The information provided is highly specific to childbearing among American families in 1988.

SPONSORSHIP

Many federal agencies were involved in planning and funding the NMIHS and specific questions were included in the questionnaire to address issues of importance to these agencies. By sharing costs and melding their data interests into the NMIHS, the need for each agency to conduct its own survey was reduced. Table 1 on the following three pages lists each agency involved and its research interest.

Table 1. Federal Agencies Involved in Planning and Funding the NMIHS

Agency	Research Interest
Agency for Toxic Substances and Disease Registry	Maternal exposure to toxic wastes and hazards during pregnancy
Center for Prevention Services/Centers for Disease Control	Effects of sexually transmitted diseases on birth outcome
Division of Diabetes Translation/Centers for Disease Control	Prevalence of gestational diabetes
Office of Minority Health/Centers for Disease Control	Racial differences in risk factors and birth outcomes
Center for Devices and Radiological Health/Food and Drug Administration	Exposure to x-rays and ultrasound during pregnancy
Center for Food Safety and Applied Nutrition/Food and Drug Administration	Infant feeding practices and maternal vitamin use

Table 1. Federal Agencies Involved in Planning and Funding the NMIHS (continued)

Health Care Financing Administration	Medicaid patients' access to prenatal care
Maternal and Child Health Bureau/Health Resources and Services Administration	Barriers and facilitators to prenatal care, causes of infant death
Indian Health Service	Health care delivery systems for 1,000 urban Indians in the natality component
Office of Minority Health/Public Health Service	Barriers to prenatal care among minorities
National Institute on Alcoholism and Alcohol Abuse	Maternal alcohol consumption and its interaction with pregnancy risk
National Institute of Child Health and Human Development	Babies born to older and younger mothers, infertility services
National Institute on Drug Abuse	Effects of cigarettes, marijuana, and cocaine on birth outcome

Table 1. Federal Agencies Involved in Planning and Funding the NMIHS (continued)

National Institute of Mental Health	Depression using Center for Epidemiologic Studies Depression (CES-D) scale
Food and Nutrition Service/United States Department of Agriculture	Use of WIC program
Texas Department of Health	Risk factors and birth outcomes of 500 additional Hispanics in Texas
National Center for Health Statistics	Melded diverse data interests; ensured continuity with previous NNSs, NMFS, and NIMS

GUIDE TO DATA AND DOCUMENTATION

File Structure

The NMIHS data tape consists of mothers' questionnaire data, imputation flags, a set of recodes, live birth/fetal death certificate data, and infant death certificate data. The live birth/death certificate data includes place of occurrence, place of residence, prenatal care, child's characteristics, and other items. The infant death certificate data includes place of occurrence, place of residence, decedent's characteristics, underlying cause of death, and multiple cause of death conditions. (A second NMIHS data tape will be released in 1993; it will contain the hospital and prenatal care questionnaire data added to the first tape. The third tape to be released in 1993 will be the Longitudinal Follow-up data linked with the NMIHS.) There are a total of 18,594 records: one record per case, and 6,436 bytes per record.

List of Available Documentation

The data set is available either on two reels of magnetic tape or one tape cartridge. A set of documentation, including the questionnaires, codebook, and survey information, is available along with the data set. Technical assistance and a list of reports available can be obtained from the Followback Survey Branch at the National Center for Health Statistics.

Contact

National Technical Information Service (NTIS)
5285 Port Royal Road
Springfield, VA 22161
(703) 487-4650

Cost

The first NMIHS data tape and all paper documentation (275 pages) together cost $590. An extra set of documentation costs $26.

BIBLIOGRAPHY

Albers, L., & Krulewitch, C. (in press). Electronic fetal monitoring in the 1990s. *Obstetrics and Gynecology*.

Banach, J., Placek, P., & Simpson, G. (1988). AMRA's role in the 1988 national maternal and infant health survey. *Journal of the American Medical Research Association, 59*(10), 28-32.

Editorial (1986, July). Maternal, infant health survey to be conducted. *Ob. Gyn. News, 21*(4).

Gonzalez, J.F., & Krauss, N.A. (in press). Estimation in the national maternal and infant health survey. *ASA Survey Research Methods Section Proceedings*.

Jeng, L., Moore, R., Kaczmarek, R., et al. (1991). How frequently are home pregnancy tests used? Results from the 1988 national maternal and infant health survey. *Birth, 18*(1), 11-13.

Keppel, K.G., & Taffel, S.M. (in press). Implications of the latest guidelines on weight gain during pregnancy for postpartum weight retention. *American Journal of Public Health*.

Kogan, M., Kotelchuck, M., Alexander, G. R., & Johnson, W.E. (in press). Racial disparities in reported prenatal care advice. *American Journal of Public Health*.

Moore, R., Jeng, L., Kaczmarek, R., et al. (1990). Use of diagnostic imaging procedures and fetal monitoring devices in the care of pregnant women. *Public Health Reports, 105*(5), 471-475.

Moss, N., & Carver, K. (in press). Pregnant women at work: Sociodemographic perspectives (NMIHS). *American Journal of Industrial Medicine*.

Moss, N., & Carver, K. (1992). Maternal employment during pregnancy: Sociodemographic perspectives from the USA. *Contemporary Review of Obstetrics and Gynaecology, 4*, 177-184.

National Center for Health Statistics. *1988 national maternal and infant health survey, tape #1*, (New Electronic Data Product Releases, Draft). Hyattsville, MD: Author.

Newsline. (1987, November-December). 1988 national maternal and infant health survey. *Public Health Reports, 102*(6).

Parker, J.D., & Abrams, B. (in press). Differences in postpartum weight retention between black and white mothers. *Obstetrics and Gynecology.*

Placek, P., Moore, R., & Jeng, L. Use of diagnostic ultrasound X-ray examinations, and electronic fetal monitoring in perinatal medicine. *Journal of Perinatology, 10*(4).

Rooks, J.P., Ernst, E.K.M., & Weatherby, N.L. (1992, July-August). National birth center study: Part 1. Methodology and prenatal care referrals (uses NMIHS as control group in a maternal weight gain comparison). *Journal of Nurse-Midwifery.*

Sanderson, M., Placek, P.J., & Keppel, K.G. (1991, March). The 1988 national maternal and infant health survey: Design, content, and data availability. *Birth, 18*(1), 26-32.

Schoendorf, K., & Kiely, J.L. (1992). Relationship of sudden infant death syndrome to maternal smoking during and after pregnancy. *Pediatrics, 90*, 905-908.

Schoendorf, K.S., Parker, J.D., Batkhan, L., & Kiely, J. (1993). Comparability of the birth certificate and the 1988 NMIHS. *Vital Health Statistics 2*(116).

Schwartz, J.B., Guilkey, D.K., Akin, J.S., & Popkin, B.M. (1993). *The WIC breast feeding report: The relationahip of WIC program participation to the initiation and duration of breastfeeding.* OAE, FNS, Washington, DC: U.S. Department of Agriculture.

Simpson, G., & Placek, P. (1989, March). Surveillance aspects of the 1988 national maternal and infant health survey (abstract). *Statistics in Medicine, 8.*

16

TREATMENT PROCESS: A PROBLEM AT THREE LEVELS, 1988

Gerald R. Patterson
Patricia Chamberlain

PURPOSE OF THE STUDY

Treatment Process: A Problem at Three Levels is a three-year investigation of the process of therapeutic intervention in the treatment of oppositional children and their parents. As part of an ongoing program of empirical investigation of treatment process variables, the investigators employ nonreactive observational measures of behavior to assess the effects of family management training on the behavior of extremely antisocial, preadolescent children. Two raw data files were generated from this research. (They comprise Data Set 35-36 in the American Family Data Archive.) The first (Data Set 35) includes therapist-client verbal interaction codes for 73 families participating in the Parent Training treatment program conducted at the Oregon Social Learning Center (OSLC). The second (Data Set 36) includes demographic data gathered during the treatment intake interview.

An additional purpose of the study was to gather information about client resistance. During the Parent Training treatment program, three phases of treatment were videotaped and verbal interactions coded with the Therapy Process Coding System (TPC), a nonreactive criterion measure developed at OSLC. TPC allows for a moment-to-moment analysis of the relationship between therapist behaviors and client resistance. Client resistance could explain the individual differences among families in their response to treatment at OSLC.

Finally, the social-learning approach used in this study stipulates that behavior patterns develop from learning experiences within the family system. The purpose of the treatment, therefore, was to train parents and other family members to alter their nonfunctional styles of interaction and to learn skills such as parental monitoring, disciplining, and problem-solving.

METHODS

Sampling Design

Eighty families were recruited and screened over a three-year period from those families of extremely antisocial, preadolescent children that were referred to the Oregon Social Learning Center for treatment. Recruitment was based on three criteria. Families were asked to participate if they had requested counseling because of child antisocial behavior, had a child in the age range of 6 to 13 years, and if they had a telephone. Families electing to participate in the study underwent two final phases of screening to determine eligibility. In Phase 1, children received the Child Behavior Checklist. Those children rated with a t-score of 70 or above on the aggression, hyperactivity, immaturity, and delinquency scales were considered eligible for the next phase of treatment. In Phase 2, three in-home observations were conducted. Using the Family Process Coding system developed at OSLC, experienced coders recorded interactions between the focal child and all other family members. From the Family Process Codes, child scores on 16 aversive behaviors were combined to create a composite measure, the Total Aversive Behavior score (TAB), for which there exist age-equivalent norms. Those children scoring above .5 standard deviations above the general population mean for TAB were considered eligible for the study.

Periodicity

Eighty families were recruited and screened during the three-year period from 1986 to 1989. Each family had its first treatment session one week after their intake interview. Treatment sessions were held weekly; the entire treatment program took place over a period of 12 to 20 weeks. Treatment was terminated when the participating family and therapist agreed that referral problems had improved or if the family wished to stop treatment.

Unit of Analysis

The family was the unit of analysis.

Response Rates

Of the 80 families screened and recruited into the study, 73 families completed five or more treatment sessions. Seven families completed four or fewer treatment sessions or elected to quit the study prior to beginning treatment.

Attrition

Not applicable.

CONTENT

Data Sources

Eligible families were scheduled for a 3-hour parent intake interview and 2-hour child interview. Parents completed a demographic questionnaire and the Minnesota Multiphasic Personality Inventory (MMPI). Past and current psychological functioning were evaluated using the Schedule for Affective Disorders and Schizophrenia. Prior to intake, families were assigned to receive treatment at either OSLC or Looking Glass, a Eugene, Oregon family therapy center oriented towards structural family therapy and Adlerian treatment.

The first treatment session took place one week after the intake interview. Treatment sessions were held weekly; the entire treatment program took place over a period of 12 to 20 weeks. Treatment was terminated when the participating family and therapist agreed that referral problems had improved or if the family wished to stop treatment. Videotapes were made of the following three phases of treatment: sessions 1 and 2, the chronological middle-two sessions, and the last 25% of the sessions. Tapes were dubbed using a date/time generator that recorded the passage of time in minutes and seconds on the tape. Data were recorded using a hand-held computer that recorded the codes onto a tape. Duration and sequence of each client-therapist interaction was recorded.

Therapy Process codes were assigned by trained coders. Coders required an average of thirty hours of training along with biweekly retraining meetings to reach and maintain a minimum of 75% agreement. Session tapes varied in length from 45 minutes to one hour. Coders were instructed to divide each session into trials. A new trial was coded when the following situations occurred:

a) twenty minutes had elapsed;
b) a new therapist or family member joined the therapy session;

c) the therapist or a family member exited the session;
d) the therapist gave a family member an assignment to do during a session.

If the therapist temporarily exited and reentered the room during a session, a time out was coded as 00000 followed by 99999; a new trial was not coded. Code 99999 was also used as a duration place holder when no codable event was occurring (e.g., silence).

Description of Variables Covered

Variables in the Therapy Process data set (Data Set 35) included who was present during a therapy session, which family member was the focus of a therapy trial, whether or not family management skills were discussed, and therapist/client interaction codes.

The Demographic data set (Data Set 36) covered the following: age of all the people in the household, biological function/development such as whether or not the child had colic as a baby, clinical activities such as the child's physical exams, education level of head of household and whether or not the child had behavioral/academic problems in school, gender of the siblings, child's physical health including medication taken and handicaps/illnesses, family/household structure and composition, marriage and divorce of the adults in the household, occupation of the head of household, parent-child relationships, religion of the head of household, receipt of health/mental health/social services by the family, and annual household income.

Number of Variables

The Therapy Process data set (Data Set 35) has 20 variables, 73 cases, and 437,855 records (each record corresponding to a coded therapist-family trial, as defined above). The Demographic data set (Data Set 36) has 113 variables and 80 cases.

Checklist of Topics Covered: Treatment Process Data

___ Gender / Gender Role
___ Race / Ethnicity
___ Age
___ Education
___ Occupation / Employment
___ Physical Health / Disease
___ Nutrition
___ Clinical Activities
___ Biological Functioning / Development
___ Mental Health / Disease
___ Psychological Functioning / Development
_X_ Guidance / Counseling
___ Personality
___ Intellectual Functioning
___ Residential Mobility
___ Dwelling
___ Neighborhood / Community
___ Region / State
___ Marriage and Divorce
___ Cohabitation
___ Family/Household Composition & Structure
___ Inter-Partner Relationships
___ Parent-Child Relationships
___ Inter-Sibling Relationships
___ Relationships with Other Kin

___ Relationships with Nonkin
___ Other Family/Household Characteristics
___ Child Care
___ Wealth / Finances / Material Things
___ Receipt of Health, Mental Health, Social Services
___ Adoption / Foster Care
___ Childbearing / Pregnancy
___ Out-of-Wedlock Pregnancy & Parenthood
___ Abortion
___ Sexuality
___ Sex Education
___ Contraception
___ Sexually Transmitted Diseases
___ Civic/Political Activities
___ Friends / Social Activities
___ Social Support
___ Dating, Courtship
___ Recreation
___ Religion
___ Crime / Delinquency / Behavior Problems
___ Substance Use
___ Agency Characteristics
___ Interview

Checklist of Topics Covered: Demographic Data

X Gender / Gender Role
___ Race / Ethnicity
X Age
X Education
X Occupation / Employment
X Physical Health / Disease
___ Nutrition
X Clinical Activities
X Biological Functioning / Development
___ Mental Health / Disease
___ Psychological Functioning / Development
___ Guidance / Counseling
___ Personality
___ Intellectual Functioning
___ Residential Mobility
___ Dwelling
___ Neighborhood / Community
___ Region / State
X Marriage and Divorce
___ Cohabitation
X Family/Household Composition & Structure
___ Inter-Partner Relationships
X Parent-Child Relationships
___ Inter-Sibling Relationships
___ Relationships with Other Kin

___ Relationships with Nonkin
___ Other Family/Household Characteristics
___ Child Care
X Wealth / Finances / Material Things
X Receipt of Health, Mental Health, Social Services
___ Adoption / Foster Care
___ Childbearing / Pregnancy
___ Out-of-Wedlock Pregnancy & Parenthood
___ Abortion
___ Sexuality
___ Sex Education
___ Contraception
___ Sexually Transmitted Diseases
___ Civic/Political Activities
___ Friends / Social Activities
___ Social Support
___ Dating, Courtship
___ Recreation
X Religion
___ Crime / Delinquency / Behavior Problems
___ Substance Use
___ Agency Characteristics
X Interview

Checklist of Key Variables: Treatment Process Data

None of the key variables apply to the Treatment Process data.

Checklist of Key Variables: Demographic Data

___ Number of family members
___ Identification of marital
    partners in family
___ Size of dwelling
___ Type of dwelling
___ Urban/rural residence
___ Region/state of residence
X Family income
X Religious affiliation
X Relation of each family
    member to:
    X Reference person
    X All other members
X Age of family members
    X Respondent
    X Others
X Sex of family members

___ Respondent
___ Others
___ Race of family members
    ___ Respondent
    ___ Others
X Marital status of family
    members
    ___ Respondent
    ___ Others
X Education of family
    members
    X Respondent
    ___ Others
X Occupation of family
    members
    X Respondent
    ___ Others

LIMITATIONS

If the user wishes to compare the file structure of the therapy process data (Data Set 35) to the demographic data (Data Set 36) he or she should keep in mind that the therapy data are hierarchical (i.e., one data set case corresponds to one unique therapy session interaction) and the demographic data are nonhierarchical (i.e., one data set case corresponds to information on one unique family member). Family ID codes, MEX36001 FAMILY IDENTIFICATION NUMBER and MEX35003 FAMILY IDENTIFICATION NUMBER, used across both data sets allow linkage.

SPONSORSHIP

The study was conducted at the Oregon Social Learning Center with funds from the National Institute of Mental Health.

GUIDE TO DATA AND DOCUMENTATION

File Structure

Machine-readable data and documentation files are available in both mainframe and microcomputer formats. Unless otherwise requested, files formatted for a mainframe computer are provided on a 9-track tape at a density of 6250 bpi, in EBCDIC character mode with IBM Standard Labels. Microcomputer files are available on CD-ROM in ISO 9660 format. A description of the contents of each file is given below.

File 1a (Therapy Process Codes, Data Set 35): Raw data file. The format of this file is described in the "data list" section of the SPSS program file (file 2).

File 1b (Demographics, Data Set 36): Raw data file. The format of this file is described in the "data list" section of the SPSS program file (file 2).

Files 2a and 2b (SPSS Programs, Data Sets 35 and 36): These files consist of SPSS program statements designed to read the raw data in files 1a and 1b, respectively, and create an SPSS active file. The SPSS program file contains data list statements, variable names and labels, and value labels.

Files 3a and 3b (SAS Programs, Data Sets 35 and 36): The files consist of SAS program statements designed to read the raw data in files 1a and 1b, respectively, and create a SAS active file. The contents of these files are analogous to the contents of the previously described files 2a and 2b. SPSS users should use files 2a and 2b; SAS users, files 3a and 3b. Users may need to add "job control language" (JCL) statements to the SAS program files to meet the requirements for their specific operating system.

Files 4a and 4b (Dictionary; Data Sets 35 and 36): Sequential list of variable and value labels. These files consist of DISPLAY DICTIONARY output describing the SPSS-X active file created by the program in files 2a and 2b, respectively. Variables are listed in sequential order. Variable names and labels, value labels, missing value designations, print formats, and write formats are clearly displayed.

Files 5a and 5b (Statistics; Data Sets 35 and 36): Unweighted frequencies or other descriptive statistics for each variable. Descriptive statistics only are provided for variables with more than 50 value categories, such as respondent identification number, etc.

List of Available Documentation

For each data set, a User's Guide which accompanies the machine-readable files provides the following information: Summary; General study overview; Description of machine-readable files and supplementary documentation; Specifications for machine-readable files; Key characteristics report; Distribution of variables by topic and type; and Data completeness and consistency report.

For each data set, paper versions of the machine-readable SPSS and SAS program files and data documentation (files 2a-5b above), and copies of the original instruments and codebooks, are available upon request (at 15 cents per page).

Contact

Sociometrics Corporation
American Family Data Archive
170 State Street, Suite 260
Los Altos, California 94022-2812
(415) 949-3282

Cost

The cost for the machine-readable data set (Data Set 35-36 of the American Family Data Archive) is $150. This price includes the raw data, SPSS program statements, the SAS program statements, the Dictionary, and the Frequencies in mainframe format, and the accompanying printed and bound User's Guide. The CD-ROM version costs $175. A paper version of the original Codebook/Instrument for the Demographic data can be obtained for $1.35.

BIBLIOGRAPHY

Chamberlain, P., et al. (1985). *The therapy process code: A multidimensional system for observing therapist and client interactions.* (Oregon Social Learning Center Technical Report, No. 1Rx). Eugene, OR: Oregon Social Learning Center.

Chamberlain, P., Patterson, G.R., Reid, J.B., Kavanagh, K., & Forgatch, M.S. (1984). Observation of client resistance. *Behavior Therapy, 15,* 144-155.

Chamberlain, P., & Ray, J. (1988). The therapy process code: A multidimensional system for observing therapist and client interactions in family treatment. In R.J. Prinz (Ed.), *Advances in behavioral assessment of children and families* (Vol 4, pp. 198-217). JAI Press.

McKean, E.A., Lang, E.L., & Card, J.J. (1992). *Treatment process: A problem at three levels, 1988. A user's guide to the machine-readable files and documentation* (Data Set 35-36). Los Altos, CA: Sociometrics Corporation, American Family Data Archive.

Patterson, G.R. (1986). Performance models for antisocial boys. *American Psychologist, 41*, 432-445.

Patterson, G.R., & Chamberlain, P. (1988). Treatment process: A problem at three levels. In L.C. Wynne (Ed.), *The state of the art in family therapy research: Controversies and recommendations* (pp. 189-223). New York: Family Process Press.

Patterson, G.R., & Chamberlain, P. (in press). Some antecedents and functions for resistance during parent training (A neobehavioral perspective). In H. Arkowitz (Ed.), *Why don't people change? New perspectives on resistance and noncompliance.* Guilford Press.

Patterson, G.R., & Forgatch, M.S. (1985). Therapist behavior as a determinant for client noncompliance: A paradox for the behavior modifier. *Journal of Consulting and Clinical Psychology, 53*, 19.

17

GENERAL SOCIAL SURVEYS, 1972-1990 (GSS)

James A. Davis and Tom W. Smith,
National Opinion Research Center

PURPOSE OF THE STUDY

The General Social Surveys (GSS) provide data for the National Data Program for the Social Sciences at the National Opinion Research Center, University of Chicago. The National Data Program for the Social Sciences is designed as a data diffusion project and a program of social indicator research. Toward the goal of functioning as a social indicator program, items which have appeared on previous national surveys between 1937 and 1978 have been replicated in the GSS. By retaining exact wording, the aim is to facilitate time trend studies as well as replication of earlier findings. A second objective is the prompt distribution of fresh, interesting, and high-quality data to a variety of users who are not affiliated with large research centers.

METHODS

Sampling Design

Each survey is an independently drawn sample of English-speaking persons 18 years of age or over, living in noninstitutional arrangements within the United States. Block quota sampling was used in 1972, 1973, and 1974 surveys and for half of the 1975 and 1976 surveys. Full probability sampling was employed in half of the 1975 and 1976 surveys and the 1977, 1978, 1980, 1982-1990 surveys.

In the original National Science Foundation grant, support was given for a modified probability sample. Samples for the 1972 through 1974 surveys followed this design. This modified probability design introduces the quota element at the block level. The NSF renewal grant, awarded for the 1976-77 surveys, provided funds for a full probability sample design, a design which is acknowledged to be superior. Having allowed for the appearance of all items in the "transitional samples design" which would provide the basis for methodological studies of the transition, the General Social Survey then switched to a full probability sample for the 1977, 1978, 1980, and 1982 through 1987 annual surveys. A similar split sample transition design was used in the 1983 survey to measure the effect of switching from the 1970 sample frame to the 1980 sample frame. A detailed empirical analysis of the 1970 and 1980 samples on the 1983 survey was prepared as part of the General Social Survey Technical Report Series.

The sample is a multistage area probability sample to the block or segment level. At the block level, however, quota sampling was used in the early surveys, with quotas based on sex, age, and employment status. The Primary Sampling Units employed are Standard Metropolitan Statistical Areas (SMSAs) or nonmetropolitan counties selected from the National Opinion Research Center's Master Sample. These SMSAs and counties were stratified by region, age, and race before selection. The third stage of selection was that of blocks, which were selected with probabilities proportional to size. The average cluster size is five respondents per cluster, which provides a suitable balance of precision and economy.

A major design change was implemented starting in 1988. Instead of rotating items across years, items began to be asked of two-thirds (1,000) of the (1,500) cases each year.

Periodicity

The General Social Surveys have been conducted during February, March, and April of 1972, 1973, 1974, 1975, 1976, 1977, 1978, 1980, 1982, 1983, 1984, 1985, 1986, 1987, 1988, 1989, and 1990.

Unit of Analysis

The individual is the natural unit of analysis.

Response Rates

There are a total of 26,265 completed interviews (1,613 in 1972, 1,504 in 1973, 1,484 in 1974, 1,490 in 1975, 1,499 in 1976, 1,530 in 1977, 1,532 in 1978, 1,468 in 1980, 1,506 in 1982, 354 in 1982 black oversample, 1,599 in 1983, 1,473 in 1984, 1,534 in 1985, 1,470 in 1986, 1,466 in 1987, 353 in 1987 black oversample, 1,481 in 1988, 1,537 in 1989, and 1,372 in 1990). These numbers represent approximately 75% of the target sample in each year.

Attrition

Not Applicable. Each year a new, nationally representative sample is drawn.

CONTENT

Data Sources

Data were collected via an in-person interview. The median length of the interview was one and a half hours. This study employed standard field procedures for national surveys, including interviewer hiring and training by area supervisors in interviewing locations when necessary. The sampling procedures were reviewed by having interviewers take a training quiz after they had studied the sampling instructions specific to this study. Around the same time, publicity materials were sent to area supervisors; these included letters to be mailed locally to the Chief of Police, the Better Business Bureau, the Chamber of Commerce, and the various news media. After these steps were completed, interviewers received materials needed for data collection (assignments, specifications, blank interview schedules). Each interviewer completed one practice interview which was evaluated at NORC. Actual interviewing then commenced; completed interviews were immediately returned to NORC where they were edited for completeness and accuracy. Twenty percent of the interviews were validated. Feedback on specific problems was given to individual interviewers and on general problems to all interviewers. Once field work was completed, the edited questionnaires were coded and keypunched, and the resulting data were cleaned.

Description of Variables Covered

The items appearing on the surveys are one of three types: Permanent questions that occur on each survey, rotating questions that appear on two out of every three surveys (1973, 1974, and 1976, or 1973, 1975, and 1976), and a few occasional questions such as split ballot experiments that occur in a single survey. Starting in 1988 items were no longer rotated across years, but appeared on two-thirds of the cases every year.

In recent years the GSS expanded in two significant ways. First, by adding annual topical modules that explore new areas or expand existing coverage of a subject. Second, by expanding its cross-national collaboration. Topical supplements were first employed in 1977 when a grant from the National Science Foundation allowed the addition of items to extend the regular scales on race relations, feminism, and abortion. In 1982 and 1984, the Ford Foundation funded a special section on the role of the military, including recruitment, training and human capital development, expectation of various forms of war and peace, and citizenship obligations. Starting in 1985 the project, in consultation with the GSS Board of Overseers, had developed an annual topical module. The 1985 module was on social networks. For 1986, the module was on the feminization of poverty. In addition to questions in this data set, factorial vignettes on public assistance for families were conducted. The vignette data are available as a companion file from the Roper Center. For 1987, the module was on sociopolitical participation. This replicated substantial sections of the 1967 Verba-Nie study of political participation. For 1988, the module was on religious socialization, behaviors, and beliefs. For 1989, the module was on occupational prestige. The occupational prestige data are being processed and occupational prestige scores for the 1980 Census codes are being calculated for future release. For 1990, the module was on race relations.

Bilateral collaboration with the Zentrum fuer Umfragen, Methoden und Analysen in the Federal Republic of Germany dates from 1982. In 1985 the first multinational collaboration was carried out the United States, Britain, Germany, Italy, and Austria. The 1985 topic was the role of government and included questions on a) civil liberties and law enforcement, b) education and parenting, c) economic regulation, and d) social welfare and inequality. The 1986 topic was social support covering information of contact with family and friends and hypothetical questions about where one would turn for help when faced with various problems. The 1987 topic was social inequality dealing with social mobility, intergroup conflicts, beliefs about reasons for inequality, and perceived and preferred income differentials between occupations. The 1988 topic was the impact on the family of the changing labor force participation of women. The 1989 topic was on work orientation.

Number of Variables

The GSS codebook lists 1,668 variables. Not all variables were asked in every survey year.

Checklist of Topics Covered

X Gender / Gender Role
X Race / Ethnicity
X Age
X Education
X Occupation / Employment
X Physical Health / Disease
___ Nutrition
___ Clinical Activities
___ Biological Functioning / Development
___ Mental Health / Disease
___ Psychological Functioning / Development
___ Guidance / Counseling
___ Personality
___ Intellectual Functioning
X Residential Mobility
X Dwelling
___ Neighborhood / Community
X Region / State
X Marriage and Divorce
___ Cohabitation
X Family/Household Composition & Structure
___ Inter-Partner Relationships
___ Parent-Child Relationships
___ Inter-Sibling Relationships
___ Relationships with Other Kin

___ Relationships with Nonkin
___ Other Family/Household Characteristics
X Child Care
X Wealth / Finances / Material Things
___ Receipt of Health, Mental Health, Social Services
___ Adoption / Foster Care
___ Childbearing / Pregnancy
___ Out-of-Wedlock Pregnancy & Parenthood
X Abortion
X Sexuality
X Sex Education
X Contraception
___ Sexually Transmitted Diseases
X Civic/Political Activities
X Friends / Social Activities
___ Social Support
___ Dating, Courtship
X Recreation
X Religion
X Crime / Delinquency / Behavior Problems
X Substance Use
___ Agency Characteristics
X Interview

17 - 5

Checklist of Key Variables

X Number of family members
___ Identification of marital
    partners in family
___ Size of dwelling
X Type of dwelling
X Urban/rural residence
X Region/state of residence
X Family income
X Religious affiliation
___ Relation of each family
    member to:
    ___ Reference person
    ___ All other members
X Age of family members
    X Respondent
    X Others
X Sex of family members

    X Respondent
    ___ Others
X Race of family members
    X Respondent
    X Others
X Marital status of family
    members
    X Respondent
    ___ Others
X Education of family
    members
    X Respondent
    X Others
X Occupation of family
    members
    X Respondent
    X Others

LIMITATIONS

The survey is intentionally thin on political behavior and labor force activity. Since children are not eligible to be respondents, no data are available on their attitudes and behaviors. The survey provides data on the number of children in the household, but only in broad age groups, and not by sex. However, the survey does provide good data on the social and psychological characteristics of the family environments of children.

SPONSORSHIP

The initial survey in 1972 was supported by grants from the Russell Sage Foundation and the National Science Foundation. The National Science Foundation provided complete support for the 1973 through 1978, 1980 and 1982 through 1987 surveys. NSF will continue to support the project through 1991. Supplemental funding for 1984-1991 has been provided by Andrew M. Greeley.

GUIDE TO DATA AND DOCUMENTATION

File Structure

The surveys are available in a cumulative data set that merges all 17 surveys into a single file with each year or survey acting as a subfile. This greatly simplifies the use of the General Social Surveys for both trend analysis and pooling. In addition, this cumulative data set contains items previously available only as supplemental data sets (e.g., the 1982 black oversample) as well as newly created variables (e.g., a poverty line code). Finally, the cumulative file contains items never before available (e.g., the 1987 module on the impact of the family of the changing labor force participation of women).

List of Available Documentation

The codebook cited in the Bibliography provides comprehensive documentation of the merged machine-readable data set.

Contact

For data tapes and documentation:

The Inter-university Consortium for Political and Social
Research
The University of Michigan
P.O. Box 1248
Ann Arbor, MI 48106
(313) 763-5010

The Roper Public Opinion Research Center
Office of Archival Development & User Services
Box 440
University of Connecticut
Storrs, CT 06268
(203) 486-4440

For substantive questions, contact:

Tom W. Smith
Director and Co-Principal Investigator,
General Social Surveys
National Opinion Research Center
1155 East 60th Street
Chicago, IL 60637
(312) 753-7877

Cost

Free to members of the Inter-university Consortium for
Political and Social Research (ICPSR). For nonmembers, the cost
depends on the format requested. Contact ICPSR for a price quote.

From The Roper Public Opinion Research Center the raw data
version of the data set costs $120 and the SPSS-X version costs $200.
Send a mainframe tape with your request. There is an additional
charge if Roper provides a tape.

BIBLIOGRAPHY

National Opinion Research Center. (1990). *General social surveys, 1972-1990: Cumulative codebook*. Chicago, IL: University of Chicago, Author.

Smith, T.W., & Arnold, B.J. (1992). *Annotated bibliography of papers using the general social surveys* (9th ed.). Ann Arbor, MI: Inter-university Consortium for Political and Social Research.

18

NATIONAL SURVEY OF BLACK AMERICANS, 1979 - 1980

James S. Jackson
M. Belinda Tucker
Gerald Gurin

PURPOSE OF THE STUDY

The purpose of this data collection was to provide an appropriate theoretical and empirical approach to concepts, measures, and methods in the study of black Americans.

Previous studies of black American adults had been restricted to limited and special populations. National data on blacks had been gathered in the course of surveys of the general population. The representativeness of such studies in regard to blacks was generally impaired because the geographical distribution of blacks is different than that of the total United States population. The typical approach to data collection on black samples in national studies also had meant that concepts, measures and methods developed in the study of the white majority had been used in the study of black Americans. There had been little theoretical or empirical concern with the appropriateness of this simple comparative approach. For the most part, prior national studies had not been informed by an awareness and appreciation for the unique cultural experience of black Americans; and, concepts, measures, and research procedures that reflected this uniqueness had not been developed or employed.

Limited to small and nonrepresentative samples of blacks, national surveys had not gone beyond superficial analyses of gross black-white comparisons. This level of analysis and the lack of attention in survey instruments and procedures to the cultural context of black life in America, served to perpetuate a simplistic view of black experiences.

In order to address these limitations in the existing research literature, the National Survey of Black Americans (NSBA) was initiated in 1977.

METHODS

Sampling Design

The multistage national probability sample was based upon the 1970 Census, and subsequent updates, of the distribution of the black population. The selection of the 76 certainty and noncertainty primary areas was done in order to maximize selection of current Survey Research Center (SRC) sample areas that met minimum size requirements of black households. The overall rate of selection was 1:2,300. Approximately 58 percent of the black sample areas were also in the 1970, SRC national sample. The sample was self-weighting and every black American household in the continental United States had the same probability of being selected. The sampling of housing units within primary areas was done in an effort to yield approximately the same level of clustering and precision of estimates as SRC household samples of comparable size. This outcome was accomplished through joint efforts of the SRC Sampling Section and the study staff.

Two new screening methods for locating black housing units (HUs) were developed in this study. The first, the Standard Listing and Screening Procedure (SLASP) was developed by SRC. The second method, the Wide Area Screening Procedure (WASP) was developed by the PIs. The SLASP method was applied in both mixed and mostly black areas and provided a unique method of identifying black households. In addition to the usual SRC procedure of listing every household in the designated sampling area, the SLASP method identified a subsample of households to serve as references for the race of occupants in the remaining households. The WASP method was developed for screening by white interviewers in areas with suspected few or no black occupied households. This procedure used the reference housing unit approach but with a modification. In the SLASP procedure the interviewer was told explicitly by SRC which HUs to contact. In the WASP, the selection of these reference HUs depended on the interviewers' assessment of the number and concentration of HUs in the area. Whereas the SLASP interviewers listed and classified each HU in a cluster as black or all other, the WASP interviewers asked the reference HUs about blacks in the area and listed only the black HUs. This procedural difference minimized the cost of screening in geographical areas of low-density black housing and was highly effective in reducing the cost and time in locating and listing black housing units. Within sample households, one person was randomly chosen from the list of eligible respondents (18 years of age or older, self-identified black, and U.S. citizen).

Twenty percent of the WASP clusters were selected for intensive screening of households to estimate the extent of undercoverage, if any. Analyses indicated that the procedure was far more effective than originally anticipated. Only eight black households in the sampled WASP clusters were missed, the majority of these in one particular cluster. The WASP procedure permitted the NSBA sample to be obtained with clustering and precision comparable to SRC household samples of comparable size for a fraction of the cost. It also appears to be an effective and generally useful screening method for future sample surveys of blacks and other rare population groups.

The sampling procedures reported here resulted in 2,107 completed interviews. The overall response rate was 67%.

Overall the national sample is fairly representative of the black population as reported by the 1980 Census. There is, however, a disparity in the proportion of women to men and a slight tendency to underrepresent younger people of both sexes and to overrepresent older women. Analyses reveal no sex differences between respondents and identified nonrespondents. Thus, the sex differences may be due to the disproportionate representation of black female-headed households in the United States. Finally, there is a slighter proportion of individuals to come from the South than their distribution in the population would indicate. These differences from expected Census distributions are relatively minor (particularly if undercount and enumeration problems in the black population are considered) in comparison with other large studies of the black population.

Periodicity

Not applicable to this study.

Unit of Analysis

The individual is the main unit of analysis. However, much information about black families is also available from these data. Every black American household in the continental United States had the same probability of being selected.

Response Rates

The overall response rate was 67%. The black population is disproportionately distributed and concentrated within urban areas, where historically response rates have been low. An average of 3.4 callbacks, with a range of 1-22, per selected household were required to complete the interviews.

Attrition

Not applicable to this study.

CONTENT

Data Sources

Face-to-face interviews were conducted with all 2,107 individuals in the sample. The all black interviewer staff, male and female, was trained and supervised by the Survey Research Center and NSBA staffs at the Institute for Social Research, the University of Michigan.

The NSBA questionnaire was developed particularly for the black population. Actual use in the field was preceded by two years of pretesting and refinement. The instrument contained both open- and close-ended items and took on average 2 hours and 20 minutes to administer.

Description of Variables Covered

The final instrument was comprehensive, encompassing several broad areas related to black American life. These areas included: a) Neighborhood—community integration, services, crime and community contact; b) Religion—role of the church, church attendance, prayer, emotional and instrumental functions of the church and religion; c) Health—physical status, health care utilization, physical disability, self-esteem and life-satisfaction; d) Employment and Unemployment—effects of job-related problems, effects of chronic unemployment, irregular economy activity, work discrimination, effects of race on work force composition, barriers to employment, effects of under- and un-employment; e) Family and Friends—degree of contact with family and friends, fictive kin, social support, loneliness, marital satisfaction, role relationships; f) Mental Health Status and Utilization—problem recognition and life-time prevalence, problem severity, symptom reports, coping strategies, informal and formal help sources, evaluation of mental health services; g) Group and Self Identity—racial attitudes, social and welfare policies, group stereotypes, racial identity and consciousness, race ideology; and h) Background—education, income and occupation, political behavior and affiliation, parental attainment, cross-race contact.

Number of Variables

There are 1,451 variables on 2,107 cases.

Checklist of Topics Covered

X Gender / Gender Role
X Race / Ethnicity
X Age
X Education
X Occupation / Employment
X Physical Health / Disease
___ Nutrition
___ Clinical Activities
___ Biological Functioning /
    Development
X Mental Health / Disease
X Psychological Functioning /
    Development
X Guidance / Counseling
X Personality
___ Intellectual Functioning
X Residential Mobility
X Dwelling
X Neighborhood /
    Community
X Region / State
X Marriage and Divorce
___ Cohabitation
X Family/Household
    Composition & Structure
X Inter-Partner Relationships
X Parent-Child Relationships
___ Inter-Sibling Relationships
X Relationships with Other Kin

X Relationships with Nonkin
X Other Family/Household
    Characteristics
X Child Care
X Wealth / Finances / Material
    Things
X Receipt of Health, Mental
    Health, Social Services
___ Adoption / Foster Care
___ Childbearing / Pregnancy
___ Out-of-Wedlock Pregnancy
    & Parenthood
___ Abortion
___ Sexuality
___ Sex Education
___ Contraception
___ Sexually Transmitted
    Diseases
X Civic/Political Activities
X Friends / Social Activities
    Social Support
X Dating, Courtship
___ Recreation
X Religion
X Crime / Delinquency /
    Behavior Problems
X Substance Use
X Agency Characteristics
X Interview

Checklist of Key Variables

X Number of family members
X Identification of marital
   partners in family
X Size of dwelling
X Type of dwelling
X Urban/rural residence
X Region/state of residence
X Family income
X Religious affiliation
X Relation of each family
   member to:
   X Reference person
   X All other members
X Age of family members
   X Respondent
   ___ Others
X Sex of family members

X Respondent
___ Others
X Race of family members
   X Respondent
   X Others
X Marital status of family
   members
   X Respondent
   ___ Others
X Education of family
   members
   X Respondent
   ___ Others
X Occupation of family
   members
   X Respondent
   X Others

LIMITATIONS

Although the response rate was 67%, the black population is disproportionately distributed and concentrated within urban areas, where historically response rates have been low. The national sample is fairly representative of the black population as reported by the 1980 Census despite some disparity in the proportion of women to men, and the slight tendency to underrepresent younger people of both sexes and to overrepresent older women. Also there are slightly fewer Southerners in the sample than their distribution in the 1980 census would indicate. These differences from expected Census distributions are relatively minor (particularly if undercount and enumeration problems in the black population are considered) in comparison with other large studies of the black population.

SPONSORSHIP

Funding for the study was provided by the Center for the Study of Minority Group Mental Health, National Institute of Mental Health.

GUIDE TO DATA AND DOCUMENTATION

File Structure

The *National Survey of Black Americans, 1979-1980* is available from the Inter-university Consortium for Political and Social Research (ICPSR) in two formats: card image and OSIRIS. The card image file contains several decks per case in a format based on 80-column punched cards. The data are sorted by case with all decks for a case together in ascending order.

The OSIRIS dictionary gives the format and other information for each variable in the OSIRIS data file. The dictionary or dictionary-codebook file is used in conjunction with the OSIRIS software package. The OSIRIS data file is constructed with a single logical record for each case. There are 1,451 variables for 2,107 cases.

The OSIRIS data file can be accessed directly through software packages or programs which do not use the OSIRIS dictionary by specifying the tape locations of the desired variables. These tape locations are given in the OSIRIS dictionary-codebook.

List of Available Documentation

Jackson, J. S., Tucker, M. B. & Gurin, G. (1987). *National Survey of Black Americans, 1979-1980.* [Machine-readable data file]. 1st ICPSR ed. Ann Arbor, MI: Inter-university Consortium for Political and Social Research (Distributor).

Contact

For data tapes, contact your school/university's official representative. They can order the data tapes through the computer network.

For codebooks contact Piper Simmons at:

The Inter-university Consortium for Political and Social Research
The University of Michigan
P.O. Box 1248
Ann Arbor, MI 48106-1248
(313) 763-5010

Cost

Two-volume codebook: $52 including shipping and handling.

Machine-readable data file: cost must be worked out on an individual basis since it depends on the customer's computer setup and affiliation.

BIBLIOGRAPHY

Antonucci, T.C., & Jackson, J.S. (1990). The role of reciprocity in social support. In I.G. Sarason, B.R. Sarason, & G.R. Pierce (Eds.), *Social support: An interactional view* (pp. 173-198). New York: John Wiley & Sons.

Bowman, P.J. (1990). Coping with provider role strain: Adaptive cultural resources among black husband-fathers. *Journal of Black Psychology, 16*(2), 1-21.

Broman, C.L. (1988). Household work and family life satisfaction of blacks. *Journal of Marriage and the Family, 50*(3), 743-748.

Broman, C.L., (1988). Satisfaction among blacks: The significance of marriage and parenting. *Journal of Marriage and the Family, 50,* 45-51.

Chatters, L.M. (1990). The family life of older black adults: Stressors and resources. *Journal of Health and Social Policy, 1*(4), 45-53.

Chatters, L.M., Taylor, R.J., & Neighbors, H.W. (1989). Size of the informal health network mobilized in response to serious personal problems. *Journal of Marriage and the Family, 51,* 667-676.

Coleman, L.M., Antonucci, T.C., Adelmann, P.K., & Crohan, S.E. (1987). Social roles in the lives of middle-aged and older black women. *Journal of Marriage and the Family, 49,* 761-771.

Demo, D.H., & Hughes, M. (1990). Socialization and racial identity among black Americans. *Social Psychology Quarterly, 53*(4), 364-374.

Ellison, C.G. (1990). Family ties, friendships, and subjective well-being among black Americans. *Journal of Marriage and the Family, 52,* 298-310.

Gibson, R.C. (1991). Race and the self-reported health of elderly persons. *Journal of Gerontology: Social Sciences, 46*(5), S235-S242.

Gibson, R.C. (1991). The subjective retirement of black Americans. *Journal of Gerontology, 46*(4), S204-S209.

Gibson, R.C., & Jackson, J.S. (1992). The black oldest old: Health, functioning, and informal support. In R. Suzman, D. Willis, & K. Manton (Eds.), *The oldest old* (pp. 505-515). New York: Oxford University Press.

Hatchett, S.J., & Jackson, J.S. (1993). African American extended kin systems: An assessment. In H. P. McAdoo (Ed.), *Family ethnicity: Strengths in diversity*. Newbury Park, CA: Sage.

Jackson, J.S. (1991). *Life in black America*. Newbury Park, CA: Sage.

Jackson, J.S., Chatters, L.M., & Taylor, R.J. (Eds.). (1993). *Aging in black America*. Newbury Park, CA: Sage.

Jackson, J.S., Jayakody, R., & Antonucci, T.C. (1993). Exchanges within black American three-generation families: The family environment context model. In T.K. Hareven (Ed.), *Aging and generational relations*. Berlin: Walter de Gruyter & Co.

Jackson, J.S., McCullough, W., & Gurin, G. (1987). Socialization environment and identity development in black families. In H. McAdoo (Ed.), *Black families*, 2nd Ed. (pp. 265-283). Beverly Hills, CA: Sage.

Jackson, J.S., & Wolford, M.L. (1992). Changes from 1980 to 1987 in the mental health status of African Americans. *Journal of Geriatric Psychiatry, 25*(1), 15-67.

Jackson, J.S., Tucker, M.B., & Gurin, G. (1987). *National survey of black Americans, 1979-1980.* [Machine-readable data file]. 1st ICPSR ed. Ann Arbor, MI: Inter-university Consortium for Political and Social Research (Distributor) (ICPSR 8512).

Lewis, E.A. (1988). Role strengths and strains of African-American mothers. *Journal of Primary Prevention, 9*(1 & 2), 77-91.

Neighbors, H.W. (1988). The help-seeking behavior of black Americans: A summary of findings from the national survey of black Americans. *Journal of the National Medical Association, 80*(9), 1009-1012.

Taylor, R.J. (1990). Need for support and family involvement among black Americans. *Journal of Marriage and the Family, 52,* 584-590.

Taylor, R.J., & Chatters, L.M. (1991). Non-organizational religious participation among elderly black adults. *Journal of Gerontology: Social Sciences, 46*(2), S103-S111.

Tucker, M.B., & Taylor, R.J. (1989). Demographic correlates of relationship status among black Americans. *Journal of Marriage and the Family, 51,* 655-666.

Wilson, K.R., & Allen, W.R. (1987). Explaining the educational attainment of young black adults: Critical familial and extra-familial influences. *Journal of Negro Education, 56*(1), 64-76.

19

THE PANEL STUDY OF INCOME DYNAMICS, 1968-1990 (PSID)

Survey Research Center,
University of Michigan

PURPOSE OF THE STUDY

The Panel Study of Income Dynamics (PSID) has been conducted annually since 1968 at the Survey Research Center, University of Michigan. The central focus of the data is economic and demographic, with substantial detail on income sources and amounts; employment; family composition changes; and residential location. The study was a supplement to the Census Bureau surveys taken for the Office of Economic Opportunity in 1966 and 1967. The intent of the 1966 and 1967 surveys was to assess the extent to which Lyndon Johnson's War on Poverty had effected the economic well-being of families. The Census Bureau surveyed approximately 30,000 households, a sample comprised of a disproportionately large number of low income households and, hence, a sizable subsample of blacks.

In 1968, the PSID was developed to continue the survey on a subsample of 1,872 low-income households from the original OEO studies, but a fresh cross-section of 2,930 households from a national sampling frame was added to provide a more representative sample of the entire population of the U.S., including poor and nonpoor households. In addition, as part of the sample, members of the families who moved away from their original households to set up new households, such as children who came of age during the study, are tracked and interviewed. The tracking of sample individuals and recording information about the people with whom they are living has increased the original sample size of 18,000 individuals in 1968 to over 36,000 by 1990 (approximately 7,100 family units). Because of its methods of tracking individuals and families, the study contains an accurate representation of the nonimmigrant U. S. population both cross-sectionally and demographically since 1968. A representative sample of 2,000 Latino households was added in 1990.

The PSID provides a wide variety of information at the family and individual level, as well as information about the areas in which sample households reside. The study investigates the effects of demographic, environmental and institutional variables on the economic well-being of families, as well as the effects of attitudes and behavior patterns. In each year, the survey measures money and nonmoney components of family income; behavior in crucial areas such as employment, residential location, assistance to and from extended family members; and some relevant attitudes.

METHODS
Sampling Design

The panel study is based on a national probability sample of approximately 5,000 families interviewed annually. Each interviewed family contains at least one member who was in one of the families originally interviewed in 1968, or a child born to an original sample member. Children born to a member of an original sample household are classified as official sample members and are eligible for interviewing as "split-offs" when they begin setting up their own households. The procedure replicates the population's household-building activity and (with the exception of recent immigration) produces an unbiased sample of families each year. Annual attrition has been modest, and new PSID families have formed when children have grown up and established separate households or when marriage partners have gone separate ways. This has resulted in growth over time in both the number of family units and the number of people residing with an original sample member at some time during the study.

The initial sample for the survey combined a cross-sectional sample and a sample of low-income families. The first sample was drawn by the Survey Research Center (SRC) and is commonly known as the SRC Sample. It was an equal probability sample of households in the coterminous United States designed to yield about 3,000 (2,930 actual) completed interviews. The second subset of responding families came from the original Census Bureau's Survey of Economic Opportunity (SEO sample) and was designed to yield interviews with about 2,000 (1,872 actual) low-income families with heads under 60 years old. The SEO sample was confined to Standard Metropolitan Statistical Areas (SMSAs) and to non-SMSAs in the Southern region.

The SEO sample involves unequal selection probabilities. Weights supplied on the data files are designed to compensate for both unequal selection probabilities and differential nonresponse in 1968 and subsequent years.

The general design of the study has remained largely unchanged over time; however, the mode of interviewing has changed. From 1968 through 1972, the PSID conducted personal interviews. In 1973, to reduce costs, the study began taking the majority of interviews by telephone instead. Since that time, in-person interviews have been conducted only with respondents (roughly 600 each year) who do not have telephones, or who have special circumstances which make a telephone interview unfeasible. To further reduce costs, and because long interviews are especially difficult over the telephone, the length of the interview was also reduced beginning in 1973. The interview averaged about one hour in length when it was conducted in-person; since the change to telephone interviewing the length has ranged from an average of 20 to 30 minutes.

A single primary adult, usually the male adult head, if there is one, serves as the sole respondent. The wife (or permanent partner, called "wife") of the head is the respondent if she agrees to grant an interview when the head does not. The single household respondent provides information about him/herself and about all other family members. The most detailed information is collected each year about the heads of family units. However, since 1976, the same amount of detail has been collected about wives and "wives." In two years (1976 and 1985) interviews were taken with all wives and "wives" (labeled wives' interview) as well as all heads.

Periodicity

Interviews have been conducted annually since 1968. As of 1990, the PSID had collected information about over 36,000 individuals spanning as much as 23 years of their lives. The data files contain the full span of information collected over the course of the study.

Unit of Analysis

The PSID allows wide variety on the choice of unit of analysis. It can be used to represent individuals, couples, families, person-years, couple-years, or ex-couple years. It can also represent the U.S. as a whole and major regions of the country. Due to its clustered sample design, it cannot represent states, cities, or similar small geographic divisions.

A major challenge of the PSID is changes to family composition over time. Nearly one-quarter of the PSID's families experience at least some type of change in a typical year, and only about one in twenty has remained completely intact for the first 18 years of the study. While consistent treatment of individuals in a family is possible, there is no consistent or acceptable definition of what constitutes a family over time. Family composition changes must be taken into consideration before longitudinal analysis or cross-sectional analysis can begin. Since the PSID tracks both family and individual, it is important to maintain clear distinction between family units and the individuals within them. Individual units are better suited to longitudinal analysis, but it is often important to consider the individual in the context of what family he or she is in at different points in time.

Response Rates

In 1968, the PSID's first year, 76 percent of the sampled households were successfully interviewed.

Attrition

In 1969 the response rate across households interviewed the previous year was 88.5 percent. Since 1969, response rates have ranged between 96.9 and 98.5 percent. As of the 1988 wave, the cumulative response rate for individuals who lived in a household interviewed in 1968 was 56.1 percent. Because there are many people entering the study over time, that may or may not be the segment of PSID individuals of interest to an analyst. Because of its survey procedures, the sample of families changes each year. The inclusion of newly formed families has caused the total sample to grow gradually despite attrition among original sample households.

CONTENT

Data Sources

The data collection for a given PSID wave in the 1968-1990 period extended from April through September using a national field staff of interviewers and supervisors dispersed across the U. S. but coordinated by the SRC Field Office in Ann Arbor. Approximately 115 interviewers and 6 to 12 supervisors worked on the survey each year.

About 92% of the PSID sample were interviewed by telephone each year, with interviewers working from their own homes. The remaining 8% of the sample were respondents interviewed face-to-face because of such circumstances as not having a telephone, hearing or health problems, and other personal factors. A proportion of each interviewer's completed cases were re-contacted by the Field supervisors to verify that the interview actually took place. The proportion varied from 5% for experienced interviewers to 10% for new interviewers.

Strategies incorporated by the PSID to maintain a high re-interview response rate are: paying respondents for interviewing and turning in change-of-address notices; mailing respondents a booklet summarizing how information from prior waves are being analyzed and used in policy debates; mailing personalized letters requesting information; obtaining names of friends or relatives who would know respondent's location should they move; maintaining accessible staff personnel for troubleshooting; maintaining continuity of interviewer-respondent matches if possible; offering the option of a telephone or personal interview; monitoring interviewer performance in the early phases of interviewing; developing a core of "elite" interviewers for the difficult field work; and mailings in between interview periods to maintain respondent interest and up-to-date information on location.

Description of Variables Covered

The PSID contains a large number of variables that have been asked each year in a similar, if not identical, manner. They constitute what is termed "core" content, and are available on the main data files. A wide variety of other topics have been covered intermittently, and while they are also available in the main data files, special data files exist to handle the finer details. A comprehensive listing of variables, listed alphabetically by topic, is available with the documentation and *User Guide* distributed by the ICPSR.

The core topics covered in the PSID [1] are:

Income Sources and Amounts
    Earning of family members
    Business/farm income
    Income from professional practice or trade
    Income from farming or gardening
    Income from roomers or boarders
    Income from rent
    Dividends, interest, trust fund, royalties
    AFDC/ADC
    SSI
    Other welfare
    Social security
    VA pension, service disability or GI bill
    Retirement pay, pensions, or annuities
    Unemployment compensation
    Alimony
    Child support
    Help from relatives/nonrelatives
    Other income

Poverty Status
    Family poverty thresholds [2]

Public Assistance in the form of Food or Housing
    Use of food stamps
    Public assistance with housing
        If in public housing project
        If rent is publicly subsidized
        Government assistance with heating bills

Other Financial Matters
    Estimate of federal taxes paid [2]
    Financial assistance to people living elsewhere

Family Structure and Demographic Measures
  Marital events and status
  Fertility events
  Adoptions of children
  Number of siblings (total and number still living)
  Ethnic group
  Race

Employment information
  Annual and monthly information on:
    Weeks worked
    Weeks unemployed
    Weeks out of labor force
    Work missed because sick
    Work missed because family members was sick
    Weeks of vacation
    Weeks on strike
  For each main job and second job:
    Occupation and industry
    Whether government worked
    Rate of pay on job
    Hours per week working
  For each main job:
    Whether union worker
    If self-employed, whether business is incorporated
  Work experience:
    Total
    Employer-specific
  Employment status:
    Employment status at time of interview
    Whether have been looking for work and if so how
  Event-history dating employment changes during past year:
    Movements between employers
    Title changes with the same employer
    Occupation and industry
    Pay and work load at start and end with each employer
    Reasons for changing employers

Housework Time

Housing
    Size and type of housing structure
    Whether own home, pay rent, or what
    House value
    Remaining mortgage

Geographic Mobility
    Moves during last year—when and why
    Plans about moving in future—how certain and why
    State and county of residence
    Where head grew up—rural vs. urban, state and county
    All states head has lived in
    Whether head ever moved to take a job

Socioeconomic Background [3]
    Education history
    Parents' completed education
    Number of siblings
    Race and ethnicity
    Father's occupation
    Parents' poverty status

Health, Religion, Military Service
    General health and disability of family members
    Religious preference
    Ever in military service

County-level Data.
    Unemployment rates
    Wage rates for unskilled workers
    Labor market demand conditions

Intermittent topics covered in the PSID and the year(s) in which they were surveyed are:

    1968-1972, 1977-1987: Housing utilities
    1969-1986: Commuting to work

1968-1972: Housing and neighborhood characteristics
Attitudes and behavior patterns
Do-it-yourself activities
Saving (crude measure)
Disability of family members
Fertility and family planning
Child care
Time use
1972 Only: Achievement motivation
Cognitive ability (sentence completion test)
1973-1974: Child care
1975: Neighborhood and housing problems
Satisfaction
Attitudes
Disability of the head
1976: Wives' interview
Employment history [4]
Fertility and family planning [5]
Characteristics of job (including training required) [4]
Attachment to labor force [4]
Child care [5]
Attitudes [4]
1977: Child care
Disability of the head
1978: Job training
How got jobs
Retirement plans and experiences
Disability of family members
1979: Do-it-yourself activities
Child care
Impact of inflation
Savings (crude measure)
Retirement plans
Disability of the head
1980: Time and money help with emergencies
Food stamp/SSI eligibility
Impact of inflation
Child care
Disability of the head

Extended family
Savings (crude measure)
1981-1983: Retirement plans and expectations (most detail in 1983)
Spells of unemployment/out of labor force
Hospitalization over the year
Disability and illness of family members
1984: Wealth (level of assets of various types)
Fringe benefits
Pension plans and rights
Retirement plans
Inheritances
Savings (crude measure)
Job training
Spells of unemployment/out of the labor force
Disability and illness of head and wife
1985: Wives' interview
Retrospective childbirth history [4]
Retrospective history of adoptions [4]
Retrospective history of substitute parenting [4]
Retrospective marital history [4]
Child care [4]
Housework [4]
Family planning [4]
Disability and illness [4]
Job training [4]
1986: General health of all family members
Activities of daily living [5]
Hospitalization over the year [5]
Height and weight [5]
Smoking and exercising behavior [5]
1988: Kinship ties
Financial situation of parents
Health of parents
Time and money help of most kinds
1989: Wealth (level of assets of various types)
Saving behavior 1984-1989
1990: Health and health care of the elderly
Links to Medicare records

Number of Variables

Most of the information from any year's data collection is categorized as family-level variables. The family-level variables include not only information that applies to the family unit as a whole (such as total family income, or number of children), but also almost all information about the head of the family unit, and if present, the wife or "wife" of the head, plus a small set of information about the current county of residence. The main PSID files contain about 1,500 family-level variables for the 1988 interviewing year.

A small set of individual-level variables is available for each individual in the family unit interviewed by the study. This set is comprised of both year-specific variables and summary variables that may span many years. About 40 year-specific individual variables are coded each year for each individual in a family unit and cover basic demographic and economic data about the individual. If the individual is the head or wife of head, these variables are available among the family-level variables. The other variables in the individual-level data sets are "summary variables" and deal with time-invariant information, cumulative counts of rare events, timing of rare events, or details about nonresponse and institutionalization. The numbers below give the counts of family-level and individual-level variables for one illustrative year of the PSID: 1988.

I. Family-Level Variables		1,408
A. Edited variables	302	
B. Unedited variables	953	
C. Generated variables	149	
D. County variables	4	
II. Individual-Level Variables		90
A. Year-Specific variables	37	
B. Summary variables	53	

Checklist of Topics Covered

X Gender / Gender Role
X Race / Ethnicity
X Age
X Education
X Occupation / Employment
X Physical Health / Disease
___ Nutrition
___ Clinical Activities
___ Biological Functioning /
     Development
___ Mental Health / Disease
___ Psychological Functioning /
     Development
___ Guidance / Counseling
___ Personality
___ Intellectual Functioning
X Residential Mobility
X Dwelling
X Neighborhood /
     Community
X Region / State
X Marriage and Divorce
X Cohabitation
X Family/Household
     Composition & Structure
___ Inter-Partner Relationships
X Parent-Child Relationships
X Inter-Sibling Relationships
X Relationships with Other Kin

X Relationships with Nonkin
X Other Family/Household
     Characteristics
X Child Care
X Wealth / Finances / Material
     Things
X Receipt of Health, Mental
     Health, Social Services
X Adoption / Foster Care
X Childbearing / Pregnancy
X Out-of-Wedlock Pregnancy &
     Parenthood
___ Abortion
___ Sexuality
___ Sex Education
___ Contraception
___ Sexually Transmitted
     Diseases
___ Civic/Political Activities
___ Friends / Social Activities
     Social Support
___ Dating, Courtship
___ Recreation
X Religion
___ Crime / Delinquency /
     Behavior Problems
___ Substance Use
___ Agency Characteristics
X Interview

Checklist of Key Variables

X Number of family members
X Identification of marital
     partners in family
X Size of dwelling
X Type of dwelling
X Urban/rural residence
X Region/state of residence
X Family income
X Religious affiliation
X Relation of each family
     member to:
     X Reference person
     X All other members
X Age of family members
     X Respondent
     X Others
X Sex of family members

X Respondent
X Others
X Race of family members
     X Respondent
     X Others
X Marital status of family
     members
     X Respondent
     X Others
X Education of family
     members
     X Respondent
     X Others
X Occupation of family
     members
     X Respondent
     X Others

LIMITATIONS

Because the original sample for the PSID was drawn from two different sources, with differing probabilities of selection for households, the full sample is representative of the U.S. population only when the probability-of-selection weights provided on PSID data files are used. These weights also correct for differential nonresponse.

In the absence of nonresponse bias, the PSID's rules for tracking individuals and families over time lead to accurate representation of the *nonimmigrant* U.S. population both cross-sectionally each year and in terms of change since 1968. Immigration since 1968, however, is problematic. Unless a post-1968 immigrant moved into a family unit containing at least one member who was living in the U.S. in 1968, he or she could not be represented in the PSID. To help correct for omissions in representing post-1968 immigrants, a representative sample of 2,043 Latino (Mexican, Cuban, and Puerto Rican) households was added in 1990.

SPONSORSHIP

The PSID has been funded principally by a collection of federal agencies, including the Office of Economic Opportunity; the Assistant Secretary for Planning and Evaluation of the Department of Health, Education and Welfare (now Health and Human Services); the National Science Foundation; the Departments of Labor and Agriculture; the National Institute of Child Health and Human Development (NICHD); and the National Institute on Aging (NIA). The Sloan, Rockefeller, and Ford Foundations provided supplementary grants. Since 1983, the National Science Foundation (NSF) has been the principal sponsor of the study, with the Office of the Assistant Secretary for Planning and Evaluation of the Department of Health and Human Services a major secondary sponsor.

The PSID routinely prepares a number of data files. Most are updated with each new wave of data collection and then made available, along with comprehensive documentation, to the public. Most PSID files contain information dating back to the study's first wave and include records for family units, individuals, or pairs of individuals. The types of files are listed in the table on the next two pages. The files fall into three major categories—main files, special public-release files, and special restricted files. The main data files contain current and past information gathered over all of the waves. The cross-year family file includes only family-level variables and contains one and only one data record for each family unit interviewed in the most recent interviewing year. The cross-year family-individual files contain data records for individuals of PSID family units, with each data record including information (dating back to 1968) both about an individual (e.g., age and sex) and about the families with which he or she has been associated. The "response" version of this file contains records for individuals who are members of PSID family units interviewed in the most recent interviewing wave. The "nonresponse" version contains information for all individuals who were members of families interviewed in the past but are not members of families interviewed in the most recent wave.

File Structure

The data files are listed in Table 1 on the next two pages. Further discussion of the files continues on page 19-18.

Table 1. PSID File Structure

Type of PSID Data Files	Is file updated with each subsequent wave of data?	Is file available from ICPSR?
Main Files		
Cross-Year Family File	Yes	Yes
Cross-Year Family-Individual Response Files	Yes	Yes
Cross-Year Family-Individual Nonresponse File	Yes	Yes
Special Public Files		
1985 Ego-Alter File [1]	No	Yes
Marital History File [1]	Yes	Yes [2]
Childbirth & Adoption History File	Yes	Yes [2]
Work-History File	Yes	Yes
Relationship File	No	Yes
1988 Time & Money Transfers File	No	Yes
1990 Health Supplement File	No	Yes [2]

19 - 16

Table 1. PSID File Structure (continued)

Type of PSID Data Files	Is file updated with each subsequent wave of data?	Is file available from ICPSR?
Special Restricted Files		
Census Tract/Enumeration District File	No	No [3]
Death Certificate File	No	No [3]

[1] The information in these files can date as far back as the early 1900s, because they contain marital and childbirth histories for PSID adults, some of whom are quite elderly.

[2] As of spring 1992, work on this file is still in process but will be made available to ICPSR as soon as it is completed.

[3] Contact Greg Duncan for availability of information.

There are several special files whose information is presented in summarized form on the main files but detailed form on these separate files. These files may have some stand-alone application but are best if merged with the main data files. Some of these files are: Ego-alter File; Marital History File; Childbirth and Adoption History File; Work History File; Relationship File; Census Track Enumeration District and Other Geographic Identifiers; Death Certificate Information; and a 1990 Health Supplement.

Historically, PSID data files have been released through the Inter-university Consortium on magnetic tape. However, a CD-ROM version of either the 1968-1987 or the 1968-1988 rectangular cross-year family-individual response and nonresponse files is also available with SAS and SPSS-X program files on the CD-ROM.

List of Available Documentation

Documentation is provided for all PSID files released to the public in a set of documentation volumes entitled *A Panel Study of Income Dynamics—Procedures and Tape Codes.* This multivolume set covers all interviewing years starting with 1968. The first five waves of data are documented in the first two volumes; for each subsequent wave a separate volume has been prepared and made available. Documentation is also available in machine readable form starting with the 1985 interviewing year. The documentation volumes contain the questionnaire, complete listing of variable names and labels, missing data codes, and description of edited variables.

Separate documentation volumes are available for PSID special files: the 1985 Ego-Alter file, the Work-History Supplement file, the Marital History file, the Childbirth and Adoption History file, the Relationship file, and the 1988 Time and Money Transfers file.

Two additional publications serve as broad-based guidebooks to the data. They are intended both as introductions to the data and for use in conjunction with the multivolume set of documentation books. The broadest introduction, which describes the origins, design, procedures, and broad analytical potential of the PSID, is provided by the monograph:

Hill, M.S. with assistance of the staff of the PSID (1992). *The panel study of income dynamics*. (Guide to Major Data Bases, Volume 2). Newbury Park, CA: Sage Publications.

More detailed instructions about how to use the data are provided in:

Survey Research Center, Economic Behavior Program (1984). *User guide to the Panel Study of Income Dynamics*. Ann Arbor: University of Michigan, Inter-university Consortium for Political and Social Research.

Both the documentation books and the *User Guide* provide an alphabetic list of variables by topic area, with variable numbers and type locations for each year and indications of any problems of year-to-year comparability. The documentation books and *User Guide* (with revisions to the latter projected for 1992) are available through ICPSR.

Contact

Most of the data files from the PSID are available through the Inter-university Consortium for Political and Social Research (ICPSR). To obtain more information, contact :

Janet Vavra
Inter-university Consortium for Political and Social
Research
P.O. Box 1248
Ann Arbor, MI 48106
(313) 763-5010

Cost

Members of the Inter-university Consortium for Political and Social Research can obtain the data sets at no cost. Ask your ICPSR campus representative for assistance. If your institution is not a member of ICPSR, contact ICPSR for a price quote.

BIBLIOGRAPHY

Duncan, G.J. (1984). *Years of poverty, years of plenty*. Ann Arbor, MI: Institute for Social Research.

Hill, M.S., with the assistance of the staff of PSID. (1992). *The panel study of income dynamics*. (Guide to Major Data Bases, Volume 2). Newbury Park, CA: Sage.

Morgan, J.N., & Duncan, G.J. (Eds.). *Five thousand American families: Patterns of economic progress*. Ann Arbor, MI: Institute for Social Research.

Survey Research Center (1993). *Publications, working papers, and government reports based on the panel study of income dynamics*. Ann Arbor, MI: Institute for Social Research.

NOTES

[1] The amount of detail for these topics is most extensive for the head and wife of the family unit, but some information is often provided for other family members as well.

[2] Estimates are generated for this information from indirect indicators collected in the annual interviews.

[3] Questions regarding an individual's socioeconomic background are asked the first year the individual appears as a head, wife, or "wife" in an interviewed family unit. This information is not updated on a regular basis, although pertinent information may have been gathered subsequently that allows for updating. If the individual switches from head one year to a wife the next, or vice versa, all of the socioeconomic background questions are re-asked. In addition, in a few waves of the study socioeconomic background information has been asked of all heads, wives, and "wives" regardless of whether they are new to that role that year.

[4] Questions asked of both head and wife/"wife"

[5] Questions asked of female head and wife/"wife"

20

TIME USE IN ECONOMIC AND SOCIAL ACCOUNTS, 1975-76 AND 1975-81 TIME USE LONGITUDINAL PANEL STUDY

F. Thomas Juster

PURPOSE OF THE STUDY

This panel study represents a unique attempt to document how American families spend both their work and leisure time. Data from several waves of interviews in 1975-1976 and again in 1981 make it possible to analyze how respondents' time use and related attitudes change over five years. Information was collected on demographic characteristics of the respondent, family and household structure, gender role attitudes, and social support. Similar information was also collected from the respondent's spouse and up to three children in each household. A major component of the study was the time diary, a detailed log of activities covering the span of an entire day, which respondents were asked to complete on four occasions during the year.

METHODS

Sampling Design

The 1975-1976 sample of respondents was designed to represent households in the coterminous United States exclusive of those on military reservations. A random sample of households was selected from both urban and rural areas with probability proportionate to population.

The methodology of the survey was based on previous research on time use conducted by the Survey Research Center at the University of Michigan. These earlier studies validated alternative techniques for the measurement of time use, and led to the conclusion that the most accurate record of time use is the diary methodology.

Four interviews were conducted at roughly even intervals over the course of a year. Respondents were first interviewed in person in October/November of 1975 (Wave 1). They were subsequently re-interviewed by telephone in February, May, and September of 1976 (Waves 2-4). Because time use patterns vary considerably from weekdays to weekend days, and from Saturdays to Sundays, time use data was collected from each household for one weekday, one Saturday, and one Sunday. A second weekday diary was taken from households with 4 successful contacts.

The total number of eligible households (those with adults over 18) where interviews were attempted was 2,300. In Wave 1 (October/November 1975), interviews were successfully completed at 1,519 of these households (66%). In 887 of these households, spouses were also interviewed. In Wave 2 (February/March 1976), 1,147 households were successfully re-contacted, with spouses being interviewed in 644 of these. The Wave 3 sample (May/June 1976) consisted of 1,007 households, 556 of which had spouses interviewed. By Wave 4 (September 1976), 947 of the original 1,519 households were successfully re-contacted, and spouses in 500 of those households were interviewed, making the response rate for the whole survey 41.2%.

In a second set of four interviews conducted in 1981, 920 respondents (heads of household) who had participated in at least three waves of the original time use study were considered eligible for re-contact. Of these, 620 were re-interviewed, or 27% of the original sample. By Wave 4, 493 interviews were conducted, or 21.4% of the original sample. Spouses were also re-contacted if they were still in the household, or they were contacted for the first time if not available in 1975-1976. Up to three children between the ages of three and seventeen living in the household were also interviewed in Waves 1 and 3.

Periodicity

There were two stages of the study. The first stage consisted of four waves of interviews between 1975-1976. The second stage consisted of an additional four interviews in 1981.

Unit of Analysis

The data collection focused on households. Respondents (heads of household) 18 years of age or older living in the coterminous U.S. were interviewed along with their spouses. In the 1981 study, up to three children between the ages of three and seventeen living in the household were included in the survey along with respondents and spouses.

Response Rates

	% of Preceding N	% of 2,300 [1]	% of 920 [2]
1975 Wave 1 N=1,519	—	66.0	—
1976 Wave 4 N=947	62.3	41.2	—
1981 Wave 1 N=620	65.5	27.0	67.4
1981 Wave 4 N=493	79.5	21.4	53.6

[1]Original Target Sample N was 2,300.

[2]The number of respondents eligible to be interviewed in 1981.

Attrition

	% of 1,519 [1]	% of 620 [2]
Feb. 1976 Wave 2 N=1,147	75.5	—
May 1976 Wave 3 N=1,007	66.3	—
Sept. 1976 Wave 4 N=947	62.3	—
Feb. 1981 Wave 1 N=620	40.8	—
May 1981 Wave 2 N=554	36.5	89.4
Aug. 1981 Wave 3 N=511	33.6	82.4
Nov. 1981 Wave 4 N=493	32.5	79.5

[1]Original number of successfully completed interviews.

[2]Number of successful re-contacts in Wave 1 of 1981 interviews.

CONTENT

Data Sources

For the 1975-1976 Time Use Study, Wave 1 data were obtained in the field through personal interviews. Data for Waves 2 through 4 were obtained via telephone from the Ann Arbor office of the Survey Research Center, allowing better quality control over the conduct of the interview. Direct Data Entry (DDE) enabled staff to bypass preparation of codesheets and punch cards. On all four waves of interviews, respondent and spouse time diaries were entered on line to direct access magnetic disk. By Waves 3 and 4, DDE was used to enter all interview data except for employment information. The entry program checked for wild codes and for one-way (skip pattern) inconsistencies. Data prepared via traditional codesheet/punch-card process (Wave 1 data except time diary; Wave 2 employment data only), were check coded and scanned for wild codes and obvious inconsistencies. No formal consistency checks were done on these data.

Wave 1 of the 1981 follow-up study consisted of personal interviews with respondents, spouses, and up to three children, ages 3-17. Parents, usually the mother, gave diary information for young children (aged 3-4) and assisted in the diaries of children aged 5-9. Caution should be used in comparative analysis of spouses between the 1975-1976 and 1981-1982 studies. In some cases, there will be data pertaining to 2 different spouses in one household, indicating that the respondent remarried between studies. Wave 2 consisted of telephone interviews with respondents and spouses. In Wave 3, personal interviews were conducted in households with children aged 5-11, but in households with very young or teenage children, telephone interviews were conducted with respondents, spouses and children. In addition, teacher ratings were obtained on the academic achievement of the children. Wave 4 interviews were done via telephone interviews with respondents and spouses.

Description of Variables Covered

One of the primary features of the survey was the 24-hour time diary, which study participants were asked to complete on four occasions during the year. Each activity recorded in the time diary was coded into one of over 200 categories. Checks were made to insure that diary entries added up to 1440 minutes (24 hours), and that no gaps in activity existed. When the respondent reported more than one primary activity at a time, such as "drinking coffee and smoking", time was apportioned between each activity. The time use data are available in three formats—daily aggregates for each wave of diary data, weekly aggregates for all cases with three or four diaries in 1975 and/or 1981, and the raw diary activity records from which time-of-day, presence of others, and secondary activity analysis can be done.

Respondent information was also gathered on the following topics: employment status of the respondent and spouse; household earnings and income for each month and year that the interview was taken; "consumption benefits", e.g. satisfaction of daily activities; personal and other resources (health status, friendships, and affiliation with associations); stock of technology available to the household; division of labor for household work and related attitudes; neighborhood and housing information; respondent reports on quality of local services (schools, playgrounds, transportation) and perceptions of various dimensions of neighborhood quality (safety, etc.); net worth and housing values; job characteristics; recreation; and characteristics of mass media usage on a typical day.

In the 1975-1976 study, along with the topics described above, data were also collected on the health and personal resources of respondent families, including: measures of health status; organizational activity; number of close friends; several measures of the respondents' investment in personal and social relationships; fertility; marriage/divorce experience; time spent as a family unit; enjoyment of family activities; nonhome activities and preferences; spouse's labor force participation; family authority structure; and sex role attitudes.

The 1981 study placed more emphasis on measures relating to the family and its functioning than did the 1975 study, although many of the economic measures from 1975 were repeated in 1981.

Number of Variables

The 1975-1976 survey contains 7,966 variables and 2,406 cases—1,519 respondents and 887 spouses. The 1981 Time Use Longitudinal Panel Study contains 7,097 variables and 1,488 cases—620 respondents, 376 spouses, and 492 children.

Checklist of Topics Covered

X Gender / Gender Role
X Race / Ethnicity
X Age
X Education
X Occupation / Employment
X Physical Health / Disease
X Nutrition
___ Clinical Activities
___ Biological Functioning / Development
___ Mental Health / Disease
___ Psychological Functioning / Development
___ Guidance / Counseling
___ Personality
___ Intellectual Functioning
___ Residential Mobility
X Dwelling
X Neighborhood / Community
X Region / State
X Marriage and Divorce
___ Cohabitation
X Family/Household Composition & Structure
___ Inter-Partner Relationships
___ Parent-Child Relationships
___ Inter-Sibling Relationships
___ Relationships with Other Kin

___ Relationships with Nonkin
X Other Family/Household Characteristics
X Child Care
X Wealth / Finances / Material Things
___ Receipt of Health, Mental Health, Social Services
___ Adoption / Foster Care
X Childbearing / Pregnancy
___ Out-of-Wedlock Pregnancy & Parenthood
___ Abortion
___ Sexuality
___ Sex Education
___ Contraception
___ Sexually Transmitted Diseases
X Civic/Political Activities
X Friends / Social Activities
___ Social Support
___ Dating, Courtship
X Recreation
X Religion
___ Crime / Delinquency / Behavior Problems
___ Substance Use
___ Agency Characteristics
X Interview

Checklist of Key Variables

X Number of family members
X Identification of marital
    partners in family
X Size of dwelling
X Type of dwelling
___ Urban/rural residence
___ Region/state of residence
X Family income
X Religious affiliation
___ Relation of each family
    member to:
    ___ Reference person
    ___ All other members
X Age of family members
    ___ Respondent
    ___ Others
X Sex of family members

    X Respondent
    X Others
X Race of family members
    X Respondent
    ___ Others
X Marital status of family
    members
    X Respondent
    X Others
X Education of family
    members
    X Respondent
    X Others
X Occupation of family
    members
    X Respondent
    X Others

LIMITATIONS

Two concerns in using data from the 1975-1981 Time Use Longitudinal Panel Study are the initial response rate and attrition. Of the original sample of 2,300 eligible respondents in the 1975 study, 1,519 (66% of 2,300) completed the first interview. By Wave 4, attrition reduced that number to 947 (62.3% of 1,519). In Wave 1 of the 1981 follow-up study, 620 (40.8% of 1,519) of the original 1975 Wave 1 respondents participated, and by Wave 4 of the study, 493 (32.5% of 1,519) of the original respondents remained, or 21.4% of total eligible sample of 2,300 (see sections on Response Rates and Attrition above). For information on response errors and problems of measurement of time use, see the journal articles mentioned below.

SPONSORSHIP

The 1975-1976 Time Use Study was sponsored by the National Science Foundation (grant numbers SOC74-20206, SOC74-20206A01, SOC74-20206A03, and RDA75-21077) and by the U.S. Department of Health, Education and Welfare (grant number RDA75-21077). The 1975-1981 Panel Study was funded by the National Science Foundation (contract numbers SES-7915368 and SES-8112784) and by the Foundation for Child Development.

GUIDE TO DATA AND DOCUMENTATION

File Structure

Data are arranged in OSIRIS Dictionary-Dataset format. The data set consists of two files: the OSIRIS dictionary-codebook which contains all technical information for each variable, and the data file. The data file for the 1975-1976 Time Study is "rectangular", constructed in OSIRIS IV format, with a single logical record of 19,866 bytes for each respondent/source record. There are 7,984 variables and 2,406 cases. The 1981 data is available in separate rectangular files for Respondents, Spouses, and children, with household variables included in each file. The files may be merged using a family ID number.

List of Available Documentation

The 1975 household data, respondent data (N=1,519), and spouse data (N=887) for the panel are contained in ICPSR 7580. The 1975-1976 time use data are also available in combination with Americans Use of Time, 1965-1966 (Phillip E. Converse and John F. Robinson) in ICPSR 7796. The 1981 Time Use Longitudinal Panel Study data are contained in ICPSR 9054. Three new parts have been added: 1975 adult activity records, 1981 adult/child activity records, and a merged file of husband/wife data for 1975 and 1981. The three new parts as well as the 1975-76 data files are all available as ICPSR file number 9054. Additional and revised documentation includes a User's Guide, 1975 subject index, occupation and industry codes, and codebooks for the new data files as well as for the 1981 household, respondent, spouse, and child data.

Contact

> Janet Vavra
> Inter-university Consortium for Political and Social Research
> P.O. Box 1248
> Ann Arbor, MI 48106
> (313) 763-5010

Cost

Members of the Inter-university Consortium for Political and Social Research can obtain the data sets at no cost. Ask your ICPSR campus representative for assistance. If your institution is not a member of ICPSR, contact ICPSR for a price quote.

BIBLIOGRAPHY

Juster, F.T. (June 1986). Response errors in the measurement of time use. *Journal of the American Statistical Association, 81*, 390-402.

Juster, F.T., Hill, M.S., Stafford, F.P., & Parsons, J.E. (1990). *1975-1981 time use longitudinal panel study, study description* (Project #466066). Ann Arbor, MI: Survey Research Center.

Juster, F.T., & Stafford, F.P., (Eds.). (1985). *Time, goods, and well-being*. Ann Arbor, MI: Institute for Social Research.

Juster, F.T., & Stafford, F.P. (1991, June). The allocation of time: Empirical findings, behavioral models, and problems of measurement. *Journal of Economic Literature, 29*, 471-522.

Stafford, F.P. (1987). *Women's work, sibling competition and children's school performance* (Working Paper 8036). Ann Arbor, MI: Institute for Social Research.

21

THE ARMY FAMILY RESEARCH PROGRAM: FAMILY FACTORS IN RETENTION, READINESS, AND SENSE OF COMMUNITY, 1986-1991

U.S. Army Research Institute
Research Triangle Institute
Caliber Associates
Human Resources Research Organization

PURPOSE OF THE STUDY

In recognizing the partnership that exists between the Army and its families, the Army has increased program efforts to support Army families in all areas, including family research. The largest of the Army's family research activities has been the *Army Family Research Program's Family Factors in Retention, Readiness and Sense of Community*, conducted under the guidance of the U.S. Army Research Institute for the Behavioral and Social Sciences (ARI). The goal of this research is to produce improved programs, policies, and practices which: (1) increase the adaptation of Army Families; (2) enhance spouse employment opportunities; (3) improve retention of qualified personnel; (4) increase soldier and unit readiness; (5) heighten the sense of identity with, and participation in, Army community life among soldiers and their families.

METHODS

Sampling Design

The Army Family Research Program (AFRP) sample design employed a sampling technique known as multistage, cluster sampling to achieve desired cost savings without negating the inferential capability of the sample. Three stages of AFRP sample selection were specified by the sample design: installations, units within selected installations, and soldiers (and their spouses) from selected units. Stratification was used at each stage to control the distribution of the samples with respect to organizational and demographic characteristics. These included region of the world at the first stage, unit of function at the second stage, and demographic categories defined by paygrade, sex, and marital status at the third stage.

Since Army personnel are stationed in hundreds of locations worldwide, the costs associated with on-site data collection at randomly selected locations would have severely restricted the number of units and persons who could be surveyed. To ensure some control of the geographic distribution of the sample, a sample of geographic locations, each containing one or more Army installations, was drawn with the requirement that the subsequent selection of units be drawn only from these locations. Further, the selection of soldiers and their spouses was confined to selected units. Approximately equal-sized samples of soldiers were drawn from each unit to facilitate the estimation of unit-specific attributes.

In the first-stage (September, 1988) sample of 43 installations from 34 geographic locations, installations were selected with probabilities proportional to a composite size measure based on weighted counts of eligible soldiers assigned to those geographic locations. Composite size measures were used to attain the desired second and third-stage sample allocations for the various subpopulations of interest. Within the selected installations, 512 eligible units were selected in stage two (November 1988) with probabilities proportional to the composite number of persons assigned to eligible units. Finally, the third-stage (December 1988 to March 1989) sample of 20,033 eligible soldiers and their spouses was selected from 528 participating units with approximately equal probabilities within each third-stage stratum. Of these, there were 11,035 participating soldiers and their spouses. In the third-stage, an over-sampling of officers, married soldiers, and females was employed to obtain an adequate representation of these strata. Because of their importance to the unit-level analyses, the commanders of all selected units were also included in the sample. At each stage, the sample selection probabilities were assigned to sampling units to yield an approximately self-weighting (i.e., equal probability) sample of soldiers and spouses within categories defined by the intersection of unit function and demographic category.

Survey Population

Due to the three-stage, hierarchical nature of the sample design, eligibility for the study was assessed at three levels: geographic location, Army units within installations, and individual soldiers and spouses.

1. A geographic location was eligible for the survey if at least 1,000 active personnel were stationed at it or within fifty miles of it in May 1988.

2. A unit was eligible if, between sample selection (February 1989 to March 1989) and data collection (February 1989 to October

1989), it was located at an eligible location, was unclassified, had more than 20 active-duty persons assigned to it and was not a transition point (i.e. pipeline) or separation unit, a medical holding or confinement unit, or a unit comprised only of trainees or students.

3. A soldier was eligible if he or she was:
    1. On active duty and assigned to an eligible unit at the time of sample collection,
    2. In paygrade E2 through O6 at the time of sample selection and data collection,
    3. Not AWOL, hospitalized, incarcerated, or detached from their unit at data collection.
    4. A spouse was eligible if, at the time of data collection, he or she was married to an eligible soldier.

The soldier questionnaire (SQ) was administered in group sessions at the installations by trained data collection teams. Unit supervisors were also surveyed, and filled out Individual Readiness Rating (IRR) Questionnaires regarding up to eight subordinate soldiers participating in the survey. Unit supervisors also completed Unit Readiness Rating (URR) Questionnaires regarding the entire unit. If supervisors were part of the selected soldier sample, they also completed the standard soldier questionnaire. The Unit Commander was asked to complete a Unit Information Form, and if he or she was in the soldier sample, was also asked to complete the soldier and supervisor questionnaires. While the survey team was at the installation, the designated project liaison completed the Installation and Community Characteristics Inventory and obtained completed Survey of Family Services forms from the appropriate service directors.

Married soldiers who completed the Soldier Questionnaire were asked to provide their spouses' names and mailing addresses. A maximum of four attempts were made to have spouses complete and return questionnaires by mail.

Periodicity

Not applicable.

Unit of Analysis

Data collection centered on individual soldiers, their spouses, and Army units.

Response Rates

Due to the delay between sample selection and field data collection approximately 28% of the soldiers sampled were excluded because they were no longer eligible at the time the data was collected. Of these, 72% had been reassigned, 24% had separated from the Army, and the remainder were ineligible for other reasons. Therefore, the sample represents a smaller proportion of the Army than originally designed.

Seventy-seven percent (11,035 of 14,371) of eligible soldiers provided a usable questionnaire. IRR data were provided for 88% of the soldiers with usable questionnaires. Fifty-two percent of the spouses responded.

Thirty-eight percent of installations/sites provided a completed Installation and Community Characteristics Inventory. Eighty-three percent of installations/sites provided one or more completed Survey of Family Service (SFS) forms completed yielding a total of 789 SFSs. Seventy-one percent of the Unit Information forms were completed and over 19,347 Unit Readiness Rating Questionnaires were completed.

Table 1 on the next three pages provides figures for the response rates.

Table 1. Response Rates

Participation Status	Count	% Within Groups	% Across Groups
Units			
Total units selected for sample	612	100.0	
Ineligible:			
All trainees	25	35.7	
Unit moved	16	22.9	
Less than 21 persons assigned	15	21.4	
Other	14	20.1	
TOTAL	70	100.0	11.4
Eligible:			
Did not participate	14	2.6	
No URR, at least one SQ	154	28.4	
URR and at least one SQ	374	69.0	
TOTAL	542	100.0	88.6

Table 1. Response Rates (continued)

Participation Status	Count	% Within Groups	% Across Groups
Soldiers in participating units			
Total soldiers selected	20,033	100.00	
Ineligible:			
Reassigned	4,066	71.8	
Separated	1,309	23.5	
Other	287	5.1	
TOTAL	5,662	100.0	28.3
Eligible:			
Did not participate [a]	1,174	8.2	
SQ's only	1,376	8.2	
IRR only	2,162	15.0	
SQ and IRR	9,659	67.2	
TOTAL	14,371	100.0	71.7

[a] Includes soldiers who were on temporary duty, leave, or were sick during data collection.

21 - 6

Table 1. Response Rates (continued)

Participation Status	Count	% Within Groups	% Across Groups
Spouses of participating soldiers			
Total spouses selected	7,792		100.0
Mailing address not provided	1,669		21.4
Mailing address provided:			
Did not participate	2,846	46.5	
Did participate	3,277	53.5	78.6
TOTAL	6,123	100.0	

Attrition

Not applicable.

CONTENT

Data Sources

The Family Services Providers Survey is a 14-item instrument measuring the need, availability, and quality of services for families in the Army, completed by appropriate service directors. The Unit Information Form is an 18-item survey completed by the Unit Commander assessing the unit's personnel and equipment, past and present performance, unit accomplishments, and family support. The Installation and Community Characteristics Inventory is a 25-item survey measuring service demands and availability in the Army unit. The soldier questionnaire is a 430-item survey measuring soldier and family Army experiences, unit climate and readiness, and career intentions. The spouse questionnaire is a 354-item survey measuring spouse and family army experiences, employment status and experience of the spouse, and commitment to the Army and the soldier's career. The supervisor's Individual Readiness Rating Questionnaire is a 12-item survey, in which the supervisor rated up to eight subordinate soldiers on soldier and unit readiness.

Description of Variables Covered

Variables cover information on three general topics: soldier and unit readiness, soldier retention in the Army, and soldier and family sense of Army community. In addition, the spouse and soldier surveys contain demographic information. There are several similar variables, e.g. concerning readiness and soldier/spouse attitudes, that can be linked for soldiers, families, units, and installations.

Variables on individual and family level data include soldier performance and readiness in performing wartime tasks under different wartime conditions; soldier retention plans and reasons for retention decisions, including factors regarding family and long-term goals; soldier and spousal experience of Army life and work, family characteristics, family life experiences, and data on other attitudes and behaviors regarding the Army; spouse's experience in the Army or with Army life, aspirations for career advancement; and couple and family data derived from creating couple variables (e.g. agreement/disagreement) on retention plans, couple communication, and couple/family affects of unit leadership practices.

Unit level data were collected on unit readiness, unit leadership, the work environment, treatment of soldiers by leaders, unit leadership practices, leaders' performance and support for soldiers and families, and availability and effectiveness of Army programs and services.

Installation level data were collected on installation and community characteristics, such as location, population, cost of living, as well as availability, quality, and effectiveness of programs.

Number of Variables

Approximately 853 (See Data Sources section above for distribution).

Checklist of Topics Covered

X Gender / Gender Role
X Race / Ethnicity
X Age
X Education
X Occupation / Employment
X Physical Health / Disease
___ Nutrition
___ Clinical Activities
___ Biological Functioning / Development
___ Mental Health / Disease
___ Psychological Functioning / Development
___ Guidance / Counseling
___ Personality
___ Intellectual Functioning
X Residential Mobility
X Dwelling
X Neighborhood / Community
X Region / State
X Marriage and Divorce
X Cohabitation
X Family/Household Composition & Structure
X Inter-Partner Relationships
X Parent-Child Relationships
X Inter-Sibling Relationships
X Relationships with Other Kin

X Relationships with Nonkin
X Other Family/Household Characteristics
X Child Care
X Wealth / Finances / Material Things
X Receipt of Health, Mental Health, Social Services
___ Adoption / Foster Care
___ Childbearing / Pregnancy
___ Out-of-Wedlock Pregnancy & Parenthood
___ Abortion
___ Sexuality
___ Sex Education
___ Contraception
___ Sexually Transmitted Diseases
___ Civic/Political Activities
X Friends / Social Activities
___ Social Support
X Dating, Courtship
___ Recreation
___ Religion
___ Crime / Delinquency / Behavior Problems
___ Substance Use
X Agency Characteristics
___ Interview

Checklist of Key Variables

X Number of family members
___ Identification of marital
    partners in family
___ Size of dwelling
X Type of dwelling
___ Urban/rural residence
X Region/state of residence
X Family income
___ Religious affiliation
___ Relation of each family
    member to:
    ___ Reference person
    ___ All other members
___ Age of family members
    ___ Respondent
    ___ Others
X Sex of family members

X Respondent
___ Others
X Race of family members
    X Respondent
    ___ Others
X Marital status of family
    members
    X Respondent
    ___ Others
X Education of family
    members
    X Respondent
    X Others
X Occupation of family
    members
    X Respondent
    X Others

LIMITATIONS

Since soldiers are often assigned to new locations and tasks, it is possible that the emotional state of a soldier and his or her attitudes toward the Army may change greatly over short periods of time. Furthermore, the acquisition of new skills and increased utility of the soldier may affect his or her attitudes toward Army life. Though these issues are addressed in the study, a series of follow-up studies of the original panel would help track how soldiers' attitudes change over time given different circumstances.

SPONSORSHIP

The Army Family Research Program, under the guidance of ARI was a five-year integrated research program initiated in November 1986. The *Army Family Research Program's Family Factors in Retention, Readiness and Sense of Community*, was sponsored under the umbrella of the U.S. Community and Family Support Center and executed by a corporate consortium of three major institutions, the Research Triangle Institution RTI, Caliber Associates, and the Human Resources Research Organization.

GUIDE TO DATA AND DOCUMENTATION

File Structure

The data are formatted in a flat file (ASCII).

List of Available Documentation

A codebook and proc contents are available along with the 6250 magnetic tape.

Contact

Defense Technical Information Center (DTIC)
Office of User Services & Marketing
Cameron Station
Alexandria, VA 22304-6145
  Main number: (703) 274-6434
  Reference Services: (703) 274-7633

Cost

The cost for one magnetic tape with hard copy materials is $40. Additional tapes cost $35 each. This data set has multiple tapes.

BIBLIOGRAPHY

Barokas, J., & Croan, G.M. (1988). *The army family research program's family factors in retention, readiness, and sense of community: The plan for research* (Contract #MDA903-87-C-0540). Research Triangle Park, NC: Research Triangle Institute.

Bell, D.B. (1990, February). *The army family research program: Project overview*. Paper presented at the Department of Defense Military Family Research Review Conference, Andrews Air Force Base, MD.

Bell, D.B., Scarville, J., & Quigley, B. (1991, March). *The army family research program: Origin, purpose and accomplishments* (Research Note). Alexandria, VA: U.S. Army Research Institute for the Behavioral and Social Sciences.

Campbell, C.H., Campbell, R.C., Ramsberg, P., Schultz, S., Stawarski, C., & Styles, M. (1988). *Model of individual and unit readiness: A review of the literature* (Research Note). Alexandria, VA: U.S. Army Research Institute for the Behavioral and Social Sciences.

Cavin, E. (1990). *Effects of family programs on retention in the marine corps*. Paper presented at Military Family Research Review, Andrews Air Force Base, MD.

Croan, G.M., et al. (1987). *Career decision-making and the military family: Towards a comprehensive model* (unpublished manuscript). Alexandria, VA: U.S. Army Research Institute for the Behavioral and Social Sciences.

Etheridge, R.M. (1989). *Family factors affecting retention: A review of the literature* (Research Report 1511). Alexandria, VA: U.S. Army Research Institute for the Behavioral and Social Sciences.

Iannacchione, V.G., & Milne, J.G. (1991). *Analyzing and adjusting for nonresponse to the AFRP spouse survey* (Technical Report). Alexandria, VA: U.S. Army Research Institute for the Behavioral and Social Sciences.

Iannacchione, V.G., & Milne, J.G. (1991, August). *Sampling weights for the AFRP core research effort* (Technical Report). Alexandria, VA: U.S. Army Research Institute for the Behavioral and Social Sciences.

Kirkland, F.R., & Katz, P. (1989). Combat readiness and the army family. *Military Review*, April, 63-74.

Oliver, L.W. (1990, February). *The relationship of family factors to readiness: What we know, what we need to know, and what we can tell policy makers*. Paper presented at the Department of Defense Military Family Review Conference, Andrews Air Force Base, MD.

Orthner, D.K. (1990). Family impacts on the retention of military personnel. In D.A. Blankinship, S.L. Bullman, & G.M. Croan (Eds.), *The policy, program, and fiscal implications of military family research: Proceedings of the 1990 military family research review* (pp. 82-98). (Contract No. MDA903-89-M-8931). Arlington, VA: Office of Assistant Secretary of Defense, Office of Family Policy and Support.

Orthner, D.K. (1990). Family adaptation in the military. In D.A. Blankinship, S.L. Bullman, & G.M Croan (Eds.), *The policy, program, and fiscal implications of military family research: Proceedings of the 1990 military family research review* (pp 21-46). (Contract No. MDA903-89-M-8931). Arlington, VA: Office of Assistant Secretary of Defense, Office of Family Policy and Support.

Orthner, D.K., & Bowen, G.L.(1991, April). *Young single soldiers and relationships* (Technical Report). Alexandria, VA: U.S. Army Research Institute for the Behavioral and Social Sciences.

Orthner, D.K., et al. (1987). *Community satisfaction and support programs: Review of the literature*. Alexandria, VA: U.S. Army Research Institute for the Behavioral and Social Sciences.

Orthner, D.K., Zimmerman, L., & Bowen, G.L. (1991). *Development of a measure of family adaptation to the Army* (Technical Report). Alexandria, VA: U.S. Army Institute for the Behavioral and Social Sciences.

Rakoff, S.H., & Doherty, S. (1989). *Army family composition and retention* (Research Report 1535). Alexandria, VA: U.S. Army Institute for the Behavioral and Social Sciences.

Sadacca, R., & DiFazio, A.S. (1991, April). *Analysis of army family research program measures of individual readiness* (Technical Report). Alexandria, VA: U.S. Army Institute for the Behavioral and Social Sciences.

22

MARITAL INSTABILITY OVER THE LIFE COURSE, 1980-1988

Alan Booth
David R. Johnson
Lynn K. White
John N. Edwards

PURPOSE OF THE STUDY

Marital Instability Over the Life Course consists of data drawn from an 8-year longitudinal study of a national sample of married individuals (not couples) 55 years of age and under. Data were collected in three waves and focused on five major dimensions of marital quality: divorce proneness (or marital instability), marital problems, marital happiness, marital interaction, and marital disagreements. Initially, the investigators devoted considerable attention to female labor force participation as it related to marital dissolution and divorce proneness. For the last two waves, the investigators drew heavily on a life course perspective to guide their investigation.

METHODS

Sampling Design

A random digit dialing procedure was used to identify households in the contiguous United States with married respondents 55 years of age or younger. It was estimated that respondents were sufficiently dispersed geographically so as not to create a design effect requiring attention in the analysis of the data. An additional random procedure was employed to select a respondent couple if more than one married couple lived in a given household and to identify the husband or wife as the respondent. The procedure yielded 2,034 interviews.

Periodicity

The three-wave survey took place in the fall of 1980, the fall of 1983, and the spring of 1988.

Unit of Analysis

The individual was the unit of analysis.

Response Rates

Among eligible households during Wave I, the response rate was 65%. Three percent provided only partial interviews, 15% refused, and 17% could not be reached after 10 or more callbacks. The table below provides more detail on these response rate-related figures.

Wave I Response Rate Breakdown for Eligible Households

	Number	Percent
Completed Interview	2,033	65%
Partial Interview	87	3%
Refusal by Respondent	373	12%
Refusal by Other	92	3%
Respondent Absent	356	11%
Non-Interview—Other Reasons	58	2%
Estimated Ring—No Answers	29	1%
Estimated Quick—Refusals	92	3%
Total	3,120	100%

Attrition

In 1983, 1,592 of the respondents to the 1980 survey were successfully re-interviewed, for a re-interview rate of 78%. The re-interview rate for the third wave of the study (1988) was 66%, with 1,341 respondents of the original sample being re-interviewed successfully.

The re-survey in 1983 yielded 1,578 interviews plus reliable marital information (which was provided by someone other than the respondent) for another 150 individuals. In 1988, 1,341 respondents were interviewed directly, and reliable marital information was obtained for an additional 94 people. Since divorce proneness was the central focus of the investigation, interviewers were instructed to obtain information on an individual's marital status even if that individual could not be reached or the interview could not be completed.

Retention Rates for Eligible Respondents

	Wave II		Wave III	
	Number	Percent	Number	Percent
Completed Interview	1,578	78%	1,331	84%
Partial Interview	15	1%	10	1%
Refusal	133	6%	153	9%
Respondent Deceased	13	1%	15	1%
Respondent Unable to Be Located	264	13%	50	3%
Respondent Not Found at Home After Maximum Callbacks	22	1%	32	2%
Respondent Too Sick to Complete Interview	1	0%	1	0%
Other	7	0%	1	0%
Total	2,033	100%	1,593	100%

CONTENT

Data Sources

    All telephone interviews were conducted from the offices of the Bureau of Sociological Research in Lincoln, Nebraska, using a National WATS line. The consolidation of interviewing provided an opportunity for very careful supervision. The Supervisor, Study Director, and others on the bureau staff were accessible so that questions from the interviewers could be handled immediately and, if necessary, the respondent could be called back. Furthermore, interviews were generally conducted within the hearing range of supervisors. This helped to identify interviewing problems and difficulties. Interviewers were required to edit their own interviews before returning them in, after which each interview was carefully edited by the field supervisor or the bureau staff. This was done on a daily basis so that errors could be brought to the attention of the interviewers immediately and corrected. If answers were recorded incorrectly or questions skipped, the interviewer was asked to call the respondent back and correct the error. Five percent of each interviewer's work was verified by a second call to the respondent by the field supervisor. The supervisor checked that the interview had indeed been given by the designated respondent, that a sample of demographic questions had been correctly recorded, and that the interviewer's manner was appropriately value-free and nonjudgmental. Computer-aided interviewing was used for the third wave, which reduced the data cleaning and entry tasks.

Between waves of data collection, efforts were made to track members of the panel. One year after the data collections, letters providing a progress report on the study were sent to all respondents. Respondents received "Address Correction Requested" forms so that those individuals who had either moved or who did not reply could be tracked.

When a respondent could not be contacted for re-interview, trackers were asked to find the respondent's new phone number. One way in which trackers located respondents was to contact the three people nominated previously by the respondent as persons who would always know the respondent's whereabouts. Trackers maintained written records of their work on tracking sheets. Once the trackers located the respondent, the case was turned over to the interviewer unless it was felt that the respondent would be lost again if not interviewed immediately. In such cases, trackers conducted the interview.

Description of Variables Covered

Variables covered in this three-wave study were: sex, age, and race of the respondent; marital status of the respondent; age at first marriage; the respondent's religion; highest school year completed and whether or not the wife is in school; husband's work status; whether wife is working for pay and working part or full-time; respondent's and spouse's involvement with friends, relatives, and voluntary organizations; family income; SMSA status in region of country; number of people in the household; size and type of dwelling; relation of each family member to referent person and others in family; and indicators of five dimensions of marital quality: divorce proneness, marital problems, marital happiness, marital interaction, and marital disagreements.

Number of Variables

A total of 1,593 variables were assessed across the three waves.

Checklist of Topics Covered

X Gender / Gender Role
X Race / Ethnicity
X Age
X Education
X Occupation / Employment
X Physical Health / Disease
___ Nutrition
___ Clinical Activities
___ Biological Functioning /
Development
X Mental Health / Disease
X Psychological Functioning /
Development
X Guidance / Counseling
X Personality
X Intellectual Functioning
X Residential Mobility
X Dwelling
X Neighborhood /
Community
X Region / State
X Marriage and Divorce
X Cohabitation
X Family/Household
Composition & Structure
X Inter-Partner Relationships
X Parent-Child Relationships
___ Inter-Sibling Relationships
X Relationships with Other Kin

___ Relationships with Nonkin
X Other Family/Household
Characteristics
X Child Care
X Wealth / Finances / Material
Things
X Receipt of Health, Mental
Health, Social Services
___ Adoption / Foster Care
X Childbearing / Pregnancy
___ Out-of-Wedlock Pregnancy
& Parenthood
___ Abortion
X Sexuality
___ Sex Education
___ Contraception
___ Sexually Transmitted
Diseases
X Civic/Political Activities
X Friends / Social Activities
Social Support
X Dating, Courtship
X Recreation
X Religion
___ Crime / Delinquency /
Behavior Problems
X Substance Use
___ Agency Characteristics
X Interview

Checklist of Key Variables

X Number of family members
X Identification of marital
partners in family
X Size of dwelling
X Type of dwelling
X Urban/rural residence
X Region/state of residence
X Family income
X Religious affiliation
X Relation of each family
member to:
  X Reference person
  ___ All other members
X Age of family members
  X Respondent
  X Others
X Sex of family members

X Respondent
X Others
X Race of family members
  X Respondent
  X Others
X Marital status of family
members
  X Respondent
  X Others
X Education of family
members
  X Respondent
  X Others
X Occupation of family
members
  X Respondent
  X Others

LIMITATIONS

The original sample was compared with national data and was found to be representative of the nation with respect to age, race, household size, presence of children, tenure, and region, although residents of large metropolitan areas are slightly underrepresented. The second and third waves are slightly less representative with respect to Blacks and Hispanics, younger respondents, renters, and those with less than a college education. However, there were no statistically significant differences between those who were re-interviewed and those who were not on the dimensions of marital quality examined in this investigation.

SPONSORSHIP

The study was co-sponsored by the National Institute on Aging and the Social Security Administration's Office of Research and Statistics.

GUIDE TO DATA AND DOCUMENTATION

File Structure

Because of the large size of the dataset, machine-readable files are only available in mainframe format or CD-ROM (microcomputer) format. Unless otherwise requested, files formatted for a mainframe computer are provided on a 9-track tape at a density of 6250 bpi, in EBCDIC recording mode with IBM Standard Labels. A description of the contents of each file is given below.

File 1 (Data): Raw data file. The format of this file is described in the "data list" section of the SPSS program file (file 2).

File 2 (SPSS Program): This file consists of SPSS program statements designed to read the raw data in file 1 and create an SPSS active file. Program statements conform to SPSS-X syntax. The SPSS program file contains data list statements, variable names and labels, value labels, and missing value declarations.

File 3 (SAS Program): The file consists of SAS program statements designed to read the raw data in File 1 and create a SAS active file. The contents of this file are analogous to the contents of the previously described File 2. SPSS users should use File 2; SAS users, File 3. Users may need to add "job control language" (JCL) statements to the SAS program file to meet the requirements for their specific operating system. For some operating systems, e.g., Unix, running the SAS program statements may result in a "segmentation violation" message from SAS due to a limit on the number of independent sets of format labels (the current limit is about 300) that can be assigned to variables. The SAS Institute plans to release an updated version of SAS early in 1993 that will correct the problem. Until then, if a segmentation violation occurs, one solution is to edit the SAS program statements to remove format (value label) assignments for all variables unrelated to the analysis at hand.

File 4 (Dictionary): Sequential list of variable and value labels. This file consists of DISPLAY DICTIONARY output describing the SPSS-X active file created by the program in File 2. Variables are listed in sequential order. Variable names and labels, value labels, missing value designations, print formats, and write formats are clearly displayed.

File 5 (Statistics): Unweighted frequencies or other descriptive statistics for each variable. Individual frequencies are provided for variables with fewer than 50 value categories. For variables with 50 or more value categories, summary descriptive statistics are provided. Users may obtain individual frequency counts for such variables by using the SPSS-X FREQUENCIES command without specifying the subcommand /FORMAT=LIMIT(50).

List of Available Documentation

A User's Guide which accompanies the machine-readable files provides the following information: Summary; General study overview; Description of machine-readable files and supplementary documentation; Specifications for machine-readable files; Key characteristics report; Distribution of variables by topic and type; and Data completeness and consistency report.

Paper versions of the machine-readable SPSS and SAS program files and data documentation (files 2-5 above), and copies of the original instrument and codebook, are available upon request (at 15 cents per page).

Contact

Sociometrics Corporation
American Family Data Archive
170 State Street, Suite 260
Los Altos, California 94022-2812
(415) 949-3282

Cost

The cost for the mainframe machine-readable data set (Data Set 22-24 of the American Family Data Archive) is $100. This price includes the raw data, SPSS program statements, SAS program statements, the Dictionary, and the Frequencies on a mainframe tape, and the accompanying printed and bound User's Guide. The CD-ROM version costs $175. A paper version of the original Instrument/Codebook can be obtained for $57.75.

BIBLIOGRAPHY

Amato, P., & Booth, A. (1991). The consequences of divorce for attitudes toward divorce. *Journal of Family Issues, 12,* 306-322.

Amato, P.R., & Booth, A. (1991). Consequences of parental divorce and marital unhappiness for adult well-being. *Social Forces, 69,* 895-914.

Bitter, R.G. (1986). Late marriage and marital instability: The effects of heterogeneity and inflexibility. *Journal of Marriage and the Family, 48*, 631-640.

Booth, A., & Amato, P. (1991). Divorce and psychological stress. *Journal of Health and Social Behavior, 32*, 396-407.

Booth, A., & Amato, P. (1992). Divorce, residential change, and stress. *Journal of Divorce and Remarriage, 18*, 205-213.

Booth, A., & Edwards, J.N. (1989). Transmission of marital and family quality over the generations: The effect of parental divorce and unhappiness. *Journal of Divorce, 13*, 41-58.

Booth, A., & Edwards, J.N. (1985). Age of marriage and marital instability. *Journal of Marriage and the Family, 47*, 67-75.

Booth, A., & Edwards, J.N. (1992). Starting over: Why are remarriages more unstable? *Journal of Family Issues, 13*, 179-194.

Booth, A., Edwards, J.N., & Johnson, D.R. (1991). Social integration and divorce. *Social Forces, 40*, 207-224.

Booth, A., & Johnson, D.R. (1988). Premarital cohabitation and marital success. *Journal of Family Issues, 9*, 255-272.

Booth, A., & Johnson, D.R. (1985). Tracking respondents in a telephone interview panel selected by random digit dialing. *Sociological Methods and Research, 14*, 53-64.

Booth, A., Johnson, D.R., White, L.K., & Edwards, J.N. (1984). Women, outside employment and marital instability. *American Journal of Sociology, 90*, 567-583.

Booth, A., Johnson, D.R., & Edwards, J.N. (1985). Measuring Marital Instability. *Journal of Marriage and the Family, 47*, 67-75.

Booth, A., Johnson, D.R., White, L.K., & Edwards, J.N. (1985). Predicting divorce and permanent separation. *Journal of Family Issues, 6*, 331-346.

Booth, A., Johnson, D.R., White, L.K., & Edwards, J.N. (1986). Divorce and marital instability over the life course. *Journal of Family Issues,* 7, 421-442.

Booth, A., Johnson, D.R., White, L.K., & Edwards, J.N. (1991). *Marital instability over the life course methodology report and codebook for three-wave panel study.* Lincoln, NE: University of Nebraska, Bureau of Sociological Research.

Edwards, J.N., Johnson, D.R., & Booth, A. (1987). Coming apart: A prognostic instrument of marital breakup. *Family Relations, 36,* 168-170.

Johnson, D.R. (1992). Stability and developmental change in marital quality: A three-wave panel analysis. *Journal of Marriage and the Family, 54,* 582-594.

Johnson, D.R., White, L.K., Edwards, J.N., & Booth, A. (1986). Dimensions of marital quality: Toward methodological and conceptual refinement. *Journal of Family Issues, 7,* 31-49.

Margolin, L. & White, L. (1987). The continuing role of physical attractiveness in marriage. *Journal of Marriage and the Family, 49,* 21-27.

Muller, K.L., Kaplan, A.S., Hickerson, M., Lang, E.L., & Card, J.J. (1992). *Marital instability over the life course, 1981-1988: A user's guide to the machine-readable files and documentation* (Data Set 22-24). Los Altos, CA: Sociometrics Corporation, American Family Data Archive.

White, L.K. (1988). Gender differences in awareness of aging among married adults ages 20 to 60. *Sociological Quarterly, 29,* 487-502.

White, L.K. (1983). Determinants of spousal interaction: Marital structure or marital happiness. *Journal of Marriage and the Family, 45,* 511-519.

White, L.K., & Booth, A. (1991). Divorce over the life course: The role of marital happiness. *Journal of Family Issues, 12,* 5-12.

White, L.K., & Booth, A. (1985). The quality and stability of remarriages: The role of stepchildren. *American Sociological Review, 50*, 689-698.

White, L.K., & Booth, A. (1985). Transition to parenthood and marital quality. *Journal of Family Issues, 6*, 435-449.

White, L.K., & Edwards, J.N. (1990). Emptying the nest and parental well-being: An analysis of national panel data. *American Sociological Review, 55*, 235-242.

White, L.K., & Keith, B. (1990). The effect of shift work on the quality and stability of marital relations. *Journal of Marriage and the Family, 52*, 453-464.

23

NATIONAL LONGITUDINAL SURVEY OF LABOR FORCE BEHAVIOR: YOUTH SURVEY AND CHILD SUPPLEMENT (THE NLSY), 1979-1992

Center for Human Resource Research,
Ohio State University

PURPOSE OF THE STUDY

In 1977, the Department of Labor decided to initiate a new youth panel of the National Longitudinal Survey of Labor Force Behavior, adding to the four panels begun in 1966 to 1968 (young men, young women, mature men, mature women). The surveys were designed primarily to analyze sources of variation in the labor market behavior and experience of Americans. Data from the new panel replicate much of the information obtained on young people in the earlier cohorts and thus support studies of changes in the labor market experience of youth. In addition, the new data on youth permitted evaluation of the expanded employment and training programs for youth established by the 1977 amendments to the Comprehensive Employment and Training Act (CETA). A supplementary sample of persons serving in the Armed Forces permitted the study of the recruitment and service experiences of youth in the military. The supplementary military sample was terminated following the 1984 survey round. While the focus of the NLSY is on labor market behavior, extensive data have also been collected regarding many issues of interest to family researchers: family background and structure, fertility, marriage and divorce, educational progress, migration, health, delinquent behavior, and financial status.

In 1986 the Department added a child supplement to the female portion of the youth panel. The purpose of the supplement was to collect child development data on the children born to female respondents in the NLSY, thereby creating a large, nationally representative data resource for the study of child outcomes. Given the rich data available about the youth participating in the National Longitudinal Survey, data about child outcomes creates an unprecedented opportunity for studying such family issues as the effects of parental characteristics and experiences on the well-being and development of young children. The 1988 through 1992 data collections continued to follow these "children of the NLSY."

METHODS

Sampling Design

The Youth panel comprises a nationally-representative probability sample of youth (equally divided by sex) aged 14-21 in 1979, plus a sample of young persons serving in the Armed Forces. Blacks, Hispanics, and disadvantaged whites were oversampled to permit detailed analyses of youth in these population groups (The disadvantaged whites were dropped from the sample following the 1990 survey round). The sampling frame was the resident, noninstitutional population of the United States and youth on active military duty. Nonmilitary respondents were selected using a multistage, stratified area-probability sample of dwelling units and group quarter units. A screening interview was administered at approximately 75,000 dwellings and group quarters in 202 primary sampling units. Two independent probability subsamples were selected using this frame: (1) a cross-sectional sample, and (2) a supplemental sample designed to produce statistically-efficient oversamples of civilian Hispanic, black, and economically-disadvantaged nonhispanic and nonblack youth. The Department of Defense provided rosters of youth aged 17-21 as of January 1, 1979, and serving in the military as of September 30, 1978, from which the military subsample was selected. A total of 12,686 persons was interviewed in the initial wave: 6111 from the cross-sectional sample, 5295 from the supplemental sample, and 1280 from the military sample.

Individual case weights were developed to permit the calculation of population estimates from the data. For the base year these weights adjust for (1) the initial probability of selection, (2) differential response rates during screening and the initial interview, and (3) sampling variation, to conform the sample to independently derived population totals. Follow-up case weights incorporate further adjustments for differential response rates in the respective follow-up surveys.

With regard to the child supplement, planners faced the substantial design challenge of studying child development in the course of a home interview using survey interviewers to conduct all tests. With funding from the Foundation for Child Development, a group of experts met to select valid measures appropriate for administration in a field survey. The goal of the advisory panel was to select a set of measures that would tap a range of child characteristics, that could be administered by interviewers without college backgrounds in child development, that would not require expensive or bulky equipment, that would be acceptable to parents, that would not be exorbitantly expensive to administer to a large sample, and that would be valid across a sample varying in social and economic characteristics. The intent was to select existing measures that were known to work well, although some modification in terms of length or manner of administration was necessary to accommodate the survey setting.

Since a majority of the children born to NLS Youth by 1986 were quite young, a majority of the measures were designed for young children. However, because 780 children—14 percent of the sample—were eight or older in 1986 and because additional interviews with the children were planned, measures appropriate for older children were also included.

Periodicity

Interviews have been conducted annually since 1979. The most recent round of interviews was conducted in 1990 and a 1992 interview will be completed this year. While future waves are contingent on funding, current prospects for continued support are good.

The initial wave of child supplement interviews was completed in 1986. Second and third waves were conducted in 1988 and 1990, in which children previously studied received modules appropriate to their current age. Newborn children were added to the sample and given age-appropriate modules. It is anticipated that additional interview waves will also be conducted at intervals.

Unit of Analysis

The individual respondent is the unit of analysis. Because much family and household information is obtained about the respondents, many analyses about family-related topics are possible. However, using the family as the unit of analysis introduces problems relating to representativeness (see LIMITATIONS section, below.)

Response Rates

The screening rates and initial response rates (based on those screened and found eligible) are presented by sample component in the first two columns of the table below.

Sample	Screening Rate	Initial (1979) Response Rate	Follow-up Rates (Base-1979)									
			1980	1981	1982	1983	1984	1985	1986	1987	1988
Cross-section	91.2	89.7	96.1	96.4	96.2	96.4	95.2	93.9	91.8	90.4	90.4
Supplement	91.9	88.7	95.8	96.5	95.2	*	*	*	*	*	*
Military	N/A	71.5	93.2	93.4	94.6	95.8	94.9				

* Rate above applies to both parts of civilian sample.

23 - 4

Attrition

The attrition rates for the three components of the sample (based on those interviewed in the base year, 1979) are presented in the third through the last column in the table on the previous page. As of 1990, the overall completion rate is 89.9 percent—91.1 percent if one excludes deceased respondents.

CONTENT

Data Sources

The majority of the data for the base year and all follow-up surveys have been collected through in-person interviews lasting about an hour. An exception was the 1987 survey round, which was a telephone survey.

In addition to the questionnaires, other instruments have been used from time to time. First, completed four-year high school transcripts have been collected for members of the civilian subsamples as they have graduated. Second, during the summer of 1980, the Armed Services Vocational Aptitude Battery was administered to all three subsamples. The battery provides information on individuals' knowledge and skills in science, mathematics, English, mechanics, and electronics. Third, the child supplement, administered in 1986, 1988, and 1990, included both a questionnaire for the mother, and direct assessment of children. (More detail is provided below.) Fourth, environmental variables for county of residence have been gathered from various sources and are available in a separate geographic micro-data file. Environmental variables in this file include those such as population size, labor force statistics, median income, educational characteristics, and crime rates.

Description of Variables Covered

The Main Surveys. Because of their labor market focus, the content of the surveys is weighted toward labor force training and experience. Among the topics covered in detail are employment (both that of the respondent and other family members), job characteristics, job satisfaction, work history, occupation, occupational training (including participation in government-sponsored training programs), military service, educational attainment and achievement, earnings, assets, finances, and sources of income (including welfare and other transfer programs). However a great deal of information relevant to the family is also collected, including information on family background, family composition, marriage history, pregnancy and birth history, contraceptive use, childrearing, child care, sex role attitudes, and maternal (including extensive data on health behaviors during pregnancy) and child health care. Questions on drug and alcohol use, delinquency, and crime are included, along with information on religion, attitudes, aspirations, expectations, self-esteem, and locus or control. Basic demographic variables in addition to those mentioned above are well covered, including age, sex, race, ethnic origin, residence, and migration.

Children of the NLSY. Beginning in 1986, and again in 1988 and 1990, information about all children born to female respondents in the NLS-Youth was obtained from mother-child pairs in the NLSY. Illustrative of constructs included in those three years are the following:

Child Assessments Administered Directly to the Children in 1988:

> Body Part (deleted in 1990)
> Memory for Location (deleted in 1990)
> Verbal Memory
> SPPC: Self-Worth and Scholastic Competence
> Memory for Digit Span
> PIAT Mathematics
> PIAT Reading Recognition
> PIAT Reading Comprehension
> Peabody Picture Vocabulary Test (Revised)

Child Assessments Completed by the Mother in 1988:
> Home Observation for Measurement of the
> > Environment-Short Form (HOME-SF)
> Temperament Subscales
> Motor and Social Development
> Behavior Problems Index

Number of Variables

Each wave of the NLSY gathers between four and five thousand variables.

Checklist of Topics Covered

X Gender / Gender Role
X Race / Ethnicity
X Age
X Education
X Occupation / Employment
X Physical Health / Disease
___ Nutrition
___ Clinical Activities
X Biological Functioning /
    Development
___ Mental Health / Disease
X Psychological Functioning /
    Development
___ Guidance / Counseling
X Personality
X Intellectual Functioning
X Residential Mobility
X Dwelling
X Neighborhood /
    Community
X Region / State
X Marriage and Divorce
___ Cohabitation
X Family/Household
    Composition & Structure
X Inter-Partner Relationships
X Parent-Child Relationships
___ Inter-Sibling Relationships
___ Relationships with Other Kin

___ Relationships with Nonkin
X Other Family / Household
    Characteristics
X Child Care
X Wealth / Finances / Material
    Things
X Receipt of Health, Mental
    Health, Social Services
___ Adoption / Foster Care
X Childbearing / Pregnancy
X Out-of-Wedlock Pregnancy &
    Parenthood
X Abortion
X Sexuality
X Sex Education
X Contraception
___ Sexually Transmitted
    Diseases
___ Civic / Political Activities
___ Friends / Social Activities
___ Social Support
X Dating, Courtship
X Recreation
X Religion
X Crime / Delinquency /
    Behavior Problems
X Substance Use
___ Agency Characteristics
X Interview

Checklist of Key Variables

X Number of family members
___ Identification of marital
    partners in family
___ Size of dwelling
X Type of dwelling
X Urban / rural residence
X Region / state of residence
X Family income
X Religious affiliation
X Relation of each family
    member to:
    X Reference person
    ___ All other members
X Age of family members
    X Respondent
    X Others
X Sex of family members

    X Respondent
    X Others
X Race of family members
    X Respondent
    ___ Others
X Marital status of family
    members
    X Respondent
    X Others
X Education of family
    members
    X Respondent
    X Others
X Occupation of family
    members
    X Respondent
    X Others

LIMITATIONS

Attrition is always a concern in a longitudinal data set. Compared to similar studies, the NLSY has kept attrition quite low. At of the completion of the twelfth (1990) interview wave, 90 percent, or 10,436 of the original 11,607 respondents still in scope were still being interviewed. Even so, researchers would be well advised to check on the possible effects of biases introduced by attrition.

Researchers attempting to generalize findings from this data set to *families*, rather than to *individuals*, should be aware of problems using the family as the unit of analysis. First, cases of individuals not living in families would have to be excluded. Second, the remaining cases would represent only families that contain respondents in the eligible age range. Third, families with more than one respondent in the eligible age range would be overrepresented in the sample in direct proportion to the number of youth the family has in that age range.

The sample of children about whom data are being collected in the child supplement are those born to an age cohort of younger parents. Consequently, they are not a nationally representative sample of children. The 1988 panel represents approximately the first 60 percent of the children that this age cohort can be expected to bear. Therefore, these children include disproportionate numbers of children born to younger parents. About a quarter of the children studied in 1988 were born when their mothers had not yet turned twenty. As additional waves of interviews are conducted (as of this writing 1986 through 1990 waves have been completed), the sample will become increasingly representative of all offspring born to a cohort of American females.

Another limitation with the child supplement data is that only children born to female respondents have been assessed and no direct information is obtained from the child's father.

SPONSORSHIP

The National Longitudinal Survey of Youth was initiated by the Department of Labor, and DOL continues to provide funding for the survey. Since the first survey in 1979, a number of other government agencies have also provided support for data collection on topics of interest to them, including the National Institute of Child Health and Human Development (NICHD), the National Institute on Drug Abuse (NIDA), the National Institute on Alcohol and Alcohol Abuse (NIAAA), and the Department of Defense.

Funding for the Child Supplements to the regular interview was provided by NICHD and by the Carnegie, Ford, Grant, Hewlett, Rockefeller, and Sloan Foundations. Data are collected by the National Opinion Research Center, Chicago, Illinois.

GUIDE TO DATA AND DOCUMENTATION

File Structure

The data are available on either mainframe tape or CD-ROM. Various versions of the files are available on tape (see the Cost section below). The most complete collection of the data are the 1979-1989 main file tape and CD-ROM. This is actually a collection of over fifty separate files that organize the data topically and by year. The different files can be linked by the respondent ID, the first variable in every record. In addition to the main files, tapes containing specialized files are also available. The 1989 NLSY is available as a single-year file. Work history data for 1979-1989 have been gathered into a single file. Detailed geographic data including data from secondary sources are available in a geocode data file for 1979-1989. And the 1986 and 1988 child assessment data together with related mother data from 1979-1988 are available as a single file.

Each CD-ROM contains the raw data files and search and retrieval software to create extract files from these data. All files are rectangular with the youth respondent defining the case. All of the data available on the 1979-1989 main file tape are included on the CD-ROM.

List of Available Documentation

Complete documentation is included with each tape order. The CD-ROM includes a user's manual, but no other paper documentation, as codebook and index information is included on the disk.

Contact

Public use tapes and tape documentation as well as a list of publications are available from the Center for Human Resource Research (see below). For specific questions, information is available from Steve McClaskie, Gale James, or Randall Olsen, Principal Investigator for the NLS, at the Center.

A child-based data tape including 1979-1988 wave data is currently available—the merged child-mother data file. This data file includes over 6,000 variables and provides rich information about the child's mother and her life, information about the child's family and household, data on prenatal care and birth, and social and economic data on the child's household during the child's life, as well as summary scores on the measures of child development. A detailed data file containing raw data from the child interviews is also available from the Center for Human Resource Research. The 1979-1990 version of this file will be available by mid-1992.

These data files and information can be obtained from:

> The Center for Human Resource Research
> The Ohio State University
> 921 Chatham Lane, Suite 200
> Columbus, OH 43221
> (614) 442-7300

Cost

Tape products and prices are as follows:

NLSY Main Files	1979-1989	$415
NLSY Single Year Files	1989 Only	140
NLSY Workhistory	1979-1989	145
NLSY Geocode Data	1979-1989	120
NLSY Child/Mother Data	1979-1988	120

The CD-ROM products and prices are as follows:

NLSY Main & Child Data	1979-1989	$15
NLSY Main/Child/Geocode	1979-1989	15
NLSY Workhistory Data	1979-1989	15

BIBLIOGRAPHY

Baker, P.C., & Mott, F.L. (1989). *NLSY child handbook: A guide to the national longitudinal survey of youth 1986-1990 child data.* Columbus, OH: Center for Human Resource Research, The Ohio State University.

Chase-Lansdale, P.L., Mott, F.L., Brooks-Gunn, J., & Phillips, D. A. (1991, November). Children of the national longitudinal survey of youth: A unique research opportunity. *Developmental Psychology, 27*(6), 919-931.

Center for Human Resource Research. (1980-1986). *Pathways to the future, volumes I to VI: A report on the national longitudinal surveys of labor market experience of youth.* Columbus, OH: The Ohio State University.

Center for Human Resource Research. (1989). *NLS annotated bibliography 1968-1989.* Columbus, OH: The Ohio State University.

Center for Human Resource Research. (1992). *NLS bibliography update 1990-1992.* Columbus, OH: The Ohio State University.

Center for Human Resource Research. (1993). *NLS handbook 1993.* Columbus, OH: The Ohio State University.

Center for Human Resource Research. (1993). *Research using NLSY data on fertility, child care, and child development: A bibliography.* Columbus, OH: The Ohio State University.

Center for Human Resource Research. (quarterly). *The NLSUPDATE Newsletter.* Columbus, OH: The Ohio State University.

Mott, F.L., & Quinlan, S.V. (1991). *Children of the NLSY. 1988 tabulations and summary discussions*. Columbus, OH: Center for Human Resource Research, The Ohio State University.

Mott, F.L., & Quinlan, S.V. (1991). *Maternal-child health data from the NLSY. 1988 tabulations and summary discussion*. Columbus, OH: Center for Human Resource Research, The Ohio State University.

Olsen, R.J. (1991, Spring). The national longitudinal surveys of labor market experience merged child-mother data. *Journal of Human Resources, 24*(2), 336-339.

Zill, N., & Peterson, J.L., (Eds). (1989). *Guide to federal data on children, youth, and families*. Washington, DC: Child Trends.

24

CURRENT POPULATION SURVEY (CPS) MARITAL AND FERTILITY SUPPLEMENTS 1971 - 1988, 1990

U. S. Bureau of the Census

PURPOSE OF THE STUDY

The Current Population Survey (CPS) is the source of official U.S. Government statistics on employment and unemployment. The CPS has been conducted monthly for over 45 years.

Although the main purpose of the survey is to collect information on the employment situation, a very important secondary purpose is to collect information on the demographic status of the population, information such as age; sex; race; marital status; educational attainment; and family structure. From time to time additional questions are included on such important subjects as health; education; income; and previous work experience. The statistics resulting from these questions serve to update similar information collected once every 10 years through the decennial census, and are used by government policy makers and legislators as important indicators of the nation's economic situation, and for planning and evaluating many government programs.

The CPS provides current estimates of the economic status and activities of the population of the United States. Because it is not possible to develop one or two overall figures (such as the number of unemployed) that would adequately describe the whole complex of labor market phenomena, the CPS is designed to provide a large amount of detailed and supplementary data. Such data are made available to meet a wide variety of needs on the part of users of labor market information. Thus, the CPS is the only source of monthly estimates of total employment (both farm and nonfarm); nonfarm self-employed persons, domestics, and unpaid helpers in nonfarm family enterprises; wage and salary employees; and, finally, estimates of total unemployment.

It provides the only available distribution of workers by the number of hours worked (as distinguished from aggregate or average hours for an industry), permitting separate analyses of part-time workers, workers on overtime, etc. The survey is also the only comprehensive current source of information on the occupation of workers and the industries in which they work. Information is available from the survey not only for persons currently in the labor force but also for those who are outside the labor force. The characteristics of such persons—whether married women with or without young children, disabled persons, students, older retired workers, etc.—can be determined. Information on their current desire for work, their past work experience, and their intentions as to job seeking are also available.

The marital and fertility supplements to the CPS are designed to provide national estimates of women's marriage and childbearing experiences, and future birth expectations.

METHODS

Sampling Design

The CPS sample is based on the civilian noninstitutional population of the United States. The sample is located in 629 sample areas comprising 1,148 counties and independent cities with coverage in every state and in the District of Columbia.

In all, some 71,000 housing units or other living quarters are assigned for interview each month; about 58,000 of them containing approximately 122,000 persons 14 years old and over are interviewed. Also included are demographic data for approximately 34,000 children zero to thirteen years old within these households. The remainder of the assigned housing units are found to be vacant, converted to nonresidential use, contain persons with residence elsewhere, or are not interviewed because the residents are not found at home after repeated calls, are temporarily absent, or are unavailable for other reasons. Approximately 13,000 noninterview households are present each month. The resulting file size is approximately 170,000 records.

For the marital and fertility supplements, the age range of women has varied from year to year; however, certain core ages have been included annually. Questions on children ever born have usually been asked of ever-married women 15 to 44 years old and of never-married women 18 to 44 years old. On occasion, the upper age limit has been extended. The questions on birth expectations have been consistently asked of women 18 to 34 years old regardless of marital status. In selected years, the upper age limit has been extended to 39 or 44 years of age. Never-married women were first introduced into the sample in June of 1976. In previous marital and fertility supplements, men were asked detailed marriage history questions. In the 1985 and 1990 supplements, however, men were only asked the number of times they had been married.

Periodicity

Except for 1989, the supplement has been conducted annually in June since 1971. Funding levels will determine the frequency of data collection in the future, but in general, the supplement will be collected at least once every two years. The next supplement is expected to be conducted in 1992. There was no 1991 fertility supplement. Questions on fertility were asked of women in June 1958 and February 1965, but these were asked of a restricted universe and are not comparable to the data obtained in the 1971 and later surveys.

Table 1 on the next page lists topics and years in which data were collected, and the years for which public use data files are currently available.

Table 1. Current Population Survey Data Files, June Supplement Survey

Topic	Years Collected	Years Available
Fertility and birth expectations	1971-88, 90	1971-77, 1979-88, 1990
Immigration (also see April and Nov.)	1986, 1988	1986, 1988
Fertility and birth expectations (June/March match)	1983	1983
Marriage and birth history	1971,1975,1980,1985,1990	1975,1980,1985, 1990
Child care	1977, 1982	1977, 1982

Unit of Analyses

The individual female is the unit of analysis. Questions on marriage are now asked of married females 15-44 years old. The fertility questions were asked of all females 15-44 years old. The birth expectation questions were asked generally of all females 18-34 years old. In prior years, fertility items were generally asked of women 18 to 44 years old.

Response Rates

The response rates are provided in Table 2 on the next page.

Table 2. Description of Current Population Survey

Time Period	Number of sample areas	Housing units eligible	
		Interviewed	Not interviewed
1990	729	57,400	2,600
1986-88	729	57,000	2,500
1985 [1]	629/729	57,000	2,500
1982-84	629	59,000	2,500
1980-81	628	65,500	3,000
1977-79	614	55,000	3,000
1973-76	461	46,500	2,500
1972	449	45,000	2,000
1971	449	48,000	2,000

[1]The CPS was redesigned following the 1980 decennial census of Population and Housing. During phase-in of the new design, housing units from the new and old designs were in the sample.

Attrition

Not applicable.   The CPSs are a series of cross-sectional surveys.

CONTENT

Data Sources

Data are collected via in-person interviews in respondents' homes.   Currently, the CPS interviews about 57,000 households monthly, scientifically selected on the basis of area of residence to represent the nation as a whole, individual states, and other specified areas.   Each household is interviewed once a month for four consecutive months one year, and again for the corresponding time period a year later.   This technique enables CPS to obtain month-to-month and year-to-year comparisons at a reasonable cost while minimizing the inconvenience to any one household.

Description of Variables Covered

Data are provided on labor force activity for the week prior to the survey.   Comprehensive data are available on the employment status, occupation, and industry of persons 14 years old and over.   Also available are personal characteristics such as age, sex, race, marital status, veteran status, household relationship, education background, and Spanish origin.

In addition, data pertaining to date of first marriage, fertility, and birth expectations are included in the files.   Date of first marriage was asked of all ever-married females 18-44 years old.   The fertility questions were asked of all female household members 18-44 years old. Questions determining the number of live born children and the date of birth of the youngest and oldest children are asked of women 18-44 years old.   The birth expectation items had to be answered by the woman herself; proxy responses were not accepted.   These questions were asked of women 18-39 years old.   The 1990 supplement contained additional questions on marital history: dates of marriage, separation, and breakups (first, second, and most recent); dates of live birth of children (one through four and last); sex of children; current residence of child(ren); and birth expectation. Marital and fertility items in 1990 were asked of women 15 to 65 years of age (except for the items on birth expectations).

Number of Variables

There are several hundred variables in each basic CPS plus a few dozen variables in each supplement.

Checklist of Topics Covered

X Gender / Gender Role
X Race / Ethnicity
X Age
X Education
X Occupation / Employment
___ Physical Health / Disease
___ Nutrition
___ Clinical Activities
___ Biological Functioning /
    Development
___ Mental Health / Disease
___ Psychological Functioning /
    Development
___ Guidance / Counseling
___ Personality
___ Intellectual Functioning
___ Residential Mobility
X Dwelling
X Neighborhood /
    Community
X Region / State
X Marriage and Divorce
___ Cohabitation
X Family/Household
    Composition & Structure
___ Inter-Partner Relationships
___ Parent-Child Relationships
___ Inter-Sibling Relationships
___ Relationships with Other Kin

___ Relationships with Nonkin
___ Other Family/Household
    Characteristics
___ Child Care
X Wealth / Finances / Material
    Things
___ Receipt of Health, Mental
    Health, Social Services
___ Adoption / Foster Care
X Childbearing / Pregnancy
X Out-of-Wedlock Pregnancy &
    Parenthood
___ Abortion
___ Sexuality
___ Sex Education
___ Contraception
___ Sexually Transmitted
    Diseases
___ Civic/Political Activities
___ Friends / Social Activities
___ Social Support
___ Dating, Courtship
___ Recreation
___ Religion
___ Crime / Delinquency /
    Behavior Problems
___ Substance Use
___ Agency Characteristics
X Interview

Checklist of Key Variables

X Number of family members
X Identification of marital
   partners in family
___ Size of dwelling
X Type of dwelling
X Urban/rural residence
X Region/state of residence
X Family income
___ Religious affiliation
X Relation of each family
   member to:
   X Reference person
   X All other members
X Age of family members
   X Respondent
   X Others
X Sex of family members

X Respondent
X Others
X Race of family members
   X Respondent
   X Others
X Marital status of family
   members
   X Respondent
   X Others
X Education of family
   members
   X Respondent
   X Others
X Occupation of family
   members
   X Respondent
   ___ Others

LIMITATIONS

The basic supplement is quite brief, and thus more detailed information on fertility-related topics is available only on an occasional basis. The variability in the age range of women eligible for the supplement in different survey years has limited comparisons over time to women 18 to 44 years old for data on children ever born and to women 18 to 34 for birth expectations data. Furthermore, fertility data for single women were not asked until 1976 and thus previous data are restricted to ever-married women.

Basic sociodemographic characteristics of women can be obtained from the supplement; however, no data is collected on the woman's earnings. The June supplement lacks the detailed income data collected on the annual March income and demographic supplement to CPS. Thus, family income is the only measure that can be used to approximate the woman's economic standing.

The child care supplements present data only for working women with pre-school children, and only for the youngest of these children. Data are collected on the type of child care payment (cash or noncash), but not the amount. Additionally, the use of nursery schools or preschools for child care may be underestimated due to June school closings.

Because of the sensitive nature of asking never-married women under 18 about their childbearing experience, these women have been excluded from the supplement until 1990. Thus, period measures of out-of-wedlock births to younger teenagers were previously not available. However, estimates of out-of-wedlock childbearing can be obtained by cohort analysis.

Only limited data on men's marital histories can be obtained from the marital and fertility history supplements conducted in June 1975, 1980, 1985, and 1990.

SPONSORSHIP

The supplemental questions on children ever born and birth expectations are sponsored and conducted entirely by the Bureau of the Census. The child care supplements in both June 1977 and 1982 were sponsored in part by the National Institute of Child Health and Human Development (NICHD), Department of Health and Human Services.

The detailed marital and fertility history supplements of June 1971, 1975, 1980, 1985, and 1990 were also funded by NICHD as was the April 1983 supplement on the fertility of foreign-born women. The Immigration and Naturalization Service sponsored the June 1986 supplement and also provided funding for the June 1988 supplement on the fertility of foreign-born women.

GUIDE TO DATA AND DOCUMENTATION

File Structure

The machine-readable data files (see Table 1 on page 3 for available years) are available on 1600 or 6250 bpi computer tape in EBCDIC or ASCII format. Each file consists of one year's data. File structure is rectangular; file sort sequence is by state rank by CMA/MSA rank by household identification number by line number.

List of Available Documentation

Technical documentation accompanies each file. Technical documentation contains an abstract, a questionnaire facsimile, code lists, and records layouts of the file. These documents may be ordered separately through Customer Services, Data User Services Division, Bureau of the Census, Washington, DC 20233.

Also available is *The Current Population Survey: Design and Methodology* (Technical Paper 40) published by the Bureau. It describes in detail the sample design and survey procedures used as well as accuracy of estimates and sampling errors. This document is available on microfiche or microfiche paper prints from Customer Services, Data User Services Division, Bureau of the Census, Washington, DC 20233.

Contact

For documentation questions:

Data User Services Division,
Data Access and Use Staff
Bureau of the Census
Washington, DC 20233
(301) 763-2074

For tape questions:

Data User Services Division
Customer Services
Bureau of the Census
Washington, DC 20233
(301) 763-4100

For subject matter questions:

Demographic Surveys Division
Bureau of the Census
Washington, DC 20233
(301) 763-5303

For further information on the availability of additional marital
and fertility reports, contact:

Subscriber Services Section
Bureau of the Census
Washington, DC 20233

Photocopies of tables showing detailed national fertility rates by socioeconomic characteristics categorized by age, race, marital status, and parity can be ordered by contacting:

Martin O'Connell
Population Division
Bureau of the Census
Washington, D.C. 20233
(301) 763-5303

Cost

Machine-readable files (1 file = 1 year) are available on 6250 or 1600 bpi tape in EBCDIC or ASCII format from Customer Services, Data User Services Division. Cost is $175 per tape. Cost per file will vary depending upon amount of data and choice of tape density. Contact Customer Services (address and phone number noted in *Contact* section above) for specific information.

Technical documentation accompanies each order. Additional copies are available for $5 each. The *Design and Methodology* (Technical Paper 40) report is $5 for two microfiche or $33 for paper prints. Both reports are available from Customer Service, Data User Services Division (address noted in *Contact* above).

The photocopies of tables, *Current Fertility Indicators* tabulation, consists of approximately 400 pages and costs $35. Orders are placed through Martin O'Connell, address noted in *Contact* above.

BIBLIOGRAPHY

U.S. Bureau of the Census. (1979). *Fertility of American women: June 1979* (Current Population Reports, Population Characteristics, Series P-20, No. 358). Washington, DC: U.S. Government Printing Office.

U.S. Bureau of the Census. (1980). *Fertility of American women: June 1980* (Current Population Reports, Population Characteristics, Series P-20, No. 375). Washington, DC: U.S. Government Printing Office.

U.S. Bureau of the Census. (1981). *Fertility of American women: June 1981* (Current Population Reports, Population Characteristics, Series P-20, No. 378). Washington, DC: U.S. Government Printing Office.

U.S. Bureau of the Census. *Childspacing among birth cohorts of American women: 1905 to 1959* (Current Population Reports, Population Characteristics, Series P-20, No. 385). Washington, DC: U.S. Government Printing Office.

U.S. Bureau of the Census. (1982). *Fertility of American women: June 1982* (Current Population Reports, Population Characteristics, Series P-20, No. 387). Washington, DC: U.S. Government Printing Office.

U.S. Bureau of the Census (1982). *Trends in child care arrangements of working mothers* (Current Population Reports, Special Studies, Series P-23, No. 117). Washington, DC: U.S. Government Printing Office.

U.S. Bureau of the Census (1983). *Child care arrangements of working mothers: June 1982* (Current Population Reports, Special Studies, Series P-23, No. 129). Washington, DC: U.S. Government Printing Office.

U.S. Bureau of the Census. (1983). *Fertility of American women: June 1983* (Current Population Reports, Population Characteristics, Series P-20, No. 395). Washington, DC: U.S. Government Printing Office.

U.S. Bureau of the Census. (1984). *Fertility of American women: June 1984* (Current Population Reports, Population Characteristics, Series P-20, No. 401). Washington, DC: U.S. Government Printing Office.

U.S. Bureau of the Census. (1985). *Fertility of American women: June 1985* (Current Population Reports, Population Characteristics, Series P-20, No. 406). Washington, DC: U.S. Government Printing Office.

U.S. Bureau of the Census. (1986). *Fertility of American women: June 1986* (Current Population Reports, Population Characteristics, Series P-20, No. 421). Washington, DC: U.S. Government Printing Office.

U.S. Bureau of the Census. (1987). *Fertility of American women: June 1987* (Current Population Reports, Population Characteristics, Series P-20, No. 427). Washington, DC: U.S. Government Printing Office.

U.S. Bureau of the Census. (1988). *Current population survey, June 1988: Fertility, birth expectations, and immigration survey technical documentation*. Washington, DC: Data User Services Division, Bureau of the Census.

U.S. Bureau of the Census. (1989). *Fertility of American women: June 1988* (Current Population Reports, Population Characteristics, Series P-20, No. 436). Washington, DC: U.S. Government Printing Office.

U.S. Bureau of the Census. (1990). *Fertility of American women: June 1990* (Current Population Reports, Population Characteristics, Series P-20, No. 454). Washington, DC: U.S. Government Printing Office.

U.S. Bureau of the Census. *Studies on American fertility* (Current Population Reports, Special Studies, Series P-23, No. 176). Washington, DC: U.S. Government Printing Office.

U.S. Bureau of the Census (1990). *Work and family patterns of American women* (Current Population Reports, Series P-23, No. 165). Washington, DC: U.S. Government Printing Office.

Zill, N., & Peterson, J.L. (Eds.) (1989). *Guide to federal data on children, youth, and families*. Washington, DC: Child Trends.

25

INTERGENERATIONAL PANEL STUDY OF PARENTS AND CHILDREN: 1962-1985

Arland Thornton
Deborah Freedman

PURPOSE OF THE STUDY

The Intergenerational Panel Study of Parents and Children is a twenty-three year panel study that began in 1962 and extends through 1985. The study includes seven waves of interviews with the mothers in the sample families between 1962 and 1985. Two waves of interviews were obtained with a sample child in each family in 1980 and 1985.

The purposes and goals of the Intergenerational Panel Study of Parents and Children have evolved over the life of the project. The original study was launched in 1962 as a prospective study of childbearing. The original interviews collected a wide range of information useful for predicting subsequent childbearing decisions, while the follow-up data collections through 1966 measured subsequent fertility experience. In 1977, the purposes of the study were expanded to investigate employment, divorce, and changing family attitudes while at the same time retaining the earlier emphasis on childbearing decisions.

In 1980 the study shifted its emphasis to the children in the family and how they were influenced by the homes in which they were reared. The project became interested in the ways in which the parental family influenced the attitudes, values, experiences, and plans of the children. Of particular interest were the children's attitudes and experiences in the domains of marriage, childbearing, school, work, living arrangements, and family relationships. The 1980 wave of interviews with the children was also designed to be a prospective study of the determinants of variations in the ways children made the transition to adulthood.

METHODS

Sampling Design

The families participating in the study were chosen to represent white couples in the Detroit metropolitan area who had just given birth to their first, second, or fourth child in 1961. The sampling frame used in the study was the birth records of white babies born in the Detroit metropolitan area (Wayne, Oakland, and Macomb counties), and the sample was drawn from the universe using systematic random procedures. The original sample size was 1,113 families. Approximately equal numbers of families from each parity group were selected.

Periodicity

The mothers of the sampled children were first interviewed in the winter of 1962 in face-to-face interviews that averaged approximately 80 minutes. Four follow-up surveys with these women were conducted by telephone in the fall of 1962, and in 1963, 1966, and 1977.

In 1980, the study was broadened to be a two-generation family study by conducting a personal interview with the children born in 1961, then 18 years of age, as well as re-interviewing the mothers by telephone. In 1985 both the personal interview with the children, then age 23, and the telephone interview with their mothers were repeated.

Unit of Analysis

Three units of analysis can be defined in this study. First, the unit of analysis can be defined as a birth cohort of children born in 1961 in the Detroit metropolitan area. Second, the unit of analysis can be defined as a group of women giving birth to a child in 1961. Finally, the unit of analysis can be conceptualized as families, or more specifically as mother-child pairs.

Response Rates

Response rates have been high throughout the study. In 1962, 92 percent of the original target sample of mothers was interviewed. Between 1962 and 1985 only 15 percent of the mothers and young adults were lost from the study. Interviews were obtained in 1985 with both the mother and child in 82 percent of the families that were interviewed in 1962.

Throughout this panel study the original respondents were reinterviewed regardless of their current location. Along with a great deal of change in residence within southeastern Michigan, many of these families moved out of Michigan during the 23-year study period.

By 1985 respondents resided in more than twenty states in the U.S. spread from coast to coast.

CONTENT

Data Sources

The first wave of interviews with the mothers was collected using face-to-face interviewing procedures. Subsequent interviews with the mothers have been conducted by telephone.

The study protocols for both the 1980 and 1985 children's interviews called for face-to-face interviews with all children who were living in Southeast Michigan at the time of the surveys. Children living outside of the Southeast Michigan area were to be interviewed by telephone. The bulk of the interviews with the children in both 1980 and 1985 were face-to-face interviews.

The 1980 and 1985 interviews with the children included both interviewer- and self-administered components. The self-administered part of the questionnaire was designed to allow the young person more privacy in answering questions that were judged to be more sensitive than others.

The 1985 interview with the children also utilized a life history calendar. The interviewer and respondent collaborated in the use of the calendar to ascertain monthly event-history data from the respondent for the period of time between the child's fifteenth birthday and the interview (at age 23).

Description of Variables Covered

The availability of seven waves of data collected from the mothers across the entire lifetimes of the participating children (23 years) provides a wealth of information about the parental family. The interviews with the mothers ascertained extensive information about the fertility experiences of the mothers, including their childbearing histories, attitudes and plans concerning family size, and contraception attitudes and experience. The mothers were also asked about their experiences with divorce and remarriage, their attitudes about marriage, cohabitation, and divorce, and the quality of their relationships with their husbands.

The interviews with the mothers contain extensive information about the standard of living in the family, including such information as income, assets, and the ownership of houses and consumer durables. Information about the mother's employment experience and reasons for work was obtained. Also ascertained was data about leisure time activities and household organization, including the division of household chores and authority. The mothers provided extensive information about their extended family networks, including the degree of contact with parents. Information was also collected from the mothers about religion and health care.

The interviews with the mothers also ascertained large amounts of prospective information about the mother's desires and expectations for the child participating in the study. Some examples of this information are aspirations for the child's education, career attainments, marriage, and childbearing. Also available is extensive information about such issues as the relationship between the mother, father, and child and the parents' willingness and ability to help the child financially.

The project also has available a broad range of information from the young adults—information collected across two waves of interviews from ages 18 through 23. Included in these data are a wide range of information about the attitudes and values of the young adults. These data focus on such life domains as childbearing, marriage, cohabitation, divorce, and the division of labor between men and women.

Also available from the children is prospective information about the plans and expectations of the young adults concerning school, work, marriage, and childbearing, as well as information about the relationships of the young adults with their mothers and fathers. Also important is information about the children's perceptions of their parents' attitudes and willingness to be of assistance.

The data set from the children includes information about their standard of living. This includes data about consumption aspirations and the ownership of consumer durables. Home ownership, vacation trips, and income are also included in the list of variables measured.

The data set contains extensive information about the children's educational experiences, both their achievements in high school as well as their attendance and completion of educational programs beyond high school. There is also extensive information in the data set about employment. Religion, politics, and leisure time activities are also included in the study. Particularly important in the latter category are relationships with friends and dating. Self esteem was ascertained in both waves of interviews with the children.

Extensive information was ascertained in the children's interviews about their relationships with their parents. The children were asked about the quality of their relationships with both mothers and fathers. In addition, the degree of communication and contact was ascertained.

A particularly novel and valuable feature of the data set is the availability of event history information for several important domains of life, including cohabitation, marriage, separation, divorce, fertility, living arrangements, education, paid employment, and military service. Monthly information was collected for each of these domains from the young adult's fifteenth birthday through the 1985 interview at age 23. To ensure the quality of the event history information, the data were collected using a life history calendar that provided both the interviewer and respondent the opportunity to discover and correct missing and discrepant data.

Number of Variables

The data set is organized into six data files, one each for the 1962-1977 data, the 1980 mother's data, the 1980 children's questionnaire data, the 1985 mother's data, the 1985 children's questionnaire data, and the 1985 life history calendar data for the children. The number of variables for the six data files are respectively as follows: 827; 211; 540; 310; 565; and 3,236.

Linking Variables

Each of the six data files contains a variable that allows linkage across the respective data sets. That variable is named "1962 family ID" on each of the files. The exact variable number can be found in the codebook for each data file.

Checklist of Topics Covered: Mothers' Surveys

X Gender / Gender Role
X Race / Ethnicity
X Age
X Education
X Occupation / Employment
___ Physical Health / Disease
___ Nutrition
___ Clinical Activities
___ Biological Functioning / Development
___ Mental Health / Disease
___ Psychological Functioning / Development
___ Guidance / Counseling
___ Personality
___ Intellectual Functioning
___ Residential Mobility
X Dwelling
___ Neighborhood / Community
___ Region / State
X Marriage and Divorce
___ Cohabitation
X Family/Household Composition & Structure
X Inter-Partner Relationships
X Parent-Child Relationships
___ Inter-Sibling Relationships
X Relationships with Other Kin

X Relationships with Nonkin
___ Other Family/Household Characteristics
X Child Care
X Wealth / Finances / Material Things
___ Receipt of Health, Mental Health, Social Services
___ Adoption / Foster Care
X Childbearing / Pregnancy
X Out-of-Wedlock Pregnancy & Parenthood
___ Abortion
___ Sexuality
___ Sex Education
X Contraception
___ Sexually Transmitted Diseases
X Civic/Political Activities
X Friends / Social Activities Social Support
___ Dating, Courtship
X Recreation
X Religion
___ Crime / Delinquency / Behavior Problems
___ Substance Use
___ Agency Characteristics
___ Interview

Checklist of Topics Covered: Children's Surveys

X Gender / Gender Role
X Race / Ethnicity
X Age
X Education
X Occupation / Employment
___ Physical Health / Disease
___ Nutrition
___ Clinical Activities
___ Biological Functioning /
      Development
___ Mental Health / Disease
___ Psychological Functioning /
      Development
___ Guidance / Counseling
___ Personality
X Intellectual Functioning
X Residential Mobility
___ Dwelling
___ Neighborhood /
      Community
___ Region / State
X Marriage and Divorce
X Cohabitation
X Family/Household
      Composition & Structure
X Inter-Partner Relationships
X Parent-Child Relationships
___ Inter-Sibling Relationships
X Relationships with Other Kin

X Relationships with Nonkin
___ Other Family/Household
      Characteristics
___ Child Care
X Wealth / Finances /
      Material Things
___ Receipt of Health, Mental
      Health, Social Services
___ Adoption / Foster Care
X Childbearing / Pregnancy
X Out-of-Wedlock
      Pregnancy & Parenthood
X Abortion
X Sexuality
___ Sex Education
X Contraception
___ Sexually Transmitted
      Diseases
___ Civic/Political Activities
X Friends / Social Activities
      Social Support
X Dating, Courtship
X Recreation
X Religion
___ Crime / Delinquency /
      Behavior Problems
___ Substance Use
___ Agency Characteristics
___ Interview

Checklist of Key Variables: Mothers' Surveys

X Number of family members
X Identification of marital
   partners in family
___ Size of dwelling
___ Type of dwelling
___ Urban/rural residence
___ Region/state of residence
X Family income
X Religious affiliation
___ Relation of each family
   member to:
   ___ Reference person
   ___ All other members
X Age of family members
   X Respondent
   X Others
X Sex of family members

X Respondent
X Others
___ Race of family members
   ___ Respondent
   ___ Others
X Marital status of family
   members
   X Respondent
   ___ Others
X Education of family
   members
   X Respondent
   X Others
X Occupation of family
   members
   X Respondent
   X Others

Checklist of Key Variables: Children's Surveys

X Number of family members
X Identification of marital
   partners in family
___ Size of dwelling
___ Type of dwelling
___ Urban/rural residence
___ Region/state of residence
X Family income
X Religious affiliation
X Relation of each family
   member to:
   X Reference person
   X All other members
X Age of family members
   X Respondent
   ___ Others
X Sex of family members

X Respondent
X Others
X Race of family members
   X Respondent
   ___ Others
X Marital status of family
   members
   X Respondent
   ___ Others
X Education of family
   members
   X Respondent
   X Others
X Occupation of family
   members
   X Respondent
   X Others

LIMITATIONS

None.

SPONSORSHIP

This study has been funded by grants from the National Institute of Child Health and Human Development.

GUIDE TO DATA AND DOCUMENTATION

File Structure

As noted above, the raw data set is arranged in six data files. Documentation and data files can be obtained from the Inter-university Consortium for Political and Social Research (ICPSR). The data set is listed in the ICPSR archives as data set number 9902.

List of Available Documentation

The documentation available from ICPSR comes in two volumes and includes data collection instruments as well as codebooks. The ICPSR material also contains a machine-readable file giving the univariate frequencies for the variables. There are also OSIRIS dictionaries available for each of the data file. Note that while the OSIRIS dictionaries are available, the data set can also be read by other software programs.

Contact

Inter-university Consortium for Political and Social Research
Institute for Social Research
426 Thompson Street
Ann Arbor, MI 48106-1248
Phone: (313) 764-2570
Fax: (313) 764-8041

Members of the Inter-university Consortium for Political and Social Research (ICPSR) can obtain the data set from ICPSR at no cost. For nonmembers, the cost depends on the format requested. Contact ICPSR (313-763-5010) for a price quote.

BIBLIOGRAPHY

Axinn, W.G., & Thornton, A. (1992, August). The relationship between cohabitation and divorce: Selectivity or causal influence? *Demography, 29*(3), 357-374.

Axinn, W.G. & Thornton, A. (1993, forthcoming) Mothers, children, and cohabitation: The intergenerational effects of attitudes and behavior. *American Sociological Review, 58*(2).

Freedman, D.S., Thornton, A., & Camburn, D. (1980, August). Maintaining response rates in longitudinal studies. *Sociological Methods and Research, 9*(1).

Freedman, D., Thornton, A, Camburn, D., Alwin, D., & Young-DeMarco, L. (1988). The life history calendar: A technique for collecting retrospective data. In C.C. Clogg (Ed.) *Sociological Methodology, Vol. 18*, San Francisco, CA: Jossey-Bass.

Freedman, D.S. & Thornton, A. (1990, March). The Consumption aspirations of adolescents: Determinants and implications. *Youth and Society, 21*(3).

Thornton, A. (1988, November). Cohabitation and marriage in the 1980s. *Demography, 25*(4).

Thornton, A. (1991, January). Influence of the marital history of parents on the marital and cohabitational experiences of children. *American Journal of Sociology, 96*(4).

Thornton, A., Axinn, W.G., & Hill, D.H. (1992, November). Reciprocal effects of religiosity, cohabitation, and marriage. *American Journal of Sociology, 98*(3), 628-651.

Thornton, A., Freedman, D.S., & Camburn, D. (1982, August). Obtaining respondent cooperation in family panel studies. *Sociological Methods and Research, 11*(1). Reprinted in D.H. Olson and B.C. Miller (Eds.) (1984), *Family Studies Review Yearbook, Vol. 2,* Beverly Hills, CA: Sage.

Thornton, A., Young-DeMarco, L., & Goldscheider, F. (1993, February). Leaving the parental nest: The experience of a young white cohort in the 1980s. *Journal of Marriage and the Family, 55,* 216-229.

26

NATIONAL FAMILY VIOLENCE SURVEY, 1975 AND 1985

Murray A. Straus
Richard J. Gelles

PURPOSE OF THE STUDY

Both the 1975 and 1985 National Family Violence Surveys explore conflict/resolution and violence in the family with the goal of demonstrating that physical violence between family members is more frequent than believed. Objectives of the 1975 survey were to determine the extent to which violence occurs between parents and children, siblings, and husbands and wives; to provide descriptive information of the violence which occurs; and to test three theories of why violence does or does not occur in intra-family relations. Objectives of the 1985 survey were to compare intra-family violence incidence in 1985 with estimates of the 1975 incidence; to generate comparisons of intra-family physical violence by race and ethnicity; and to generate state-by-state estimates of intra-family violence which could be included in inter-state analysis.

METHODS

Sampling Design: The 1975 Survey

Response Analysis Corporation generated a national probability sample of individuals to be interviewed. The sequence of the steps used in the development of the sample included:

1. Selection of a national sample of 103 primary areas (counties or groups of counties) stratified by geographic region, type of community, and other population characteristics.

2. Selection of 300 interviewing locations, or secondary areas (Census enumeration districts or block groups) from the national sample for use on this study.

3. Field counts by trained interviewers to divide interviewing locations into sample segments of ten to twenty-five housing units.

4. Selection of specific sample segments in each interviewing location for field administration of the survey.

5. Random selection of the eligible person to be interviewed using a specific scheme assigned for each sample household. First, the number of "couples" in a household was obtained, and then a couple was designated for interview. Half of the time the older couple was selected, and half of the time the younger was selected. Once the couple was selected, half of the time the male member was designated as the respondent, and half of the time the female was designated. To be eligible, both members of the couple had to be over 18 years old and the respondent had to be under 70 (although there were three respondents age 70).

Sampling Design: The 1985 Survey

A national probability sample of individuals to be interviewed was generated using the following steps:

1. A national sample of primary areas (counties or groups of counties) was selected; the sample was stratified by geographic region, type of community, and other population characteristics.

2. Within each stratum, counties were selected as the primary sampling units (PSU). These PSUs were selected in proportion to the distribution of the population within the stratum.

3. Specific households within a PSU were selected by using a random digit dialing technique.

4. Households were screened for eligibility. To be eligible, there had to be at least one adult in the household who was (1) married or living with a member of the opposite sex; or (2) a single parent with at least one child under 18; or (3) had lived with a member of the opposite sex within the past two years. It was also determined how many adults in the household fell into these categories.

5. The eligible person to be interviewed was randomly selected using a specific scheme assigned for each sample household. First, the number of eligible respondents in a household was

obtained, and then a respondent was randomly designated for the interview. If the selected respondent was part of a "couple", half of the time the male member was designated as the respondent, and half of the time the female was designated.

Black, Hispanic, and State Oversampling: The 1985 Survey

The number of black and Hispanic respondents expected from a national cross-section of approximately 4,000 qualifying family units was not considered to be large enough to provide sufficient sampling precision for comparison of incidence by race and ethnicity. Hence, the study design called for additional interviews with approximately 500 qualifying black respondents and 500 qualifying Hispanic respondents. The procedure for identifying a national sample of qualifying black and Hispanic units was similar to the procedure described for the main sample. Households were contacted and screened for race/ethnicity. There were a total of 502 blacks included in the black oversample and 510 Hispanics included in the Hispanic oversample.

In order to generate state-by-state estimates of incidence of intra-family physical violence, it was necessary for the investigators to conduct additional interviews to oversample states which were not adequately represented in the main sample. The state specific oversample differed from the Hispanic and black oversamples in that it was not developed on the basis of a national probability sampling frame. The state oversample was developed to yield state-by-state estimates of the incidence of family violence. Although these state estimates would fall considerably short of the precision of national estimates, they would allow inter-state analysis of factors related to incidence rates.

Periodicity: The 1975 and 1985 Surveys

Interviewing for the 1975 survey took place from January to June 1976. The main cross-sectional survey for the 1985 survey was conducted between June 10 and August 13, 1985. The black oversample survey was conducted between August 9 and August 30, 1985; the Hispanic oversample between August 9 and September 15, 1985; and the State oversample between August 6 and August 29, 1985.

Unit of Analysis: The 1975 and 1985 Surveys

The individual is the unit of analysis.

Response Rates: The 1975 Survey

The response rates for the 1975 survey break down as follows:

Eligible respondents	3,296
Refused, other incomplete	990
Eligibility undeterminable	112
Completed interviews	2,194
Eliminated prior to processing (wrong respondent, spouse less than 18)	51
Total interviews included in analysis	2,143 (65% of eligible respondents)

Response Rates: The 1985 Survey

The response rates for the 1985 survey are shown in Table 1 on the next three pages.

Table 1. Response Rates: The 1985 Survey

Sample Disposition

	Main Sample	State Oversample	Black Oversample	Hispanic Oversample
Sample Drawn	28,518	6,192	5,753	9,218
No Household Reached	15,811	3,787	3,326	5,512
Business	2,067	330	307	597
Not in Service	6,837	1,064	1,451	2,040
No Answer (4 attempts)	4,000	944	935	1,744
Constant Busy (4 attempts)	527	140	138	270
Callback status at end of field period	2,380	309	495	861
Unable to Screen for Eligibility	4,059	581	677	849

Table 1. Response Rates: The 1985 Survey (continued)

		Sample Disposition		
	Main Sample	State Oversample	Black Oversample	Hispanic Oversample
Screened Ineligible	3,846	677	1,164	2,241
No adult in household	36	9	5	17
No eligible units in household	2,672	469	961	1,969
Designated respondent speaks language other than English or Spanish	239	23	27	54
Designated respondent incapacitated	467	55	73	81
Designated respondent away for duration of field period	262	78	62	66
Duplicate case	6	1	6	11
Other ineligible	209	42	30	43

Table 1. Response Rates: The 1985 Survey (continued)

Sample Disposition

	Main Sample	State Oversample	Black Oversample	Hispanic Oversample
<u>Screened Eligible</u>	4,802	1,147	592	622
Complete	**4,032**	**958**	**502**	**510**
Refused	182	38	23	21
Terminate	588	151	61	85
Completion Rate: Completed interviews as a proportion of total eligible	84.0%	83.5%	85.8%	83.0%

Total sample included in data set: Main Sample + State Oversample + Black Oversample + Hispanic Oversample = **6,002 cases.**

Note: For several categories in the "Sample Disposition" Table (above), the sum of entries within a category does not match the category total. For example, under the column heading "Black Oversample" the category total for "Screened Eligible" is 592, although the entries for that category, 502 (complete) + 23 (Refused) + 61 (Terminate), sum only to 586 (a discrepancy of about 1%). In most cases, the discrepancy between a category total and the sum of its entries is less than 2%. The discrepancies are due to inconsistencies reported by a subcontractor organization which collected the original data. Despite repeated requests by the original investigators, the subcontractor has not provided corrected values.

Attrition

Not applicable.

CONTENT

Data Sources: The 1975 Survey

Interviews were conducted among households in which at least one couple resided. The final questionnaire was translated into Spanish so that Spanish-speaking respondents could be interviewed with the same degree of accuracy as English-speaking respondents.

There was a post-interview questionnaire consisting of ten items which asked the respondent how accurate his/her responses were (e.g., were some responses exaggerated, or did the marital situation come out seeming different than it really was).

Respondents were also asked to complete a self-administered questionnaire containing two sets of questions. The first set included questions rating both the respondent and his/her spouse on aspects of personality; the second set asked the respondent if certain problems had occurred in the respondent's life in the past year.

Data Sources: The 1985 Survey

For the 1985 survey, telephone interviews were conducted. The first few pages of the questionnaire served as a screener questionnaire to establish eligibility. The remaining questions were administered by an interviewer. There were no self-administered questionnaires like those for the 1975 survey.

Description of Questionnaires and Variables Covered: The 1975 Survey

The first page of the main 1975 survey asked for information on members of the household over eighteen. The instrument then contained questions on the respondent's and spouse's educational and occupational history/status. There were also questions on children in the household. Other questions were asked about conflict resolution between the children and their siblings or parents, the respondent's marriage with respect to marital responsibility and decisions, the strength of the marital relationship, and the amount of disagreement between the couple. Information was also gathered about the respondent's parents, their employment and educational history, and marital violence while the respondent was growing up. Respondents provided demographic information and an assessment of their quality of life and satisfaction with their present standard of living.

Two additional questionnaires were administered. The first consisted of a post-interview questionnaire of ten items which asked the respondent how accurate his/her responses were (e.g., were some responses exaggerated; did the marital situation come out seeming different than it really was).

The second was a self-administered questionnaire containing two sets of questions. The first set included questions rating both the respondent and his/her spouse on aspects of personality, such as "Influences other people or takes charge of things", and "Loses his or her temper". The second set of questions asked the respondent if certain problems had occurred in the past year, such as "Troubles with the boss", and "Child got caught doing something illegal".

The original investigators constructed many variables using the Conflict Tactics Scales (CTS); [1] seventy-five of these variables in the original SPSS export file were eliminated by Sociometrics because the original investigator felt that they were not sufficiently documented to be included in the public-use data set.

Description of Questionnaire and Variables Covered: The 1985 Survey

The 1985 survey included questions on the respondent's and spouse's educational and occupational history/status, questions on children in the household, and questions about conflict resolution between the children and the respondent. The respondent was asked if there was ever any physical violence in his/her household when he/she was a teenager, conflict between respondent and his/her partner and if so was the violence severe enough to need medical treatment. Respondents were then asked about things they had done to stop their partner from hurting or threatening them and whom they had sought help for personal problems. There were questions about the respondent's mental and physical health and substance use, and demographic information was requested.

There were approximately 175 variables included in the original SPSS export file sent by the investigators which were constructed by using the Conflict Tactics Scales (CTS). Approximately 100 of these variables were eliminated by Sociometrics because the original investigator felt that they were not sufficiently documented to be included in the archived data set. The remaining 75 CTS variables were left in the data set at the request of the original investigator. (See note at the end of this chapter.)

Number of Variables: The 1975 and 1985 Surveys

The 1975 survey contains 737 variables and 2,143 cases. The 1985 survey contains 567 variables and 6,002 cases.

Checklist of Topics Covered: The 1975 Survey

X Gender / Gender Role
X Race / Ethnicity
X Age
X Education
X Occupation / Employment
X Physical Health / Disease
___ Nutrition
___ Clinical Activities
___ Biological Functioning /
    Development
X Mental Health / Disease
X Psychological Functioning /
    Development
X Guidance / Counseling
X Personality
X Intellectual Functioning
X Residential Mobility
___ Dwelling
X Neighborhood /
    Community
X Region / State
X Marriage and Divorce
___ Cohabitation
X Family/Household
    Composition & Structure
X Inter-Partner Relationships
X Parent-Child Relationships
X Inter-Sibling Relationships
X Relationships with Other Kin

X Relationships with Nonkin
X Other Family/Household
    Characteristics
X Child Care
X Wealth / Finances /
    Material Things
___ Receipt of Health, Mental
    Health, Social Services
___ Adoption / Foster Care
X Childbearing / Pregnancy
___ Out-of-Wedlock
    Pregnancy & Parenthood
___ Abortion
X Sexuality
___ Sex Education
___ Contraception
___ Sexually Transmitted
    Diseases
___ Civic/Political Activities
X Friends / Social Activities
___ Social Support
___ Dating, Courtship
___ Recreation
X Religion
X Crime / Delinquency /
    Behavior Problems
X Substance Use
___ Agency Characteristics
X Interview

Checklist of Topics Covered: The 1985 Survey

X Gender / Gender Role	X Relationships with Nonkin
X Race / Ethnicity	___ Other Family/Household
X Age	Characteristics
X Education	X Child Care
X Occupation / Employment	X Wealth / Finances /
X Physical Health / Disease	Material Things
___ Nutrition	___ Receipt of Health, Mental
___ Clinical Activities	Health, Social Services
___ Biological Functioning /	X Adoption / Foster Care
Development	X Childbearing / Pregnancy
X Mental Health / Disease	___ Out-of-Wedlock
X Psychological Functioning /	Pregnancy & Parenthood
Development	___ Abortion
X Guidance / Counseling	X Sexuality
X Personality	___ Sex Education
___ Intellectual Functioning	___ Contraception
X Residential Mobility	___ Sexually Transmitted
___ Dwelling	Diseases
___ Neighborhood /	___ Civic/Political Activities
Community	X Friends / Social Activities
X Region / State	___ Social Support
X Marriage and Divorce	___ Dating, Courtship
___ Cohabitation	___ Recreation
X Family/Household	X Religion
Composition & Structure	X Crime / Delinquency /
X Inter-Partner Relationships	Behavior Problems
X Parent-Child Relationships	X Substance Use
___ Inter-Sibling Relationships	___ Agency Characteristics
X Relationships with Other Kin	X Interview

Checklist of Key Variables: *The 1975 Survey*

_X_ Number of family members
_X_ Identification of marital
partners in family
___ Size of dwelling
___ Type of dwelling
___ Urban/rural residence
_X_ Region/state of residence
_X_ Family income
_X_ Religious affiliation
_X_ Relation of each family
member to:
  _X_ Reference person
  ___ All other members
_X_ Age of family members
  _X_ Respondent
  _X_ Others
_X_ Sex of family members

  _X_ Respondent
  _X_ Others
___ Race of family members
  _X_ Respondent
  ___ Others
_X_ Marital status of family
members
  _X_ Respondent
  _X_ Others
___ Education of family
members
  _X_ Respondent
  _X_ Others
___ Occupation of family
members
  _X_ Respondent
  _X_ Others

Checklist of Key Variables: *The 1985 Survey*

_X_ Number of family members
_X_ Identification of marital
partners in family
___ Size of dwelling
___ Type of dwelling
___ Urban/rural residence
_X_ Region/state of residence
_X_ Family income
_X_ Religious affiliation
_X_ Relation of each family
member to:
  _X_ Reference person
  ___ All other members
___ Age of family members
  _X_ Respondent
  _X_ Others
___ Sex of family members

  _X_ Respondent
  _X_ Others
___ Race of family members
  _X_ Respondent
  ___ Others
_X_ Marital status of family
members
  _X_ Respondent
  _X_ Others
___ Education of family
members
  _X_ Respondent
  _X_ Others
___ Occupation of family
members
  _X_ Respondent
  _X_ Others

LIMITATIONS

The 1975 Survey

For the 1975 survey, case-weights were calculated to compensate for differences in interview completion rate among interviewing locations. The weight factor for each location was proportional to the number of eligible households in that location divided by the number of completed interviews. Locations where the weight factor would be more than twice the average weight were combined with other similar locations, and weights were recalculated for the combined locations.

Weights were also assigned to adjust for observed differences in interview completion rates by sex of respondent. In all, 960 men and 1,183 women were interviewed. Since the sexes are equally represented in the universe of couples, weights were assigned to men to bring them into their proper proportion. The gender weight received from the original investigators was missing important decimal information and, therefore, cannot be used in analysis. The user can approximate the gender weight by assigning all women the value of 1.0 and all men the value of 1.232 (which is the ratio of interviewed women to men or 1,183/960).

The 1985 Survey

The main sample represents a self-weighting sample of American telephone households composed of current couples, single parents, or recently coupled persons. The sample construction, household screening and respondent selection methods should produce a representative national sample of the target population. In the absence of Census information on certain qualifying characteristics of this sample, e.g., recently coupled, it is not possible to test or correct sample bias.

Black, Hispanic, and state oversamples cannot be merged with the main sample for national population estimates without correction for the disproportionate sampling between the cross-sectional sample and the oversample. Hence, in order to combine oversample cases with main sample cases, it was necessary to derive case weights.

There are seven possible combinations of the main sample and oversamples which require adjustment for disproportionate sampling. The variables needed to make the proper adjustments are listed below:

VARIABLE   ADJUSTS FOR:

MEX32449   Cross-section + State Oversample
MEX32453   Cross-section + Black Oversample
MEX32455   Cross-section + Hispanic Oversample
MEX32450   Cross-section + State Oversample + Black
            Oversample
MEX32452   Cross-section + State Oversample + Hispanic
            Oversample
MEX32454   Cross-section + Black Oversample +
            Hispanic Oversample
MEX32451   Cross-section + State Oversample + Black
            Oversample + Hispanic Oversample

These case weights must be used when one wishes to combine oversamples with the national sample for national population projections. The black subsample from the main survey can be combined with the black oversample, without weighting, for unbiased national estimates of the black population. The same is true for the Hispanic subsample. The subsample from an individual state in the main survey can be combined with the state oversample from that state for unbiased estimates of that state's population. However, all other combinations require the use of the case weights listed above.

SPONSORSHIP

The 1975 National Family Violence Survey was funded by the National Institute on Mental Health. The 1985 Survey was funded by the National Institute on Mental Health and the National Science Foundation. Both surveys were conduction with assistance from Response Analysis Corporation.

File Structure

       Machine-readable data and documentation files are available in mainframe tape, microcomputer disk, and CD-ROM formats for the 1975 survey and mainframe tape and CD-ROM formats for the 1985 survey. Unless otherwise requested, files formatted for a mainframe computer are provided on a 9-track tape at a density of 6250 bpi, in EBCDIC recording mode with IBM Standard Labels. Files formatted for a microcomputer disk are provided in ASCII format on high-density 5¼" or 3½" diskettes. CD-ROM files are in ISO 9660 format. A description of the contents of each file is given below.

File 1 (Data): Raw data files. The format of this file is described in the "data list" section of the SPSS program file (file 2).

File 2 (SPSS Program): This file consists of SPSS-X program statements designed to read the raw data in file 1 and create an SPSS-X active file. The SPSS-X program file contains data list statements, variable names and labels, value labels, and missing value declarations.

File 3 (SAS Program): This file consists of SAS program statements designed to read the raw data in file 1 and create a SAS active file. The contents of this file are analogous to the contents of the previously described file 2. SPSS Users should use file 2; SAS users, file 3. Users may need to add "job control language" (JCL) statements to the SAS program file to meet the requirements for their specific operating system. For some operating systems, e.g., Unix, running the SAS program statements may result in a "segmentation violation" message from SAS due to a limit on the number of independent sets of format labels (the current limit is about 300) that can be assigned to variables. The SAS Institute plans to release an updated version of SAS early in 1993 that will correct the problem. Until then, if a segmentation violation occurs, one solution is to edit the SAS program statements to remove format (value label) assignments for all variables unrelated to the analysis at hand.

File 4 (Dictionary): Sequential list of variable and value labels. This file consists of DISPLAY DICTIONARY output describing the SPSS-X active file created by the program in File 2. Variables are listed in sequential order. Variable names and labels, value labels, missing value designations, print formats, and write formats are clearly displayed.

File 5 (Statistics): Unweighted frequencies or other descriptive statistics for each variable. Descriptive statistics only are provided for variables with more than 50 value categories, such as respondent identification number, zip codes, etc.

List of Available Documentation

For each data set, a User's Guide which accompanies the machine-readable files provides the following information: Summary; General study overview; Description of machine-readable files and supplementary documentation; Specifications for machine-readable files; Key characteristics report; Distribution of variables by topic and type; and Data completeness and consistency report.

For each data set, paper versions of the machine-readable SPSS and SAS program files and data documentation (files 2-5 above), and copies of the original instruments and codebooks, are available upon request (at 15 cents per page).

Contact

>Sociometrics Corporation
>American Family Data Archive
>170 State Street, Suite 260
>Los Altos, California 94022-2812
>(415) 949-3282

Cost

The cost for the machine-readable data sets (Data Set 31 and Data Set 32 of the American Family Data Archive) is $100 each. This price includes the raw data, SPSS program statements, the SAS program statements, the Dictionary, and the Frequencies in mainframe format, and the accompanying printed and bound User's Guide. The

CD-ROM versions cost $175 each. A paper version of the original 1975 survey Codebook/Instrument is $7.20; for the 1985 survey, $19.05.

BIBLIOGRAPHY

Bachman, R. (1992). *Death and violence on the reservation: A study of homicide, family violence and suicide in American Indian populations*. Westport, CT: Auburn House.

Bachman-Prehn, R., & Pillemer, K. (1991). Retirement: Does it affect marital conflict and violence? *Journal of Elder Abuse and Neglect, 3*(2), 75-88.

Carmody, D.C., & Williams, K.R. (1987, Spring). Wife-assault and perceptions of sanctions. *Violence and Victims, 2*, 25-38.

Cervi, D.D. (1991). *Violence inside and outside of the home: New evidence for the person-situation debate*. Paper presented at the 1991 meeting of the Eastern Sociological Society. Durham, NH: Family Research Laboratory, University of New Hampshire.

Feld, S.L. (1988). *Violence as a strategy of the weak against the strong: The case of siblings*. Durham, NH: Family Research Laboratory, University of New Hampshire.

Gelles, R.J., & Harrop, J.W. (1989, December). Violence, batterings, and psychological distress among women. *Journal of Interpersonal Violence, 4*, 400-420.

Gelles, R.J., & Straus, M.A. (1987, June). Is violence toward children increasing? *Journal of Interpersonal Violence, 2*, 212-222.

Gelles, R.J., & Straus, M.A. (1988). *Intimate violence: The causes and consequences of abuse in American families*. New York, NY: Simon and Schuster.

Hampton, R.L., & Gelles, R.J. (1988). Is violence in black families increasing? A comparison of 1975 and 1985 national survey rates. *Journal of Marriage and the Family, 51*, 969-980.

Hotaling, G.T., & Sugarman, D.B. (1990). Prevention of wife assault. In R.T. Ammerman & M. Hersen (Eds.), *Treatment of family violence*. New York, NY: John Wiley & Sons.

Kaplan, A.S., Peterson, E.C., Lang, E.L., & Card, J.J. (1992). *1975 national study of family violence: A user's guide to the machine-readable files and documentation*. Los Altos, CA: Sociometrics Corporation, American Family Data Archive.

Kaplan, A.S., Peterson, E.C., Lang, E.L., & Card, J.J. (1992). *1985 national study of family violence: A user's guide to the machine-readable files and documentation*. Los Altos, CA: Sociometrics Corporation, American Family Data Archive.

Kaufman Kantor, G. (1991, November). *Ethnicity, drinking, and wife abuse: A structural and cultural interpretation*. Paper presented at the 42nd annual meeting of the American Society of Criminology, Baltimore, MD.

Larzelere, R.E. (1986, March). Moderate spanking: Model or deterrent of children's aggression in the family. *Journal of Family Violence, 1*, 27-36.

Margolin, L., & Larson III, O.U. (1988). Assessing mothers' and fathers' violence toward children as a function of their involuntary participation in family work. *Journal of Family Violence, 3*, 209-224.

Stets, J.E. (1990, May). Verbal and physical aggression in marriage. *Journal of Marriage and the Family, 52*, 501-514.

Straus, M.A. (1991). Conceptualization and measurement of battering: Implications for public policy. In M. Steinman (Ed.), *Woman battering: Policy responses* (pp. 19-47). Cincinnati, OH: Anderson.

Straus, M.A. (1991). Physical violence in American families: Incidence rates, causes and trends. In D.D. Knudsen & J. Miller (Eds.), *Abused and battered: Social and legal responses to family violence*. New York, NY: Aldine de Gruyter.

Straus, M.A. (1991, September). *Children as witness to marital violence: Risk factor for life-long problems among a nationally representative sample of American men and women.* Paper presented at Ross Roundtable on "Children and Violence", Washington, DC.

Straus, M.A. (1992). Family violence. In E.F. Borgatta & M.L. Borgatta (Eds.), *Encyclopedia of Sociology,* Vol. 2, (pp. 682-689). New York, NY: Macmillan.

Straus, M.A., & Bachman-Prehn, R. (1990). *Alcohol, stress, and violence in American Indian families.* Paper presented at the 1990 meeting of the American Society of Criminology.

Straus, M.A., & Sweet, S. (1992). Verbal/symbolic aggression in couples: A national survey. *Journal of Marriage and the Family, 54.*

Suitor, J.J. (1991). Marital quality and satisfaction with the division of household labor across the family life cycle. *Journal of Marriage and the Family, 53,* 3221-3230.

Vissing, Y.M., Straus, M.A., Gelles, R.J., & Harrop, J.W. (1991). Verbal aggression by parents and psychosocial problems of children. *Child Abuse and Neglect, 15,* 223-238.

NOTES

[1]To request a manual on the CTS, or journal articles on the CTS written by the original investigators, please contact the Family Research Laboratory, University of New Hampshire, Durham, NH 03824. (603) 862-1888. There is a fee for any material requested.

27

NATIONAL SURVEY OF FAMILY GROWTH, CYCLE IV, 1988 (NSFG)

National Center for Health Statistics

PURPOSE OF THE STUDY

The National Survey of Family Growth (NSFG) is one of the data systems of the National Center for Health Statistics (NCHS) and has been conducted periodically since 1973. The overall objective of the NSFG is to supplement the vital statistics of fertility and of family formation and dissolution, with more detailed data on the "intermediate variables" which shape these trends and on the health and socioeconomic contexts in which they occur. In more concrete terms, the NSFG collects data on trends and socioeconomic differences in American fertility, on family planning practices and services, and on health factors related to childbearing.

The uses of the data gathered in the NSFG are broad, though mostly in the health and demographic fields. They may be described in two general classes: program and administrative applications, and research applications. For program and administrative purposes, the NSFG is the primary or sole source for numerous national estimates used for both "needs assessment" and program evaluation, such as: (a) pregnancies classified by outcome and planning status, (b) period estimates of family planning visits classified by type of service and type of provider, or (c) estimates of the sexually active population classified by contraceptive status. Among the research applications, the NSFG provides data for detailed analytical studies, such as (a) the use-effectiveness of contraceptive methods and its socioeconomic correlates, (b) contraceptive practices and their relation to the number and spacing of children, and (c) the sources and content of sex education in relation to the onset of sexual activity, the use of contraception, and the chances of unwanted adolescent pregnancies.

METHODS

Sampling Design, Weighting

The 8,450 women interviewed for the NSFG, Cycle IV, were drawn from households in which someone had been interviewed for another NCHS survey, the National Health Interview Survey, or NHIS, between October of 1985, and March of 1987. If the woman selected for the NSFG had moved since the NHIS interview, she was followed, or tracked, to her new address, and interviewed there.

Different numbers of women were available in the NHIS in 1985, 1986, and 1987, so the sampling procedure differed somewhat in each of these years. The NSFG sampling plan was designed to (1) select more black women than would have fallen into the sample by chance, in order to increase the reliability of the data for black women; and (2) increase the reliability of the data for nonblack women by reducing the variations in the sampling rates for nonblack women. The NSFG sampled only one woman per household, even if more than one eligible woman lived there. The NSFG selected households in the following way:

> For the entire period (December 1985-March 1987), all NHS sample households containing one or more eligible black women but no nonblack women were selected; some other sample households were selected as described in the report.

A simple random sample of women 15-44 in the U. S. would mean that every women 15-44 would have the same chance of being selected for the sample—regardless of where she lived or what her characteristics were. The NSFG sample is not a simple random sample for two reasons: (1) only some areas were selected to be in the sample, while the other areas were not; and (2) within the areas included in the sample, women were sampled at different rates. For example, black women were sampled for the NSFG at a higher rate than other women, so that reliable statistics could be produced for black women. As a result, interviews were completed with 2,771 black women and 5,679 women of other races. Certain other women (described in the report) were also sampled at higher rates. Therefore the NSFG data must be weighted, and estimates of sampling errors should be made using the techniques discussed below.

The response rate to the NHIS, on which the NSFG was based, was 96 percent. Of the sampled women selected from responding NHIS households for the NSFG, the simple response rate to the NSFG was 80 percent. However, this simple response rate does not take into account the subsampling for nonresponse (described in the report) which was a part of the intensive follow-up—the last stage of interviewing. NCHS prefers to take this subsampling into account when calculating the response rates. When this is taken into account, the response rate to the NSFG was 82 percent of the women in the NHIS. Thus, the total response rate is 96 percent times 82 percent, or about 79 percent.

The NSFG is intended to produce national estimates of the number, as well as the percentage, of women with certain characteristics—such as the number using the pill; the number infertile; or the number who used family planning services in the last year. In order to produce these national estimates, each woman interviewed was given a sampling weight, which is the number of women in the population that she represents. The weights were made in four main steps: the first is the baseweight, which is the reciprocal of the probability that the woman was selected for the sample. For example, if the probability that a certain woman was selected was one out of 6,000, her baseweight would be 6,000. The second stage of weighting was trimming; cases with very large weights were reduced to a maximum value. The third stage of weighting was an adjustment for nonresponse. Certain categories of women were less likely than others to be found at home and interviewed, so adjustment for nonresponse attempts to correct for this. The fourth state is called post-stratification; this is adjusting the NSFG totals to a known number of women by age, race, marital status, and parity (the number of live births the woman has had) obtained from the U. S. Bureau of the Census.

The preliminary weights as well as the final post-stratified weight appear on the Public Use Tape in TL 2540-2574 in the Respondent file (women respondents) and TL 338-372 in the Interval file (pregnancy intervals).

Periodicity

The NSFG provides data that continue a statistical time-series on American fertility patterns that was initiated during the early years of the "baby boom". The Growth of American Families surveys took place in 1955 and 1960 and were continued by the National Fertility Studies of 1965 and 1970. Cycles I, II, and III of the NSFG were fielded in 1973, 1976, and 1982, respectively. Cycle IV went into the field in January of 1988.

Data on the sexual and fertility behavior of adolescent females were obtained in 1971, 1976, and 1979 by Drs. John Kantner and Melvin Zelnik of the Johns Hopkins University. Comparable data on adolescent females were obtained in the NSFG in 1982 and 1988.

After the 1988 survey, respondents were re-interviewed by telephone every seventeen months, to provide more up-to-date information on U.S. sexual, contraceptive, and fertility patterns, to evaluate the reliability of selected data items, and to obtain additional information on reproductive health topics.

Unit of Analysis

The individual woman is the unit of analysis. For some purposes, the individual birth may also be the unit of analysis.

Response Rates

The response rate to the National Health Interview Survey (NHIS), on which the NSFG was based, was 96%. Of the sampled women selected from responding NHIS households for the NSFG, the response rate to the NSFG was 80 percent. This sample response rate does not take into account the subsampling for nonresponse which was part of the intensive follow-up, the last stage of the interviewing. Taking this subsampling into account when calculating the response rate, the response rate to the NSFG was 82 percent of the women in NHIS. Thus, the response rate is 96 percent times 82 percent, or about 79 percent.

Attrition

Not applicable. The NSFG, Cycle IV, is the fourth in a series of periodic, cross-sectional surveys of women 15-44 years of age.

CONTENT

Data Sources

Data were collected from personal interviews with a probability sample of 8,450 women (5,354 white women; 2,771 black women; and

325 women of other races) representative of the civilian, noninstitutionalized population in the entire U. S. These interviews were conducted between January and August of 1988 by Westat, Inc. (under a contract with NCHS). Separate questionnaires were designed for women under 25 and women 25 and older.

Description of Variables Covered

The interview focused on the woman's pregnancy history; her past and current use of contraception; ability to bear children (fecundity and infertility); use of medical services for family planning, infertility, and prenatal care; her marital history, occupation and labor force participation, and a wide range of social, economic, and demographic characteristics. Information on sexually transmitted diseases and extended information on adoption have been added to Cycle IV of the NSFG.

Number of Variables:

Respondent records	8,450
Pregnancy Interval records	15,760
Total records	24,210

Checklist of Topics Covered:

X Gender / Gender Role
X Race / Ethnicity
X Age
X Education
X Occupation / Employment
X Physical Health / Disease
X Nutrition
X Clinical Activities
X Biological Functioning / Development
X Mental Health / Disease
___ Psychological Functioning / Development
X Guidance / Counseling
X Personality
X Intellectual Functioning
X Residential Mobility
___ Dwelling
___ Neighborhood / Community
X Region / State
X Marriage and Divorce
X Cohabitation
X Family/Household Composition & Structure
___ Inter-Partner Relationships
___ Parent-Child Relationships
___ Inter-Sibling Relationships
___ Relationships with Other Kin

___ Relationships with Nonkin
___ Other Family/Household Characteristics
X Child Care
X Wealth / Finances / Material Things
X Receipt of Health, Mental Health, Social Services
X Adoption / Foster Care
X Childbearing / Pregnancy
X Out-of-Wedlock Pregnancy & Parenthood
X Abortion
X Sexuality
X Sex Education
X Contraception
X Sexually Transmitted Diseases
___ Civic/Political Activities
___ Friends / Social Activities Social Support
X Dating, Courtship
___ Recreation
X Religion
___ Crime / Delinquency / Behavior Problems
___ Substance Use
X Agency Characteristics
X Interview

Checklist of Key Variables

X Number of family members
X Identification of marital
   partners in family
___ Size of dwelling
___ Type of dwelling
X Urban/rural residence
X Region/state of residence
X Family income
X Religious affiliation
___ Relation of each family
   member to:
   ___ Reference person
   ___ All other members
___ Age of family members
   ___ Respondent
   ___ Others
X Sex of family members

X Respondent
___ Others
X Race of family members
   X Respondent
   X Others
___ Marital status of family
   members
   X Respondent
   X Others
X Education of family
   members
   X Respondent
   X Others
X Occupation of family
   members
   X Respondent
   X Others

LIMITATIONS

Since the focus of the survey is on fertility, the range of information on children under 15 and males 15-19 is limited. Under-reporting of abortion occurs in this, as in other household surveys. Also, since this is a survey of women, children living only with their fathers are not represented.

SPONSORSHIP

The survey was sponsored by the National Center for Health Statistics, Division of Vital Statistics, Family Growth Survey Branch. Funding for the 1988 survey was provided by NCHS as well as the Center for Population Research, NICHD; the Office of Population Affairs, OASH; the National Center for Health Statistics, CDC; and the Administration for Children, Youth, and Families, all within the Department of Health and Human Services.

GUIDE TO DATA AND DOCUMENTATION

File Structure

A public use tape is available from the National Technical Information Service. [1] Tape characteristics are as follows:

Label:	Standard Label
Tracks:	9
Density:	6250 bpi
Record Length:	3,553
Block Size:	31,977
Number of Records:	8,450 Respondent records
	15,760 Interval records
	24,210 Total records

List of Available Documentation

Documentation for the public used tape is included with purchase:

National Center for Health Statistics (1990). *National survey of family growth, cycle IV, 1988.* [Public Use Data Tape Documentation]. Hyattsville, MD.

Contact

To purchase the Public Use Tape and documentation, contact:

National Technical Information Service
5285 Port Royal Road
Springfield, VA 22161
(703) 487-4650

Individuals and educational institutions may obtain single copies of publications free of charge by writing:

Scientific and Technical Information Branch
National Center for Health Statistics
6525 Belcrest Road
Hyattsville, MD 20782

A current listing of NSFG, Cycle IV publications and copies of the Cycle IV questionnaire may be obtained by writing to:

Family Growth Survey Branch
Division of Vital Statistics
National Center for Health Statistics
6525 Belcrest Road
Hyattsville, MD 20782

Cost

The data tape and documentation cost $220.

Bachrach, C., London, K., & Maza, P. (1991, August). On the path to adoption: Adoption seeking in the U.S., 1988. *Journal of Marriage and the Family, 53*(3), 705-718.

Bachrach, C., Stolley, K., & London, K. (1992, January/February). Relinquishment of premarital births: Evidence from national survey data. *Family Planning Perspectives, 24*(1), 27-32.

Forrest, J., & Singh, S. (1990). The sexual and reproductive behavior of American women, 1986-1988. *Family Planning Perspectives, 22*(5), 206-214.

Goldscheider, C., & Mosher, W. (1991, March/April). Patterns of contraceptive use in the United States: The importance of religious factors. *Studies in Family Planning, 22*(2), 102-115.

Jones, E., & Forrest, J. (1992, January/February). Contraceptive failure rates based on the 1988 NSFG. *Family Planning Perspectives, 24*(1), 12-19.

Judkins, D., Mosher, W., & Botman, S. (1991). *National survey of family growth, cycle IV: Design, estimation and inference.* (Vital and Health Statistics, Series 2, No. 109). Hyattsville, MD: National Center for Health Statistics.

Kahn, J., & Anderson, K. (1992, February). Intergenerational patterns of teenage fertility. *Demography, 29*(1), 39-57.

Kahn, J., & London, K. (1991). Premarital sex and the risk of divorce. *Journal of Marriage and the Family, 53*(4), 845-855.

Kost, K., & Forrest, J. (1992, November/December). American women's sexual behavior and exposure to sexually transmitted diseases. *Family Planning Perspectives, 24*(6), 244-254.

London, K. (1990). *Cohabitation, marriage, marital dissolution, and remarriage: United States, 1988.* (Advance Data from Vital and Health Statistics, No. 194). Hyattsville, MD: National Center for Health Statistics.

McNally, J., & Mosher, W. (1991, May). *AIDS-related knowledge and behavior among women 15-44 years of age: United States, 1988.* (Advance Data from Vital and Health Statistics, No. 200). Hyattsville, MD: National Center for Health Statistics.

Mosher, W. (1990). Contraceptive practice in the United States, 1982-1988. *Family Planning Perspectives, 22*(5), 198-205.

Mosher, W. (1990). *Use of family planning services in the United States: 1982 and 1988.* (Advance Data from Vital and Health Statistics, No.184). Hyattsville, MD: National Center for Health Statistics.

Mosher, W., & McNally, J. (1991, May/June). Contraceptive use at first premarital intercourse: United States, 1965-1988. *Family Planning Perspectives, 23*(3), 108-116.

Mosher, W., & Pratt, W. (1990). *Fecundity and infertility in the United States, 1965-1988.* (Advance Data from Vital and Health Statistics, No. 192). Hyattsville, MD: National Center for Health Statistics.

Mosher, W., Williams, L., & Johnson, D. (1992). Religion and fertility in the United States: New patterns. *Demography, 29*(2), 199-214.

National Center for Health Statistics (1990). *National survey of family growth, cycle IV, 1988.* [Public Use Data Tape Documentation]. Hyattsville, MD.

National Center for Health Statistics (1991). Premarital sexual experience among adolescent women: United States, 1970-1988. *Morbidity and Mortality Weekly Report, 39*(51), 932.

Schwarz, S.M., Crutchfield, J. Jr., & Card, J.J. (1991). *National survey of family growth, cycle IV, 1988: A user's guide to the machine-readable files and documentation* (Data Set G7-G9). Los Altos, CA: Sociometrics Corporation, Data Archive on Adolescent Pregnancy and Pregnancy Prevention.

Seidman, L., Mosher, W., & Aral, S. (1992, October). Women with multiple sexual partners: United States, 1988. *American Journal of Public Health, 82*(10), 1388-1394.

Ventura, S., Taffel, S., Mosher, W., & Henshaw, S. (1992, November). *Trends in pregnancies and pregnancy rates, United States, 1980-88.* (Monthly Vital Statistics Report, Vol. 41. No. 6, Supplement). Hyattsville, MD: National Center for Health Statistics.

Wilcox, L., & Mosher, W. (1993, January/February). Factors associated with obtaining health screening among women of reproductive age. *Public Health Reports, 108*(1), 76-86.

Williams, L.B. (1991, September/October). Determinants of unintended childbearing among ever married women in the United States: 1973-1988. *Family Planning Perspectives, 23*(5), 212-215.

NOTES

[1]Alternately, users may purchase a slightly edited version of this data set from the Data Archive on Adolescent Pregnancy and Pregnancy Prevention, Sociometrics Corporation. Sociometrics received from NCHS a two volume tape containing a hierarchical data file, which included data for the respondent and data on each pregnancy the respondent experienced. To facilitate data analysis by nonexperts, DAAPPP staff created a rectangular data file containing all information for the respondent and a significant extract of the pregnancy history data: information on the first four pregnancies and the last pregnancy. Variable names were changed to reflect the indexing system employed by the DAAPPP archive. Additional machine-readable statements to document the data base's variables and valid values, and to transform the raw data file into an analysis file capable of being analyzed with SPSS, have been added by DAAPPP staff.

The data set (*DAAPPP Data Set No. G7-G9*) is available on mainframe tape or microcomputer floppy diskettes for a cost of $150. The files consist of: (1) the raw data;

and (2) SPSS program statements (SPSS-X for mainframe, SPSS/PC and SPSS/PC+ for microcomputer) designed to read the data file. A User's Guide accompanies each order. For ordering information contact: Sociometrics Corporation, 170 State Street, Suite 260, Los Altos, CA, 94022, (415) 949-3282.

28

NATIONAL SURVEY OF FAMILIES AND HOUSEHOLDS, 1988

James Sweet
Larry Bumpass
Vaughn Call

PURPOSE OF THE STUDY

The National Survey of Families and Households 1988 (NSFH) is a national survey designed to look at the causes and consequences of changes in American family and household structure. In each household, a primary respondent was interviewed, as was the spouse or cohabiting partner of the primary respondent, if such a person lived there. Survey questions covered a wide variety of topics, including basic demographic information, life history information, family process, effects of divorce, and child custody and child support arrangements following divorce.

NSFH 1988 addresses the limitations of previous sources of data on the American family by focusing almost exclusively on family issues, covering a broad range of family variables, addressing issues of importance to researchers working from a variety of theoretical perspectives, sampling a large enough group to permit subgroup comparisons and reliable statistical estimation, and selecting a sample representative of the total U.S. population. The survey permits not only the testing of competing hypotheses concerning a variety of aspects of the American family, but also the description of the current state of the family. The survey, while providing a cross-sectional look at American family life, will be the first round of a longitudinal survey. [1]

METHODS

Sampling Design

There were five stages of selection in the sample design. In Stage 1, 100 U.S. counties/county groups were selected with probability-proportional-to-size sampling. "Size" was based on 1985 population projections. These counties/county groups are referred to as Primary Sampling Units, or PSUs. In stage 2, subdistricts were selected within these PSUs. The number of subdistricts selected within a particular PSU depended on the population size of the PSU. The total number of subdistricts selected was 1,700, making the average 17 per PSU. These subdistricts are referred to as Secondary Sampling Units, or SSUs. In stage 3, one listing area was selected from each SSU. Listing areas contained 45 or more households. In stage 4, a "lister" was sent to each of the 1,700 listing areas to list all addresses within the listing area boundaries. Approximately 20 addresses in each listing area were selected for inclusion in the sample. Half of the households selected in this stage were randomly assigned to be in the main sample, and half to be in the oversample. In stage 5, interviewers screened each of these households, obtained a listing of all household members and determined one primary respondent.

The study included a national probability sample of approximately 9,643 households in the United States. An oversample of 3,374 households was taken for six household types: (1) African-American households; (2) Hispanic households; (3) households with children and one parent/guardian absent; (4) households with children who have a step parent; (5) households with children and both parents absent; and (6) households with couples married since January 1, 1982. A sample of secondary respondents was selected to complete self-administered questionnaires. Two groups of secondary respondents were sampled: spouses and cohabiting partners of respondents (in the same household); and other nonspouse, noncohabiting partner adults (in the same household).

For the main sample, respondents were selected randomly from the adult members of the household. The screening interview used to make this selection involved ascertaining the number of people who lived in the household, [2] and listing (in order of age) all members who were eligible for selection as the respondent. The respondent to be interviewed was then randomly selected from among the eligible adults by means of a pre-printed selection table.

For the oversample, the screener had to determine whether the household was eligible for inclusion in the oversample. The screener listed everyone in the household. The following four inquiries were conducted (where appropriate) to determine eligibility for the oversample: (1) the "informant's" race; (2) whether any children in the household under age 18 had a parent who died or no longer lived in the household; (3) whether any household member had been married since January 1, 1982; and (4) whether any couple (age 19 or older) lived together without being married. If the household met any one of these oversample selection criteria, the household was deemed eligible for inclusion in the study. [3] An adult member of the household was then randomly selected as the primary respondent. [4]

Periodicity

Interviews were conducted between March 1987 and May 1988.

Unit of Analysis

The individual was the unit of analysis.

Response Rates

The interview response rate was computed as completed interview/(successful screens—no eligible respondent). This was 73.5% for the main sample and 76.8% for the oversample.

Attrition

Not applicable.

CONTENT

Data Sources

Up to three interviews could be completed in a sampled household: in-person interview of the "primary" respondent; completion of a self-administered questionnaire from a primary respondent's spouse or cohabiting partner; and completion of a self-administered questionnaire from another nonspouse adult (head of household labelled "tertiary respondent" when the primary respondent was not the head of household).

Description of Questionnaire and Variables Covered

Spouse/Partner Questionnaire. There were two significant differences between these two questionnaires. First, in the spouse questionnaire, questions 50-68 deal with marriage and cohabitation prior to marriage. This section was replaced in the partner questionnaire with the following: dates of birth for all children; times married; (if previously married) how the prior marriage ended; and information on the current cohabitation relationship (date cohabitation started and marriage plans). Second, in the series of questions on parenting, cohabiting respondents were treated exactly like married persons. In other sections, however, cohabiting respondents were treated like persons living with nonrelatives. This is the case for questions about income, assets, and debt. Cohabiting partners were asked only about their own economic situation and not about the situation of their partner or other household members.

Tertiary Respondent Questionnaire. A goal of the National Survey of Families and Households was to gather information about households and the family and household experience of individuals. In most cases, the adult respondent was the householder or spouse of the head of household. However, in some cases the respondent is an adult son, daughter, or relative of or someone not related to the head of household. These three situations represent about 8 percent of all respondents. In these cases, asking for proxy reports from the respondent (about incomes, for example) about other members of the household was not reasonable. Accordingly, the investigators established a tertiary respondent questionnaire which was completed by the head of household in situations where the primary respondent was the adult son, daughter, or other relative of the householder. In situations where the respondent was a nonrelative (about 1 percent of the sample), the investigators did not ask the head of household to complete a questionnaire because of the diversity of this particular householder population. The questions on the tertiary respondent questionnaire assessed the perceived quality of the relationship between the primary and tertiary respondent, the economic exchanges involved, and sources of both problems and satisfactions in such living arrangements.

Number of Variables

NSFH 1988 contains 4,321 variables and 13,017 cases.

Checklist of Topics Covered

<u>X</u> Gender / Gender Role
<u>X</u> Race / Ethnicity
<u>X</u> Age
<u>X</u> Education
<u>X</u> Occupation / Employment
<u>X</u> Physical Health / Disease
___ Nutrition
___ Clinical Activities
___ Biological Functioning / Development
<u>X</u> Mental Health / Disease
<u>X</u> Psychological Functioning / Development
___ Guidance / Counseling
<u>X</u> Personality
___ Intellectual Functioning
<u>X</u> Residential Mobility
<u>X</u> Dwelling
<u>X</u> Neighborhood / Community
<u>X</u> Region / State
<u>X</u> Marriage and Divorce
<u>X</u> Cohabitation
<u>X</u> Family/Household Composition & Structure
<u>X</u> Inter-Partner Relationships
<u>X</u> Parent-Child Relationships
<u>X</u> Inter-Sibling Relationships
<u>X</u> Relationships with Other Kin

<u>X</u> Relationships with Nonkin
<u>X</u> Other Family/Household Characteristics
<u>X</u> Child Care
<u>X</u> Wealth / Finances / Material Things
<u>X</u> Receipt of Health, Mental Health, Social Services
<u>X</u> Adoption / Foster Care
<u>X</u> Childbearing / Pregnancy
<u>X</u> Out-of-Wedlock Pregnancy & Parenthood
___ Abortion
<u>X</u> Sexuality
___ Sex Education
<u>X</u> Contraception
___ Sexually Transmitted Diseases
<u>X</u> Civic/Political Activities
<u>X</u> Friends / Social Activities
___ Social Support
<u>X</u> Dating, Courtship
<u>X</u> Recreation
<u>X</u> Religion
<u>X</u> Crime / Delinquency / Behavior Problems
<u>X</u> Substance Use
___ Agency Characteristics
<u>X</u> Interview

Checklist of Key Variables

X Number of family members
X Identification of marital
  partners in family
X Size of dwelling
X Type of dwelling
X Urban/rural residence
X Region/state of residence
X Family income
X Religious affiliation
X Relation of each family
  member to:
  X Reference person
  ___ All other members
X Age of family members
  X Respondent
  X Others
X Sex of family members

X Respondent
X Others
X Race of family members
  X Respondent
  X Others
X Marital status of family
  members
  X Respondent
  X Others
X Education of family
  members
  X Respondent
  X Others
X Occupation of family
  members
  X Respondent
  X Others

LIMITATIONS

Sample weights were computed which take into account the sample design with the oversampling of members of minority groups and certain strategic family types, differential probability of selection within sample households depending on the number of adults in the household, differential screening response rates, differential response rates when screening was successful, and a post-stratification adjustment to align the weighted distributions by age, race/ethnicity, sex and region from the NSFH sample with those from the March 1988 Current Population Survey.

SPONSORSHIP

The survey was funded by the Center for Population Research of the National Institute of Child Health and Human Development and carried out by the Center for Demography and Ecology at the University of Wisconsin.

GUIDE TO DATA AND DOCUMENTATION

File Structure

Machine-readable data and documentation files are available in mainframe tape format or on CD-ROM for microcomputer. A description of the contents of each file is given below.

File 1a and 1b (Data): Raw data files. Tape 1 contains a raw data file with cases 1 to 8,000. Tape 2 contains a raw data file with cases 8,001 to 13,017. The format of both files is identical, and is described in the "data list" section of the SPSS program file (file 2). These two raw data files will need to be concatenated prior to analysis.

File 2 (SPSS Program): This file consists of SPSS-X program statements designed to read the raw data in file 1a and 1b, respectively, and create an SPSS-X active file. The SPSS-X program file contains data list statements, variable names and labels, value labels, and missing value declarations.

File 3 (SAS Program): This file consists of SAS program statements designed to read the raw data in file 1a and 1b, respectively, and create a SAS active file. The contents of this file are analogous to the contents of the previously described file 2. SPSS Users should use file 2; SAS users, file 3. Users may need to add "job control language" (JCL) statements to the SAS program file to meet the requirements for their specific operating system. For some operating systems, e.g., Unix, running the SAS program statements may result in a "segmentation violation" message from SAS due to a limit on the number of independent sets of format labels (the current limit is about 300) that can be assigned to variables. The SAS Institute plans to release an updated version of SAS early in 1993 that will correct the problem. Until then, if a segmentation violation occurs, one solution is to edit the SAS program statements to remove format (value label) assignments for all variables unrelated to the analysis at hand.

File 4 (Dictionary): Sequential list of variable and value labels. This file consists of DISPLAY DICTIONARY output describing the SPSS-X active file created by the program in File 2. Variables are listed in sequential order. Variable names and labels, value labels, missing value designations, print formats, and write formats are clearly displayed.

File 5 (Statistics): Unweighted frequencies or other descriptive statistics for each variable. Descriptive statistics only are provided for variables with more than 50 value categories, such as respondent identification number, zip codes, etc.

List of Available Documentation

A User's Guide which accompanies the machine-readable files provides the following information: Summary; General study overview; Description of machine-readable files and supplementary documentation; Specifications for machine-readable files; Key characteristics report; Distribution of variables by topic and type; and Data completeness and consistency report.

Paper versions of the machine-readable SPSS and SAS program files and data documentation (files 2-5 above), and copies of the original instrument and codebook, are available upon request (at 15 cents per page).

Contact

> Sociometrics Corporation
> American Family Data Archive
> 170 State Street, Suite 260
> Los Altos, California 94022-2812
> (415) 949-3282

Cost

The cost for the machine-readable data set (Data Set 01-05 of the American Family Data Archive) is $150. This price includes the raw data, SPSS program statements, the SAS program statements, the Dictionary, and the Frequencies on mainframe tape, and the accompanying printed and bound User's Guide. The CD-ROM version costs $175. Paper versions of the original NSFH Main Instrument cost $24.45; the Self-Enumerated Instrument, $9.75, and the Secondary Partner Instrument, $7.20. The original Codebook can be obtained for $160.20.

BIBLIOGRAPHY

Aquilino, W.S. (1991). *Effects of interview privacy on the collection of marital quality data* (NSFH Working Paper No. 46). Madison, WI: Center for Demography and Ecology.

Bumpass, L., & Sweet, J. (1989, November). National estimates of cohabitation. *Demography, 26*(4), 615-625.

Bumpass, L., Sweet, J., & Cherlin, A. (1991, November). The role of cohabitation in declining rates of marriage. *Journal of Marriage and Family, 53*(4), 913-927.

Bumpass, L., Castro Martin, T., & Sweet, J. (1991). The impact of family background and early marital factors on marital disruption. *Journal of Family Issues, 12*(1), 22-42.

Krecker, M.L. (1992). *Work history data in the national survey of families and households: An overview and preliminary assessment* (NSFH Working Paper No. 56). Madison, WI: Center for Demography and Ecology.

Lu, H. (1992). *Sibling contact among elderly Americans: Trends, patterns and determinants* (NSFH Working Paper No. 51). Madison, WI: Center for Demography and Ecology.

Manning, W. (1992). *The linkage between cohabitation and premarital fertility in the United States* (NSFH Working Paper No. 52). Madison, WI: Center for Demography and Ecology.

Marks, N. (1992). *Caregiving across the lifespan: A new national profile* (NSFH Working Paper No. 55). Madison, WI: Center for Demography and Ecology.

Marks, N. (1992). *Contemporary social demographics of American midlife parents* (NSFH Working Paper No. 54). Madison, WI: Center for Demography and Ecology.

Marks, N.F. (1992). *Remarried and single parents in middle adulthood: Differences in psychological well-being and relationships with adult children* (NSFH Working Paper No. 47). Madison, WI: Center for Demography and Ecology.

Marks, N.F., & McLanahan, S.S. (1992). *Gender and family structure differences in social integration among parents with resident children* (NSFH Working Paper No. 48). Madison, WI: Center for Demography and Ecology.

Seltzer, J.A., & Brandreth, Y. (1992). *What fathers say about involvement with children after separation* (NSFH Working Paper No. 57). Madison, WI: Center for Demography and Ecology.

Stone, V.E., Crutchfield, J.H., Colella, U.A., & Card, J.J. (1992). *National survey of families and households 1988: A user's guide to the machine-readable files and documentation.* Los Altos, CA: Sociometrics Corporation, American Family Data Archive.

Sweet, J., Bumpass, L., & Call, V.. (1988). *The design and content of the national survey of families and households* (NSFH Working Paper No. 1). Madison, WI: Center for Demography and Ecology.

Sweet, J. (1989). *Differentials in secondary respondent response rates* (NSFH Working Paper No. 7). Madison, WI: Center for Demography and Ecology.

Sweet, J. (1990). *Differentials in precision of reporting of dates of marital events in the national survey of families and households* (NSFH Working Paper No. 20). Madison, WI: Center for Demography and Ecology.

Sweet, J.A., & Bumpass, L. (1992). Young adults' views of marriage, cohabitation, and family. In S.J. South and S.E. Tolnay, (Eds.), *The changing American family*. Boulder, CO: Westview Press.

Sweet, J., & Bumpass, L. (1992). Disruption of marital and cohabitation relationships: A social-demographic perspective. In T. Orbuch (Ed.), *Close relationship loss: Theoretical approaches* (pp. 67-89). New York: Springer-Verlag.

Thomson, E. (1992). *Work schedules and time with children* (NSFH Working Paper No. 53). Madison, WI: Center for Demography and Ecology.

Thomson, E., & Li, M. (1992). *Family structure and children's kin* (NSFH Working Paper No. 49). Madison, WI: Center for Demography and Ecology.

Van Hook, J.V.W., & Thomson, E. (1992). *Occupation, parental goals, and children's academic attainment* (NSFH Working Paper No. 50). Madison, WI: Center for Demography and Ecology.

Wu, L.L., & Martinson, B.C. (1991). *Family structure and the risk of a premarital birth* (NSFH Working Paper No. 45). Madison, WI: Center for Demography and Ecology.

NOTES

[1]The investigators plan a five-year longitudinal follow-up. The five-year follow-up will permit analyses of the effects of experience, characteristics, and attitudes measured in the initial survey on subsequent life course transitions. The investigators hope that respondents of all ages can be followed to permit analyses of life events. Topics include leaving the parental home; marriage; first and subsequent births; marital disruption; and retirement.

[2] Questions about whether any household members were away at school or in the armed forces were also included in the screening interview. Those who resided in barracks (versus a dorm) were eligible to be respondents.

[3] The eligibility for selection as the respondent was slightly different in the two samples. In the oversample, members of the household who lived away from home in dorms or military barracks were not eligible for selection as the primary respondent; neither were persons age 18 living in households with no one age 19 or older.

[4] The randomly selected adult respondent was not *necessarily* a person who had any of the oversample characteristics. For example, the primary respondent could be a white person married to a Mexican American "informant," or may be a noncohabiting person in a multi-adult household which included a cohabiting couple.

29

VITAL STATISTICS ON MARRIAGE AND DIVORCE, 1968-1988

National Center for Health Statistics

PURPOSE OF THE STUDY

The National Center for Health Statistics promotes uniform collection of birth, death, fetal death, marriage and divorce records in a national registration system; analyzes and interprets official vital statistics; integrates technical and legal aspects of the vital registration system; conducts surveys to expand the scope of national vital statistics beyond the data usually available from vital records; uses actuarial methods to construct annual life tables, and investigates the quality and reliability of data methodology.

Marriage and divorce statistics are based on information from two sources: (1) complete counts of events obtained from all states and (2) data on characteristics from marriage and divorce certificates from states meeting certain reporting criteria. The latter are available from the years 1968-1988 in machine-readable form. These data provide information on marriages and divorces and on the people involved in marriages and divorces (including children involved in divorce) for the largest possible number of states.

METHODS

Sampling Design

Registration areas for the collection of marriage and divorce statistics were established in 1957 and 1958 respectively. These areas include states with adequate programs for collecting marriage and divorce statistics. Criteria for participation in the registration areas are:

A central file of marriage and divorce records

A statistical report form conforming closely in content to the U. S. Standard License and Certificate of Marriage or Standard Certificate of Divorce, Dissolution of Marriage or Annulment

Regular reporting to the state office by all local areas in which marriages or divorces are recorded

Tests for completeness and accuracy of marriage or divorce registration carried out in cooperation with NCHS.

Marriage data are classified by state of occurrence. From 1968-1970, the marriage-registration area included 39 states and the District of Columbia; two additional states were included in 1971; one additional state was included in 1979 and there has been no further change through 1988. Data are not classified for counties or cities.

Divorce data are classified by state of occurrence. The divorce-registration area included 26 states in 1968, 28 states for 1969-1970, 29 states for 1971-1977, 28 states in 1978, 30 states for 1979-1980, and 31 states for 1981-1988, and 31 states and the District of Columbia for 1986-1988. Data are not classified for counties or cities.

The marriage sample was designed to yield estimates of state totals as well as frequency distributions by characteristics of the bride and groom. These estimates were made for the total MRA and each state in the MRA. A sampling rate was designated for each of the MRA states so that the selected sample for it would consist of at least 2,500 records. Five different sampling rates were used: All records, 1/2, 1/5, 1/10, and 1/20. Sampling procedures for the divorce sample parallel those for the marriage sample. Overall, in 1981 about 39 percent of all marriages in the MRA were included in the sample, and about 46 percent of all divorces in the DRA were included.

Samples of marriage records for the entire United States (except Arizona, New Mexico, and Oklahoma) are available for the census years of 1970 and 1980.

Periodicity

Data tapes for both marriage and divorce certificate data are available for the individual years from 1968 to 1988.

Unit of Analysis

The unit of analysis is the marriage or divorce event.

Response Rates

Not applicable to this study.

Attrition

Not applicable to this study.

CONTENT

Data Sources

Marriage data include all marriages occurring in states that meet reporting criteria for inclusion in the marriage-registration area. Marriages occurring outside the marriage-registration area are not included. Data are obtained from certificates of marriages occurring in each registration state. Records of each state in the marriage-registration area were sampled at one of five sampling rates used in processing 1968-88 data. Data are weighted, based on the sampling fraction of the reporting state.

Divorce data include all divorces occurring in states that meet reporting criteria for inclusion in the divorce-registration area. Divorces occurring outside the divorce-registration area are not included. Data are obtained from certificates of divorces occurring in each registration state. Records of each state in the divorce-registration area were sampled at one of five sampling rates used in processing 1968-87 data. Data are weighted, based on the sampling fraction of the reporting state.

Description of Variables Covered

The Marriage Data Tape is a microdata computer file consisting of marriage certificate records that include data for bride and groom, including age, date of birth, race, education, previous marital status, number of this marriage, date of last marriage, state of birth, state of marriage, state of residence, type of ceremony, and related characteristics.

List of Variables in 1968-88 Marriage Data Tapes

1. Data year
2. Age of:
   - Bride
   - Groom
3. Date of birth (month/year):
   - Bride
   - Groom
4. Date of marriage (month/day)
5. Day of week of marriage
6. Date of last marriage ended [1] (month/year) (1970-88):
   - Bride
   - Groom
7. Education [1] (1970-88):
   - Bride
   - Groom
8. Interval from last marriage to present marriage [1] (1970-88):
   - Bride
   - Groom
9. Number of this marriage: [1]
   - Bride
   - Groom
10. Previous marital status: [1]
    - Bride
    - Groom
11. Race: [1]
    - Bride (three categories)
    - Groom (three categories)
12. State of birth [1] (1969-88):
    - Bride
    - Groom
13. State of residence: [2]
    - Bride
    - Groom
14. Type of Ceremony [1] (1972-88)
15. Record Weight
16. State, Division and Region of Marriage

The Divorce Data Tape is a microdata computer file consisting of divorce certificate records that include data for date of marriage, date of separation, plaintiff, state of marriage, state of divorce, total number of living children, and for each husband and wife: age at decree, age at separation, date of birth, education, race, number of this marriage, number of previous marriages, and related items.

List of Variables in 1968-88 Divorce Data Tapes

1. Data year
2. Age at decree and at marriage:
    Husband
    Wife
3. Age at separation [1] (1970-87):
    Husband
    Wife
4. Date of birth (month/year):
    Husband
    Wife
5. Petitioner (1974-88)
6. Date of marriage (month/year)
7. Date of separation [1] (month/year; 1970-88)
8. Duration of marriage
9. Interval from marriage to separation
10. Interval from separation to decree
11. Education [1] (1970-88):
    Husband
    Wife
12. Month of Divorce
13. Number of children under 18 years of age
14. Number of this marriage: [1]
    Husband
    Wife
15. Number of previous marriages ended by death [1] (1970-88):
    Husband
    Wife
16. Number of previous marriages ended by divorce [1] (1970-88):
    Husband
    Wife

17. Race (three categories): [1]
    Husband
    Wife
18. State of marriage [1] (1972-88)
19. State of divorce
20. State of residence (1976-88):
    Husband
    Wife
21. Total number of living children [1] (1970-88)
22. Record Weight

Number of Variables

There are approximately 2 dozen variables in each file.

Checklist of Topics Covered

X Gender / Gender Role
X Race / Ethnicity
X Age
X Education
___ Occupation / Employment
___ Physical Health / Disease
___ Nutrition
___ Clinical Activities
___ Biological Functioning / Development
___ Mental Health / Disease
___ Psychological Functioning / Development
___ Guidance / Counseling
___ Personality
___ Intellectual Functioning
___ Residential Mobility
___ Dwelling
___ Neighborhood / Community
X Region / State
___ Marriage and Divorce
___ Cohabitation
___ Family/Household Composition & Structure
___ Inter-Partner Relationships
___ Parent-Child Relationships
___ Inter-Sibling Relationships
___ Relationships with Other Kin

___ Relationships with Nonkin
___ Other Family/Household Characteristics
___ Child Care
___ Wealth / Finances / Material Things
___ Receipt of Health, Mental Health, Social Services
___ Adoption / Foster Care
___ Childbearing / Pregnancy
___ Out-of-Wedlock Pregnancy & Parenthood
___ Abortion
___ Sexuality
___ Sex Education
___ Contraception
___ Sexually Transmitted Diseases
___ Civic/Political Activities
___ Friends / Social Activities
___ Social Support
___ Dating, Courtship
___ Recreation
___ Religion
___ Crime / Delinquency / Behavior Problems
___ Substance Use
___ Agency Characteristics
___ Interview

Checklist of Key Variables

<u>X</u> Number of family members
<u>X</u> Identification of marital
    partners in family
___ Size of dwelling
___ Type of dwelling
___ Urban/rural residence
<u>X</u> Region/state of residence
___ Family income
___ Religious affiliation
___ Relation of each family
    member to:
    ___ Reference person
    ___ All other members
<u>X</u> Age of family members
    <u>X</u> Respondent
    ___ Others
<u>X</u> Sex of family members

    <u>X</u> Respondent
    ___ Others
<u>X</u> Race of family members
    <u>X</u> Respondent
    ___ Others
<u>X</u> Marital status of family
    members
    <u>X</u> Respondent
    ___ Others
<u>X</u> Education of family
    members
    <u>X</u> Respondent
    ___ Others
___ Occupation of family
    members
    ___ Respondent
    ___ Others

LIMITATIONS

Many states are not included in the MRA and DRA.

SPONSORSHIP

Data on marriages and divorces and of the persons involved for the states that constitute the marriage-registration area (MRA) and the divorce-registration area (DRA) are based on information from two sources. For some states, samples of records are drawn by the National Center for Health Statistics (NCHS) from microfilm copies of the original certificates received from the state registration offices. Other states submit computer tapes to NCHS through the Vital Statistics Cooperative Program (VSCP). For these states the complete file is used. Statistical data for 1988 for both marriages and divorces were provided through the VSCP by eight states—Illinois, Missouri, Nebraska, New York, (Except New York City marriages), Rhode Island, South Carolina, Vermont, and Virginia. Precoded marriage data were also provided by Florida, Maine, Montana, and New Hampshire.

GUIDE TO DATA AND DOCUMENTATION

File Structure

Data tapes are available for individual years from 1968 to 1988. The marriage and divorce data files are fixed length, blocked files. Specific characteristics for each file and year are listed in Table 1 on the next page.

Table 1. File Structure

Data year	Marriage File				Divorce File			
	Record length	Block size	Number of records	Number of reels	Record length	Block size	Number of records	Number of reels
1968	85	1,700	183,165	1	85	1,700	62,078	1
1969	85	1,700	189,919	1	85	1,700	72,272	1
1970	140	2,800	192,609	1	140	2,800	80,898	1
1971	140	2,800	211,096	1	140	2,800	91,431	1
1972	140	2,800	287,241	2	140	2,800	98,981	1
1973	140	2,800	302,809	2	140	2,800	107,160	1
1974	140	2,800	297,817	2	140	2,800	114,445	1
1975	140	2,800	494,312	3	140	2,800	169,904	1
1976	140	2,800	553,893	3	140	2,800	194,658	1
1977	140	2,800	667,945	3	140	2,800	245,693	2
1978	140	2,800	682,470	3	140	2,800	247,504	2
1979[1]	140	14,000	706,302	1	140	2,800	273,819	1
1980	140	14,000	749,691	1	140	14,000	271,180	1
1981	140	14,000	732,261	1	140	14,000	279,513	1
1982	140	14,000	747,233	1	140	14,000	272,683	1
1983	140	14,000	748,047	1	140	14,000	272,327	1
1984	140	14,000	762,597	1	140	14,000	273,224	1
1985	140	14,000	747,711	1	140	14,000	277,400	1
1986	140	14,000	787,926	1	140	14,000	279,251	1
1987	140	14,000	788,317	1	140	14,000	281,246	1
1988	140	14,000	784,211	1	140	14,000	277,434	1

[1] Started recording at 6250 bpi.

List of Available Documentation

The data tape package contains the necessary documentation, including tape content and technical information, needed to access the marriage and divorce data. Control total tables are also included for both data sets.

Contact

For data tapes, diskettes and documentation, contact:

The National Technical Information Service (NTIS)
5285 Port Royal Road
Springfield, VA 22161
(703) 487-4650

For substantive questions or to obtain reports that relate to the data, contact:

Barbara Foley Wilson
Natality, Marriage, and Divorce Statistics Branch
National Center for Health Statistics
6525 Belcrest Road
Hyattsville, MD 20782
(301) 436-8954

Cost

The prices listed in Table 2 on the next page were current as of 1990.

Table 2. Price List

Data year	VITAL STATISTICS, MARRIAGE			VITAL STATISTICS, DIVORCE		
	Accession No.	Price (U.S.)	(Foreign)	Accession No.	Price (U.S.)	(Foreign)
1968	PB-235645	$220	$440	PB-238824	$220	$440
1969	PB-235646	220	440	PB-238825	220	440
1970	PB80-186331	220	440	PB80-186745	220	440
1971	PB80-186356	220	440	PB80-187164	220	440
1972	PB80-185887	340	680	PB80-187180	220	440
1973	PB80-186273	340	680	PB80-187149	220	440
1974	PB80-185846	340	680	PB80-187123	220	440
1975	PB80-185903	450	900	PB80-186786	220	440
1976	PB80-185861	450	900	PB80-186760	220	440
1977	PB80-185804	450	900	PB80-186729	340	680
1978	PB81-164733	450	900	PB81-100216	340	680
1979	PB81-238743	450	900	PB81-238800	220	440
1980	PB83-261610	450	900	PB83-242644	220	440
1981	PB84-164201	450	900	PB84-164185	220	440
1982	PB85-221646	450	900	PB85-179430	220	440
1983	PB86-185923	450	900	PB86-165248	220	440
1984	PB87-197109	450	900	PB87-125506	220	440
1985	PB88-181987	450	900	PB88-127865	220	440
1986	PB89-221709	450	900	PB89-209415	220	440
1987	PB90-501842	450	900	PB90-501891	220	440
1988	PB92-500743	240	480	PB91-507731	240	480

BIBLIOGRAPHY

National Center for Health Statistics. (1987). *Vital statistics of the United States, 1987, Vol. 3 - marriage and divorce* (DHHS Publication No. (PHS) 91-1103). Washington, DC: U.S. Government Printing Office.

National Center for Health Statistics. (1990). *Catalog of electronic data products* (DHHS Publication No. (PHS) 90-1213). Washington, DC: U.S. Government Printing Office.

National Center for Health Statistics. (1991). Advance report of final marriage statistics, 1988. *Monthly Vital Statistics Report, 40*(4, Supplement) (DHHS Publication No. (PHS) 91-1120). Washington, DC: U.S. Government Printing Office.

National Center for Health Statistics. (1991). Advance report of final divorce statistics, 1988. *Monthly Vital Statistics Report, 39*(12, Suppl. 2) (DHHS Publication No. (PHS) 91-1120). Washington, DC: U.S. Government Printing Office.

National Center for Health Statistics, London, K.A. (1989). Children of divorce. *Vital and Health Statistics, 21*(46) (DHHS Publication No. (PHS) 89-1924). Washington, DC: U.S. Government Printing Office.

National Center for Health Statistics, Wilson, B.F. (1989). Remarriages and subsequent divorces, United States. *Vital and Health Statistics, 21*(45) (DHHS Publication No. (PHS) 89-1923). Washington, DC: U.S. Government Printing Office.

National Center for Health Statistics, Wilson, B.F. (1985). Teenage marriage and divorce, United States, 1970-1981. *Vital and Health Statistics, 20*(43) (DHHS Publication No. (PHS) 85-1921). Washington, DC: U.S. Government Printing Office.

NOTES

[1]Applicable only for those states having information on the certificate.

[2]Beginning in 1970 the place of residence for brides or grooms who were nonresidents of the United States has been coded to the country of residence (8 categories). Formerly these persons were considered resident brides or grooms of the place of occurrence.

30

THE AMERICAN FAMILY DATA LIBRARY

Josefina J. Card
Sociometrics Corporation

OVERVIEW

A library collection of state-of-the-art research data on the status and well-being of the American family is now available through Sociometrics Corporation. The *American Family Data Archive* (AFDA) consists of 3 CD-ROMs with machine-readable raw data and documentation from 36 data sets spanning over a dozen nationally recognized studies. Brief descriptions of each data set in the collection are included below. The reader is also directed to the more detailed abstracts contained in the preceding chapters of this book.

Each of the approximately 20,000 variables in the Archive has been coded into one of fifty topics (e.g., Adoption, Child Care, Health, Occupation, Sexuality), and one of seventeen types (e.g., Attitude, Behavior, History). The code for each variable's topic, type, and study of origin are embedded in that variable's unique 8-character name. Each variable has been labelled in standard format and the set of included variables can be searched by topic, type, study of origin, variable label (question), value label (answer), or any combination thereof. Five standard files are provided for each data set: raw data, program statements for use with the SPSS statistical analysis software package, program statements for use with the SAS statistical analysis software package, SPSS Dictionary of all variables, and SPSS frequencies and univariate statistics of all variables.

A User's Guide for each archived study describes: an overview of the study's purpose and methods, a description of the machine-readable files, a report on data completeness and consistency, and a list of all variables sorted by topic and type. Copies of the original data collection questionnaires and instruments are available for separate, optional purchase.

A unique search & retrieval software program, developed at Sociometrics, is included with the collection. This software is capable of searching for variables by topic, type, keyword, and data source, and building customized SPSS and SAS program statements to extract data subsets meeting user-defined criteria.

Data Set Nos. 01-05: National Survey of Families and Households, 1988 (James Sweet, Larry Bumpass, & Vaughn Call).

The **National Survey of Families and Households, 1988** is a national survey designed to look at the causes and consequences of changes in the American family and household structure. It includes interviews with a probability sample of 13,017 respondents conducted between March of 1987 and May of 1988. The sample includes a main cross-section sample of 9,643 households in the United States, plus a double sampling of blacks, Puerto Ricans, Mexican Americans, single-parent families, families with stepchildren, and cohabiting or recently married couples. In each household, a primary respondent was interviewed, as was the spouse or cohabiting partner of the primary resident, if such a person lived there. Survey questions covered a wide variety of topics, such as basic demographic information, life history information, family process, stepparenting, attitudes towards cohabitation without marriage, sibling relationships, effects of divorce, child custody and child support arrangements following divorce. There are a total of 4,321 variables, and the response rate was 73.5% in the main sample and 76.8% in the oversample. Chapter 27 in this book describes this study in more detail.

Data Set Nos. 06-12: 1976-1987 National Survey of Children: Waves 1, 2, and 3 (Nicholas Zill, James L. Peterson, Kristin A. Moore, & Frank F. Furstenberg, Jr.)

A three-wave longitudinal study was carried out by the Foundation for Child Development in 1976 (Wave 1) and by Child Trends, Inc. in 1981 and 1987 (Waves 2 and 3) in which the child was the focus of a personal interview with parents and children themselves. The purpose of Wave 1 was to assess the physical, social, and psychological well-being of different groups of American children; develop a profile of the way children live and the care they receive; permit analysis of the relationships between the condition of children's lives and measures of child development and well-being; and replicate items from previous national studies of child and parents to permit analysis of trends over time. Wave 2 focused on the effects of marital conflict and disruption on children. The third wave of data examined the social, psychological, and economic well-being of sample members as they became young adults. Further, for the first two waves, a teacher from the child's school answered questions on the child's academic performance and atmosphere. A total of 4,118 variables provide data on 1,423 children. Chapter 5 in this book describes this study in more detail.

Data Set Nos. 13-14: National Child Care Survey 1990: Parent Study (Sandra L. Hofferth, April Brayfield, Sharon Deich, Pamela Holcomb, & Frederic Glantz).

The **National Child Care Survey** is a nationally representative study of 4,392 households with one or more children under age 13 conducted in late 1989 and early 1990. The study consisted of a survey of parents in randomly selected households with children under age 13 (the Parent Study), a survey of individuals who provide child care in their own homes, a survey of child care providers used by the respondents in the Parent Study, a low-income substudy, and a military substudy. This data set includes only data from the Parent Study. The low-income substudy has been archived separately as AFDA Data Set Nos. 20-21. This study focused on the issue of child care arrangements, how child care affects parental employment patterns, how parents make decisions about child care, and the characteristics of the settings in which child care is provided. Extensive data on employment history were gathered, including the relationship between work and child care in the past. Basic demographic information such as income, education, and ethnic group is also included. There are 1,418 variables in all. The questionnaire was administered over the telephone with the interviewer using a CATI (Computer Aided Telephone Interview) system. Interviewers successfully screened 82.6% of the households contacted, and completed interviews at 69.4% of the eligible households, making the overall response rate 57.4% (69.4% X 82.6%). Chapter 1 in this book describes this study in more detail.

Data Set Nos. 15-16: A Profile of Child Care Settings: Home-Based Program, 1990 (Ellen Eliason Kisker & Valarie Piper).

The **Profile of Child Care Settings** Study was conducted for the U.S. Department of Education with the primary objective of determining the levels and characteristics of early education and care that are available in the United States. Telephone interviews were conducted with nationally representative samples of regulated home-based family day care providers and center-based early education and care programs between October 1989 and February 1990 using computer-assisted telephone interviewing (CATI) methods. The final samples included 583 regulated home-based family day care providers and 2,089 center-based programs (archived as AFDA Data Set Nos. 17-18). This data set focuses on the survey of 583 home-based programs.

The survey of home-based family care programs collected extensive data on a number of topics including care provided, children's activities, costs and income, help with child care, health and safety, and caregiver characteristics. There are 633 variables in all, seven of which provide demographic information about the counties where the home-based programs are located. The 583 cases on file represent an 87.1% completion rate among sampled programs eligible for the study. Chapter 2 in this book describes this study in more detail.

Data Set Nos. 17-18: A Profile of Child Care Settings: Center-Based Programs, 1990 (Ellen Eliason Kisker & Valarie Piper).

The **Profile of Child Care Settings** Study was conducted for the U.S. Department of Education with the primary objective of determining the levels and characteristics of early education and care that are available in the United States. Telephone interviews were conducted with nationally representative samples of regulated home-based family day care providers and center-based early education and care programs between October 1989 and February 1990 using computer-assisted telephone interviewing (CATI) methods. The final samples included 583 regulated home-based family day care providers (archived as AFDA Data Set Nos. 15-16), and 2,089 center-based programs. This data set focuses on the survey of 2,089 center-based programs.

The survey of center-based early education and care programs collected extensive data on a number of topics including general characteristics, admission policies and vacancies, types of children served, subsidies, staff, curriculum and activities, meals, health and safety, and operating experiences. There are 887 variables in all, seven of which provide demographic information about the counties where the center-based programs are located. The 2,089 cases on file represent an 88.7% completion rate among sampled programs eligible for the study. Chapter 2 in this book describes this study in more detail.

Data Set No. 19: National Commission on Children: 1990 Survey of Parents and Children (Kristin A. Moore).

The 1990 Survey of Parents and Children was sponsored by the National Commission on Children, and is a national telephone interview opinion survey conducted among 1,738 parents in the continental United States who live with their children. The survey collected nationally representative data on the current state of family life, the quality of the relationship between parents and their children and their interactions with the major institutions affecting the family, such as, schools, the workplace, neighborhoods, and religious and civic organizations. Subjects were identified from a national random sample of telephone numbers plus supplemental random samples of families with Black and Hispanic children. The response rate was 71% for parents, and approximately 81% for child interviews within these families. Chapter 4 in this book describes this study in more detail.

Data Set Nos. 20-21: National Child Care Survey 1990: Low-Income Substudy (Sandra L. Hofferth, April Brayfield, Sharon Deich, Pamela Holcomb, & Frederic Glantz).

The study is a nationally representative survey of 972 households with total annual incomes below $15,000 and one or more children under age 13. The survey was conducted in February-July of 1990 and focused on what kinds of child care arrangements respondents used, how those arrangements were chosen, and how they were paid for. The survey included a schedule of when the respondent and his or her spouse or partner was at work, and a schedule of when each child was at each child care arrangement to provide a detailed picture of the correspondence between child care arrangements and work. Extensive data on employment history were gathered, including the relationship between work and child care in the past. Basic demographic information such as income, education, and ethnic group is also included. There are 1,419 variables in all.

The questionnaire was administered over the telephone with the interviewer using a CATI (Computer Aided Telephone Interview) system. The Low-Income Substudy was designed to supplement the number of low-income households included in a larger "main" child care study (archived separately as AFDA Data Set Nos. 13-14). A total of 430 parent interviews were completed with eligible low-income households as part of the low-income substudy, resulting in an interviewer completion rate among eligible households of 78%. Combining these 430 interviews with the 672 low-income interviews from the main study yields a total of 1,102 low-income parent interviews. Of these, only 974 actually had family incomes under $15,000 and are included in this substudy. Chapter 1 in this book describes this study in more detail.

Data Set Nos. 22-24: Marital Instability Over the Life Course: 1981-1988 (Alan Booth, David J. Johnson, Lynn K. White, & John N. Edwards).

This study consists of data drawn from a three-wave panel study on marital instability. Five major dimensions of marital quality formed the foci of the study: divorce proneness (or marital instability), marital problems, marital happiness, marital interaction, and marital disagreements. Initially, the investigators devoted considerable attention to female labor force participation as it related to marital dissolution and divorce proneness. For the last two waves, the investigators drew heavily on a life course perspective to guide their investigation. Life course theories emphasize the extent to which social behaviors are a product of individuals' relative positions along a developmental continuum. A total of 2,033 cases and 1,593 variables were assessed across the three waves. Topics addressed in the study include: demographics (i.e., household characteristics, race, income, religion, education, etc.); marital/divorce history; pre-marital courtship history; marital behavior (e.g., division of labor, quarreling/violence); mental and physical health of husband and wife; employment (history, status, attitudes, and aspirations); attitudes about children; satisfaction about various aspects of life (e.g., marriage, home, community, etc.); problem areas in marriage; divorce/separation (including previous discussions of and current behavior, attitudes about divorce); and involvement with friends, relatives, voluntary associations, and the community. Chapter 22 in this book describes this study in more detail.

Data Set Nos. 25-27: Stanford Child Custody Study: Family, 1984-1990 and **Data Set Nos. 28-30: Stanford Child Custody Study: Child, 1984-1990** (Eleanor E. Maccoby, Robert H. Mnookin, & Charlene E. Depner).

The Stanford Child Custody Project embodies two studies. Study I focuses on the evolution of child custody arrangements in divorcing families and is comprised of two data sets ("Family" focused and "Child" focused). Study II is a follow-up of adolescents from the Study I sample. Study II data are still being analyzed by the original investigators as of this writing and are not yet publicly available. The data set archived by Sociometrics concerns the family-focused data from Study I.

The Stanford Child Custody Study, 1984-1990 (Study I) is a three-wave, longitudinal study of post-divorce child custody arrangements. The study is based on a sample of 1,124 families who filed for divorce in two California counties between September 1984 and April 1985. The first interview, conducted shortly after the divorce filing, provided information on family background; number, age, and sex of children; financial resources; and education, occupation, and work schedule of the two parents. It also inquired extensively into the negotiation and dispute-resolution process the couple engaged in as they tried to arrive at an agreement on financial and custodial matters. Particular attention was given to the involvement of attorneys, mediators, and other professionals. In addition, the questions explored the degree of conflict between the former spouses, any logistical problems associated with maintaining custodial and visitation arrangements, the children's reaction to the divorce, and the presence or absence of coordination between the parents with respect to the child's upbringing. In Wave II (conducted one year after the filing) and Wave III (conducted three years after the filing), many Wave I items were replicated, several items were dropped, and new items were added, including several items taken from court records and additional items on the payment of child support and legal events in the divorce process. Because Wave III interviews were conducted three years after the initial filing, most divorce cases were either completed or in their final phases. At this point, both retrospective and prospective information was valuable, as parents moved into new family/partner relationships and settled into new household routines. Chapter 6 in this book describes this study in more detail.

Data Set No. 31: 1975 National Family Violence Survey (Murray A. Straus & Richard J. Gelles).

The **1975 National Family Violence Survey** explores conflict/resolution and violence in the family. The survey was conducted by Family Research Laboratory at University of New Hampshire, and interviews were conducted among households in which at least one couple resided using a national probability sampling technique. The survey was designed to show that physical violence between family members is more frequent than believed. There are a total of 2,143 cases and 807 variables included in the study. Topics in the study include: demographics, (household characteristics and composition, race, income, religion, education, etc.); marital/divorce history; marital behavior (conflict/violence and resolution); employment (history, status); and satisfaction/attitudes about various aspects of life. A similar study (AFDA Data Set No. 32) was conducted in 1985 to track changes in the occurrence of family violence between 1975 and 1985. Chapter 25 in this book describes this study in more detail.

Data Set No. 32: 1985 National Family Violence Survey (Murray A. Straus & Richard J. Gelles).

The **1985 National Family Survey** was conducted by Family Research Laboratory at the University of New Hampshire and explores conflict/resolution and violence in the family. It is a national cross-sectional survey which can be compared to a similar study conducted by the investigators in 1975 (AFDA Data Set No. 31). The Survey was designed to show that physical violence between family members is more frequent than believed. One objective of the 1985 survey was to generate comparisons of the incidence of intra-family physical violence by race and ethnicity. Another objective was to generate state-by-state estimates of family violence. There are a total of 6,002 cases and 567 variables included in the study. Topics in the study include: demographics (household characteristics and composition, race, income, religion, education, etc.); marital and divorce history; marital behavior (conflict/violence and resolution); employment (history, status); and satisfaction/attitudes about various aspects of life. Chapter 25 in this book describes this study in more detail.

Data Set Nos. 33-34: National Health Interview Survey on Child Health, 1988 (National Center for Health Statistics).

The **1988 National Health Interview Survey on Child Health** (NHIS-CH) was conducted by the National Center for Health Statistics (NCHS), and cosponsored by the National Institute for Child Health and Human Development and the Health Resources and Services Administration. The U.S. Census Bureau directed field work for the survey. The National Health Interview Survey (NHIS) is a continuous, cross-sectional survey representing the household population of the United States. Each year the NHIS collects basic health and demographic information by face-to-face interviews with a sample of about 122,000 family members in about 47,000 families. For the 1988 NHIS-CH, additional information was collected for one randomly selected child zero to seventeen years of age in each NHIS sample household.

Topics covered in the 1988 NHIS-CH interview included child care, marital history of the child's parents, geographic mobility, circumstances of the pregnancy and birth, injuries, impairments, acute conditions, chronic conditions, passive smoking, sleep habits, school problems, developmental problems, and use of health care services. The resulting data set for this survey includes 1,347 variables and 17,110 cases. Chapter 13 in this book describes this study in more detail.

Data Set Nos. 35-36: Treatment Process: A Problem at Three Levels, 1988 (Gerald R. Patterson & Patricia Chamberlain).

This study investigates the process of therapeutic intervention in the treatment of oppositional children and their parents. As part of an ongoing program of empirical investigation of treatment process variables, Patterson and Chamberlain employ nonreactive observational measures of behavior to assess the effects of family management training on the behavior of extremely antisocial, preadolescent children.

This data set is comprised of two separate raw data files generated from this research. Data Set No. 35 includes therapist-client verbal interaction codes for 73 families participating in the Parent Training treatment program conducted at the Oregon Social Learning Center (OSLC). Three phases of treatment were videotaped. Verbal interactions were coded with the Therapy Process Coding System developed at OSLC. Data Set No. 36 includes demographic data gathered during the treatment intake interview. Chapter 16 in this book describes this study in more detail.

EDUCATIONAL TOOLKIT

Also included in the collection is a *Family Research Toolkit* which provides an introduction to secondary analysis of archived data. The *Toolkit* includes a workbook and machine-readable data extracted from AFDA Data Set Nos. 06-12, the **1976-1987 National Survey of Children.** The exercises in the workbook allow the novice researcher or student to use survey data to answer questions about the experiences of children, adolescents and young adults in the United States. In the process, the user learns how to prepare data for analysis, masters basic statistical techniques, and learns SPSS, one of the most widely-used computer statistics packages. An Instructor's Manual contains the solutions to questions asked in the workbook.

CONTACT AND COST INFORMATION

Contact

For general information contact:

Dr. Josefina J. Card, Principal Investigator
Sociometrics Corporation
American Family Data Archive
170 State Street, Suite 260
Los Altos, California 94022-2812
(415) 949-3282

For research support contact:

Dr. Eric L. Lang, Director, Research Support Group
Sociometrics Corporation
170 State Street, Suite 260
Los Altos, CA 94022-2812
(415) 949-5315

Cost

The cost of the collection is $950 for the PC CD-ROM version, and $850 for the Macintosh CD-ROM version. Included for this price are:

PC Data Library

Three Machine-Readable CD-ROMs

1, 2 Data and Documentation (5 Files) and User's Guides for Data Set Numbers 1-36
3 Search and Retrieval & Extract Files and Programs

PC Data Library (continued)

Seventeen Printed and Bound Publications

1   User's Manual for CD-ROMs
14   User's Guides to the Data Sets
1   Student Workbook and disk for *Family Research Toolkit: The National Survey of Children*
1   Instructor's Manual for *Family Research Toolkit: The National Survey of Children*

Macintosh Data Library

Two Machine-Readable CD-ROMs

1, 2   Data and Documentation (5 Files) and User's Guides for Data Set Numbers 1-36

Seventeen Printed and Bound Publications

1   User's Manual for CD-ROMs
14   User's Guides to the Data Sets
1   Student Workbook and disk for *Family Research Toolkit: The National Survey of Children*
1   Instructor's Manual for *Family Research Toolkit: The National Survey of Children*

Original study instruments for each data set are available for optional purchase, priced as follows in Table 1 on the next two pages.

Table 1.
Cost of Original Study Instruments, American Family Data Archive

Data Set Nos.	Data Set Title	Cost of original study instrument (priced at $.15 per page)
01-05	Nat'l Survey of Families and Households, 1988	$41.40
06-12	1976-87 Nat'l Survey of Children: Waves 1, 2, & 3	62.40
13-14	Nat'l Child Care Survey, 1990: Parent Study	12.00
15-16	A Profile of Child Care Settings: Home-Based Programs, 1990	6.45
17-18	A Profile of Child Care Settings: Center-Based Programs, 1990	8.70
19	Nat'l Commission on Children: 1990 Survey of Parents and Children	14.40

Table 1.
**Cost of Original Study Instruments,
American Family Data Archive (continued)**

Data Set Nos.	Data Set Title	Cost of original study instrument (priced at $.15 per page)
20-21	Nat'l Child Care Survey 1990: Low-Income Survey	$12.00
22-24	Marital Instability Over the Life Course 1981-1988	57.75
25-27	Stanford Child Custody Study: Family, 1984-1990	42.15
28-30	Stanford Child Custody Study: Child, 1984-1990	42.15
31	1975 Nat'l Family Violence Survey	7.20
32	1985 Nat'l Family Violence Survey	19.05
33-34	Nat'l Health Interview Survey on Child Health, 1988	14.40
35-36	Treatment Process: A Problem at Three Levels, 1988	9.00

Cost (continued)

All prices include first-class postage and handling. You may order by mail or telephone. Payments may be made by credit card (Mastercard or VISA) or check. Please make checks payable to Sociometrics Corporation. If you wish to be billed, the order must be accompanied by an official purchase order or signed letter on business or organization's letterhead. Mail your order to:

> Sociometrics Corporation
> American Family Data Archive
> 170 State Street, Suite 260
> Los Altos, CA 94022-2812

To place an order by telephone, call the order line 1-800-846-DISK (3475).

AUTHOR/ORGANIZATION INDEX
(Numbers in index are chapter numbers)

A

Abraham, S.Y., 8
Abrams, B., 15
Abt Associates, Inc., 1
Aday, L., 13
Adelman, C., 9
Adelmann, P.K., 18
Akin, J.S., 15
Albers, L., 15
Albiston, C.R., 6
Alexander, G.R., 15
Allen, W.R., 18
Alwin, D., 25
Amato, P., 22
Anderson, K., 27
Antonucci, T.C., 18
Aquilino, W.S., 28
Aral, S., 27
Archer, L., 12
Arnold, B.J., 17
Atkinson, J.W., 11
Axinn, W.G., 25

B

Bachman, R., 26
Bachman-Prehn, R., 26
Bachrach, C., 27
Baker, P.C., 23
Banach, J., 15
Barokas, J., 21
Batkhan, L., 15
Beck, P.A., 10
Bell, D.B., 21

Berendes, H.W., 14
Bitter, R.G., 22
Bloom, B., 13
Booth, A., 22
Bowen, G.L., 21
Bowman, P.J., 18
Botman, S., 27
Bradby, D., 8
Brandreth, Y., 28
Broman, C.L., 18
Brooks-Gunn, J., 23
Brayfield, A., 1
Bryant, F.B., 11
Buchanan, C., 6
Bumpass, L., 28
Burkheimer, G.J., 9

C

Cain, V.S., 13
Caliber Associates, 21
Call, V., 28
Camburn, D., 25
Campbell, B., 7
Campbell, C.H., 21
Campbell, R.C., 21
Card, J.J., 1, 2, 4, 6, 13, 14, 16, 22, 26, 27, 28, 30
Carmody, D.C., 26
Carnegie Foundation, 23
Carroll, C.D., 7, 9
Carver, K., 15
Castro Martin, T., 28
Cavin, E., 21
Center for Demography and Ecology, 28
Center for Human Resource Research, 23
Center for the Study of Minority Group Mental Health, 18
Centers for Disease Control, 13
Cervi, D.D., 26
Chamberlain, P., 16

Chase-Lansdale, P.L., 23
Chatters, L.M., 18
Cherlin, A., 28
Child Trends, Inc., 5
Chou, S.P., 12
Cooksey, E.C., 9
Colella, U.A., 28
Coleman, L.M., 18
Corman, H., 13
Croan, G.M., 21
Crockett, H., 11
Crohan, S.E., 18
Crohan, S.W., 11
Crutchfield, J.H., 1, 27, 28

D

Daley, H.M., 4
Danforth Foundation, 10
Data User Services Division, 3
Davis, J.A., 17
Dawson, D.A., 12, 13
DeBakey, S.F., 12
Defense Technical Information Center (DTIC), 21
Deich, S., 1
Demo, D.H., 18
Department of Defense (DOD), 23
Department of Labor (DOL), 23
Depner, C.E., 6, 11
DiFazio, A.S., 21
Divine-Hawkins, P., 1
Doherty, S., 21
Dornbusch, S.M., 6
Douvan, E., 11
Duncan, G.J., 19

E

Eagle, E., 7, 9
Edwards, J.N., 22
Ellison, C.G., 18
Ernst, E.K.M., 15
Etheridge, R.M., 21

F

Family Research Laboratory, 26
Farquhar, E., 1, 2
Feld, S.C., 11
Feld, S.L., 26
Fitzgerald, R.A., 7, 9
Ford Foundation, 5, 19, 23
Forgatch, M.S., 16
Forrest, J., 27
Foundation for Child Development (FCD), 5, 20, 23
Frankel, M.R., 8
Freedman, D.S., 25
Furstenberg, F.F., Jr., 5

G

Gallaudet University, 8
Gelles, R.J., 26
Gibson, R.C., 18
Gifford, A., 7, 9
Glantz, F., 1
Glusberg, M., 7
Goldscheider, C., 27
Goldscheider, F., 25
Gonzalez, J.F., 15
Gordon, H., 7
Grant, B.F., 12
Grant Foundation, 23
Greeley, A.M., 17

Guilkey, D.K., 15
Gurin, G., 11, 18

H

Hafner, A., 8, 9
Hagy, A.P., 2
Hampton, R.L., 26
Hardy, A.M., 13
Harford, T.C., 12
Harrop, J.W., 26
Hasin, D.S., 12
Hatchett, S.J., 18
Hawkins, P., 2
Head Start Bureau of the Administration for Children, Youth, and
        Families of the U.S. Department of Health and Human
        Services, 1
Health Resources and Services Administration, 13, 14
Hendershot, G.E., 14
Henderson, L.B., 9
Henshaw, S., 27
Hewlett Foundation, 23
Hickerson, M., 22
Hill, D.H., 25
Hill, M.S., 19
Hoachlander, E.G., 8
Hofferth, S.L., 1, 2
Hoffman, H.J., 14
Holcomb, P., 1
Holmes, B.C., 13
Horn, L., 8
Hotaling, G.T., 26
Howes, C., 2
Hughes, M., 18
Human Resources Research Organization, 21
Hunt, E., 7
Hyde, K.A., 9

I

Iannacchione, V.G., 21
Immigration and Naturalization Service, 24
Ingels, S.J., 8
Institute for Survey Research, 5, 18
Inter-university Consortium for Political and Social Research (ICPSR),
    7, 9, 10, 11, 17, 18, 19, 20, 25

J

Jackson, J.S., 18
Jayakody, R., 18
Jeng, L., 15
Jennings, M.K., 10
Johnson, D., 27
Johnson, D.R., 22
Johnson, W.E., 15
Joint Commission on Mental Illness and Health, 11
Jones, E., 27
Judkins, D., 27
Juster, F.T., 20

K

Kaczmarek, R., 15
Kaestner, R., 13
Kahn, J., 27
Kane, J., 9
Kaplan, A.S., 6, 13, 22, 26
Karr, R., 8
Katz, R., 21
Kaufman, P., 7, 8
Kaufman Kantor, G., 26
Kavanagh, K., 16
Keith, B., 22
Keppel, K.G., 15
Kiely, J.L., 15

Kirkland, F.R., 21
Kisker, E.E., 1, 2
Knepper, P.R., 7, 9
Knight, S., 7
Kogan, M., 15
Kost, K., 27
Kotelchuck, M., 15
Kovar, M.G., 14
Krauss, N.A., 15
Krecker, M.L., 28
Krulewitch, C., 15
Kulka, R., 11

L

Lang, E.L., 1, 2, 4, 6, 13, 16, 22, 26
Langton, K.P., 10
Larson III, O.U., 26
Larzelere, R.E., 26
Lee, R., 8
Levinson, J.R., 9
Lewis, E.A., 18
Li, M., 28
Lindmark, J.T., 8
London, K., 27, 29
Looking Glass Family Therapy Center, 16
Lu, H., 28

M

Maccoby, E.E., 6
Manning, W., 28
Marcus, G.B., 10
Margolin, L., 22, 26
Marks, N., 28
Marks, N.F., 28
Martinson, B.C., 28
Maza, P., 27

McCollough, W., 18
McKean, E.A., 16
McLanahan, S.S., 28
McNally, J., 27
Michael, R.T., 9
Milne, J.G., 21
Moore, K.A., 4, 5
Moore, R., 15
Morgan, J.N., 19
Morgan, P., 5
Mosher, W., 27
Moss, A.J., 13, 14
Moss, N., 15
Mott, F.L., 23
Mnookin, R.H., 6
Myers, S.L., 8
Muller, K.L., 22

N

National Association for the Education of Young Children
    (NAEYC), 1
National Center for Education Statistics (NCES), 7, 8, 9, 12, 13
National Center for Health Statistics (NCHS), 12, 13, 14, 15, 27, 29
National Commission on Children, 4
National Institute of Child Health and Human Development
    (NICHD), 5, 19, 23, 24, 27, 28
National Institute of Mental Health (NIMH), 5, 16, 18, 26
National Institute on Aging (NIA), 10, 19, 22
National Institute on Alcohol Abuse and Alcoholism (NIAAA), 12, 23
National Institute on Drug Abuse (NIDA), 23
National Institutes of Health (NIH), 6
National Opinion Research Center (NORC), 7, 8, 9, 15, 17, 23
National Science Foundation (NSF), 8, 10, 17, 19, 20, 26
National Technical Information Service (NTIS), 12, 15, 27, 29
Neighbors, H.W., 18
Newacheck, P.W., 13
Niemi, R.G., 10
Nord, C.W., 5

O

Office of Economic Opportunity (OEO), 19
Ohio State University, 23
Oliver, L.W., 21
Olsen, R.J., 23
Oregon Social Learning Center (OSLC), 16
Orthner, D.K., 21
Overpect, M.D., 13, 14
Owings, J.A., 8, 9

P

Parker, D.A., 12
Parker, J.D., 15
Parsons, J.E., 20
Patterson, G.R., 16
Peterson, E.C., 4, 26
Peterson, J.L., 3, 5, 7, 14, 23, 24
Phillips, D.A., 2, 23
Pickering, R.P., 12
Pillemer, K., 26
Piper, V., 2
Place, C., 9
Placek, P., 15
Poe, G., 14
Pollack, J.M., 8
Popkin, B.M., 15
Pratt, W., 27
Public Health Service, 13

Q

Quigley, B., 21
Quinlan, S.V., 23
Quinn, P., 8

R

Rakoff, S.H., 21
Ramsberg, P., 21
Rasinski, K.A., 8
Ray, J., 16
Reid, J.B., 16
Research Triangle Institute (RTI), 9, 21
Response Analysis Corporation, 26
Reuman, D., 11
Rhoads, A., 5
Riccobono, J., 9
Rindfuss, R.R., 9
Ritter, P.L., 14
Robert Wood Johnson Foundation, 5
Rock, D., 8
Rockefeller Foundation, 19, 23
Rooks, J.P., 15
Roper Public Opinion Research Center, 17
Russell Sage Foundation, 17

S

Sadacca, R., 21
Sanderson, M., 15
Scarville, J., 21
Schoenborn, C.A., 12, 13
Schoendorf, K.S., 15
Schneider, B., 8
Schultz, S., 21
Schwartz, J.B., 15
Schwarz, S.M., 27
Scott, L.A., 8
Sebring, P., 7
Seidman, L., 27
Seltzer, J.A., 28
Simpson, G., 15

Singh, S., 27
Sloan Foundation, 19, 23
Smith, T.W., 17
Social Security Administration's Office of Research and Statistics, 22
Sociometrics Corporation, 1, 2, 4, 5, 6, 13, 14, 16, 22, 26, 28, 30
Spencer, B.D., 7, 8
Spizman, L., 9
Stafford, C.E., 9
Stafford, F.P., 20
Stanford Center for Research on Families, Children, and Youth, 6
Stawarski, C., 21
Steffens, R.A., 12
Stets, J.E., 26
Stevenson, D., 8
Stinson, F.S., 12
Stolley, K., 27
Stone, V.E., 1, 28
Straus, M.A., 26
Styles, M., 21
Sugarman, D.B., 26
Suitor, J.J., 26
Survey Research Center (SRC), 11, 18, 19, 20
Sweet, J., 28
Sweet, S., 26

T

Taffel, S.M., 15, 27
Taylor, R.J., 18
Thomson, E., 28
Thornton, A., 25
Tourangeau, R., 8, 9
Tucker, M.B., 18

U

U.S. Army Research Institute, 21
U.S. Bureau of the Census, 3, 12, 13, 14, 19, 24

U.S. Department of Agriculture's Women, Infants, Children (WIC) Program, 15
U.S. Department of Education, 2, 7, 8
U.S. Department of Education's Office of Bilingual Education and Minority Language Affairs (OBEMLA), 8
U.S. Department of Health and Human Services, 1, 3, 13, 19, 20, 27
University of Michigan, 18, 19
University of Wisconsin, 28

V

Van Hook, J.V.W., 28
Ventura, S., 27
Veroff, J., 11
Vissing, Y.M., 26
Voran, M., 2

W

Weatherby, N.L., 15
West, J., 7, 8
White, L.K., 22
Whitebook, M., 2
Willer, B., 1, 2
Williams, K.R., 26
Williams, L., 27
Williams, L.B., 27
Willis, R.J., 9
Willms, J.D., 7
Wilcox, L., 27
Wilson, B.F., 29
Wilson, K.R., 18
Wolford, M.L., 18
Wu, L.L, 28
Wu, S.C., 8

XYZ

Young-DeMarco, L., 25
Zill, N., 3, 5, 7, 13, 14, 23, 24
Zimmerman, L., 21
Zuma, J., 7, 9

SUBJECT INDEX

Note: The topics in this Index have been derived from keywords used in each chapter. The numerical entries are chapter numbers and not page numbers. Because each chapter describes one data set, the Index can be used to see if a given data set has information on a particular topic of interest. However, other data sets besides those cited in the Index may also have information on the topic, as the abstracts do not contain an exhaustive list of the hundreds of variables included in each data set. Thus the reader is encouraged to peruse related topics/keywords and related data sets for maximal coverage of a particular topic of interest. Related data sets are grouped as follows (see the Table of Contents):

A

Abortion: 5, 15, 17, 23, 25, 27
 attitudes about, 17
 decision making about, 5
Achievement Motivation, 19
Actuarial Methods, 29
Adolescents, see Youth
Adoption/Foster Care, 5, 9, 14, 15, 19, 26, 27, 28
Aid to Families with Dependent Children (AFDC), 3, 5
AIDS, 17
Alcohol, 12, 17, 23
Alcohol Consumption Patterns, 12
Alimony, 3, 9
Age: 1, 2, 3, 4, 5, 6, 7, 8, 9, 10, 11, 12, 13, 14, 15, 16, 17, 18, 19, 20, 21, 22, 23, 24, 25, 26, 27, 28, 29
 at decree of divorce, 29
 at first marriage, 22

Biases: 9
    sex, 9
    race, 9
Biological Functioning/Development, 2, 5, 6, 13, 14, 15, 16, 23, 27
Birth: 1, 5, 11, 13, 14, 15, 23, 24, 28, 29
    characteristics at, 5
    date of for children, 28
    date of for husband and wife, 29
    events, 14
    expectations, 24
    first and most recent, 5
    history, 5, 23
    place of, 1, 11, 29
    weight, 13, 15
Black Americans, 18
Breastfeeding, 14

C

Center-Based Childcare Programs, 1
Center for Epidemiologic Studies Depression Scale (CES-D), 15
CD-ROM, 1, 2, 4, 5, 6, 7, 8, 13, 14, 16, 22, 23, 26, 28
Child: 5, 13
    bedtime schedule of, 13
    current age of, 13
    ordinal position of, 5
    wantedness of, 5
Childbearing, 3, 5, 7, 9, 11, 12, 13, 14, 15, 19, 20, 22, 23, 24, 25, 26, 27, 28
Childrearing Practices, 5
Child Care, 1, 2, 4, 5, 6, 8, 9, 11, 12, 13, 14, 15, 17, 18, 19, 20, 21, 22, 23,
    24, 25, 26, 27, 28
Child Care Settings, 1, 2
Child Custody: 5, 6, 9, 28
    arrangements following divorce, 28
    evolution of arrangements in divorcing families, 6
    gender role difference about, 6
    joint-custody arrangements, 6
    legal conflict about, 6
    maintenance and change of, 6

noncash benefits, 3
migration, 3
monthly demographic and labor force data, 3
work experience, 3
Current Population Survey (CPS) Child Support and Alimony
Supplement, 3
size of female population with children affected by divorce or
separation, 3
Current Population Survey (CPS) Marital and Fertility Supplement, 24

D

Data Archive on Adolescent Pregnancy and Pregnancy Prevention
(DAAPPP), 14, 27
Dating and Courtship, 5, 6, 18, 21, 22, 23, 25, 27, 28
Delinquency, 4, 5, 6, 7, 8, 14, 17, 18, 23, 26, 28
Development: 9
educational, 9
factors that affect, 9
personal, 9
vocational, 9
Disability, 12, 13, 14, 18
Disabled Persons, 24
Divorce: 1, 2, 3, 4, 5, 6, 7, 8, 9, 10, 11, 12, 13, 14, 15, 16, 17, 18, 19, 20, 21,
22, 23, 24, 25, 26, 27, 28, 29
compliance with agreements, 6
conflict, 5
custody and visitation of children, 5
degree of conflict and cooperation between divorced parents,
5, 6
disengagement or continued involvement of noncustodial
parent, 6
effects of, 28
evolution and maintenance of residence, 6
evolution and maintenance of visitation arrangements, 6
family reorganization due to, 6
financial arrangements after, 5
interval from separation to decree, 29
legal process leading to settlement, 6

month of, 29
nature of disruption, 5
records, 29
registration area, 29
relationship between child and parent living outside the
    home, 5
relationship with former spouse, 5
remarriage after, 6
Divorce-Registration Area (DRA), 29
Do-it-Yourself Activities, 19
Drug(s): 5, 23
    discussion of, 5
    use history, 5, 23
Dwelling: 1, 2, 3, 4, 5, 6, 7, 8, 11, 12, 13, 14, 17, 18, 19, 20, 21, 22, 23,
    24, 25, 28
    ownership, 25
    size of, 5, 7, 8, 12, 14, 18, 19, 20, 22, 28
    type of, 1, 2, 3, 5, 6, 12, 13, 14, 17, 18, 19, 20, 21, 22, 23, 24, 28

E

Economic Accounts, 20
Economic Well-Being: 19, 24
    of families, 19
    nation's, 24
Education: 1, 2, 3, 4, 5, 6, 7, 8, 9, 10, 11, 12, 13, 14, 15, 16, 17, 18, 19, 20,
    21, 22, 23, 24, 25, 26, 27, 28, 29
    aspirations and expectations for, 5, 8, 25
    attainment, 3, 9, 23, 24
    attitude toward, 7, 9
    child development courses taken, 1
    college plans, 7
    dropout history, 5, 7
    family involvement with, 8
    financial aid for future, 8
    graduate programs, 7
    history, 26
    home educational support system, 8
    influence of peers, parents, and teachers on goals for, 7

level attained by head of household, 16
levels and characteristics of early, 2
need for special resources, 5
parent/child plans for child's future, 4, 7, 8, 9, 10
policy-relevant data, 7
post-secondary participation, 8, 9, 25
progress, 23
teacher practices in, 8
teacher rating of students, 7, 8
transcript information about, 7
status, 26
Educational Testing Service (ETS), 9
Employment: 1, 3, 4, 5, 6, 7, 8, 9, 10, 11, 12, 13, 14, 15, 16, 17, 18, 19, 20, 21, 22, 23, 24, 25, 26, 27, 28
barriers to, 18
effects of job-related problems, 18
full-time, 4
history of, 1, 5, 9, 26
irregular economic activity and, 18
job satisfaction, 23
monthly estimates of total, 3, 24
parent/child plans for child's, 4
part-time, 4
place of, 1
spouse's, 21
status, 1, 4, 13, 20, 24, 26
Ethnic Group, 1, 3, 9, 19
Ethnicity, see Race
Event History Information, 25

F

Family: 1, 2, 3, 4, 5, 6, 7, 8, 9, 10, 11, 12, 13, 14, 15, 16, 17, 18, 19, 20, 21, 22, 23, 24, 25, 26, 27, 28, 29, 30
assistance to and from extended, 19
background, 23
causes and consequences of changes in, 28
composition changes in, 19

follow-up to the National Longitudinal Surveys of Labor Force
Behavior: Youth Survey and Child Supplement
(The NLSY), 23
follow-ups (Wave 2 and 3) for the 1976 National Survey of
Children (NSC), 5
1991 longitudinal follow-up of mothers of the 1988 National
Maternal and Infant Health Survey (NMIHS), 15
three follow-ups to High School and Beyond Sophomore and
Senior Cohorts (HS&B), 7
Friends/Social Support, 1, 4, 5, 7, 8, 10, 11, 17, 18, 20, 21, 22, 25, 26, 28
Future Birth Expectations, 24

G

Gender, 1, 2, 3, 4, 5, 6, 7, 8, 9, 10, 11, 12, 13, 14, 15, 16, 17, 18, 19, 20, 21,
22, 23, 24, 25, 26, 27, 28, 29
Gender Role: 6, 17, 20
attitudes about, 20
differentation, 6
women's, 17
General Social Surveys (GSS), 17
Geographic Mobility, 13
Goal Expectations, 9
Government Role: 17
in civil liberties and law enforcement, 17
in economic regulation, 17
in education and child rearing, 17
in social welfare and inequality, 17
Group: 18
identity, 18
stereotypes, 18
Growth, 27
Guidance/Counseling, 4, 5, 6, 7, 8, 11, 15, 16, 18, 22, 26, 27

H

Health: 1, 2, 3, 4, 5, 6, 7, 8, 11, 12, 13, 14, 15, 16, 17, 18, 19, 20, 21, 22, 23, 24, 25, 26, 27, 28
    accidental injuries, 12, 13, 14
    acute illness, 12, 13, 14
    alcohol consumption patterns, 12
    attitude toward sources of assistance, 11
    care, 25
    child, 13, 14, 15, 16, 23
    chronic condition and impairments, 12, 13, 14
    disability, 12, 13, 14, 18
    eyes and teeth, 14
    factors related to childbearing, 27
    growth or developmental delays, 13
    height, 13
    hospitalization and surgery, 14
    infant feeding practices, 15
    limiting conditions, 5
    maternal, 23
    missed school due to, 13
    national and regional information on major issues of, 12
    of the elderly, 19
    passive smoking and, 13
    past and present, 11
    physical status of, 18, 20
    prenatal care, 5, 13, 15
    receipt of services for, 1, 3, 5, 6, 7, 8, 11, 12, 13, 14, 15, 16, 18, 19, 21, 22, 23, 27, 28
    social effects of ill health, 14
    vaccinations, 15
    visits to doctors, dentists, hospitals, 13
    weight, 13, 14, 15
    utilization of health care services, 12, 13, 14, 18
Help with Emergencies, 19
High School and Beyond Sophomore and Senior Cohorts, 7
Home-Based Childcare Programs: 2
    counties where located, 2
Hospitalization: 14, 15
    and surgery, 14

experience, 7, 9, 10
recruitment, 17
service, 25
training and human capital development, 17
war and peace, 17
Military Substudy, 1
Minnesota Multiphase Personality Inventory (MMPI), 16
Mobility: 1, 3, 5, 6, 10, 13, 14, 17, 18, 19, 21, 22, 23, 25, 26, 27, 28
     residential, 1, 3, 5, 6, 10, 13, 14, 17, 18, 19, 21, 22, 23, 25, 26, 27, 28
     social, 17
Motor Development, 14
Multi-State, Cluster Sampling, 21
Multistage Probability Design, 12, 13

N

National Child Care Survey (NCCS), 1
National Commission on Children: 1990 Survey of Parents and Children, 4
National Data Program for the Social Science: 17
     data diffusion program, 17
     social indicator research, 17
National Educational Longitudinal Study of 1988 (NELS88), 8
National Family Violence Survey, 26
National Health Interview Survey (NHIS), 12, 13, 14, 27
National Health Interview Survey on Alcohol (NHIS-A), 12
National Health Interview Survey on Child Health (NHIS-CH), 14
National Health Survey Act of 1956, 12
National Longitudinal Study of the High School Class of 1972 (NLS-72), 9
National Longitudinal Survey of Labor Force Behavior: Youth Survey and Child Supplement (NLSY), 23
National Maternal and Infant Health Survey (1988) (NMIHS), 15
National Registration System: 30
     birth records in, 30
     death records in, 30
     divorce records in, 30
     fetal death records in, 30

marriage records in, 30
National Survey of Black Americans (NSBA), 18
National Survey of Children: Waves I, II, and III (NSC), 5
National Survey of Family Growth, Cycle IV (NSFG), 27
National Survey of Families and Households (NSFH), 28
Neighborhood, 1, 2, 4, 5, 8, 11, 12, 13, 14, 18, 19, 20, 21, 22, 23, 24, 26, 28
    cost of housing in, 5
    participation in programs in, 8
    problems of, 5, 19
    quality of, 5
Noncash Benefits, 3
Nonfunctional Style of Interaction, 16
Nonimmigrant U.S. Population, 19
Nonreactive Observational Measures of Behavior, 16
Nutrition, 2, 14, 15, 20, 27

O

Occupation, 1, 2, 3, 4, 5, 6, 7, 8, 9, 10, 11, 12, 13, 14, 15, 16, 17, 18, 19, 20,
    21, 22, 23, 24, 25, 26, 27, 28
Occupational: 17, 23, 26
    history, 26
    prestige, 17
    training, 23
    status, 26
Out-of-Wedlock: 5, 9, 15, 19, 23, 24, 25, 27
    births, 5, 24
    pregnancy and parenthood, 5, 9, 15, 19, 23, 24, 25, 27

P

Panel Study, 10, 19, 20
Panel Study of Income Dynamics, 1968-1990 (PSID), 19
Parental: 16
    disciplining, 16
    monitoring, 16
    problem solving, 16
Parenthood, 11

smoking, drinking, drug use during, 15
source of payment for, 15
total number visits, 15
WIC participation, 15
Primary Sampling Units (PSUs), 2, 11, 17, 26, 28
Profile of Child Care Settings, 2
Psychological Functioning/Development, 4, 5, 6, 7, 8, 9, 11, 13, 18, 22, 23, 26, 28
Public Assistance, 19

Q

Quality of Life, 11, 26
Quality of Parent-Child Relationship, 4

R

Race, 1, 2, 3, 4, 5, 6, 7, 8, 9, 10, 11, 12, 13, 14, 15, 17, 18, 19, 20, 21, 22, 23, 24, 25, 26, 27, 28, 29
Race Relations, 17
Racial: 18
    identity, 18
    attitudes, 18
Random Digit Dialing Procedure, 22
Readiness of Army Personnel, 21
Recreation, 5, 6, 7, 8, 11, 15, 17, 20, 22, 23, 25, 28
Region/State, 1, 2, 3, 4, 5, 7, 8, 10, 11, 12, 13, 14, 15, 17, 18, 19, 20, 21, 22, 23, 24, 26, 27, 28, 29
Relationship(s): 1, 4, 5, 6, 7, 8, 9, 10, 11, 12, 13, 14, 16, 18, 19, 21, 22, 23, 24, 25, 26, 28
    between child and parent living outside the home, 5
    each family member to each other, 1, 4, 5, 6, 7, 8, 10, 11, 12, 13, 14, 16, 18, 19, 22, 23, 24, 25, 26, 28
    inter-partner, 4, 5, 6, 9, 10, 18, 19, 21, 22, 23, 25, 26, 28
    inter-sibling, 4, 5, 9, 19, 21, 23, 26, 28
    parent-child, 4, 5, 6, 8, 9, 10, 11, 13, 16, 18, 19, 21, 22, 23, 25, 26, 28
    with former spouse, 5

with nonkin, 4, 5, 6, 8, 11, 18, 19, 21, 25, 26, 28
with other kin, 4, 5, 6, 8, 18, 19, 21, 22, 25, 26, 28
role, 18
social, 11
Religion, 1, 4, 5, 6, 7, 8, 9, 10, 11, 16, 17, 18, 19, 20, 22, 23, 25, 26, 27, 28
church attendance, 11, 18
emotional and instrumental functions of the church and
religion, 18
prayer, 18
role of the church in, 18
Religious: 1, 4, 5, 6, 7, 8, 10, 11, 16, 17, 18, 19, 20, 22, 23, 26, 27, 28
affiliation, 1, 4, 5, 6, 7, 8, 10, 11, 16, 17, 18, 19, 20, 22, 23, 25, 26,
27, 28
behaviors, 17
beliefs, 17
preference, 1, 4, 11
training, 5
socialization, 17
Residence: 1, 3, 4, 5, 7, 8, 10, 11, 12, 14, 15, 17, 18, 19, 22, 23, 24, 27, 28
community of, 4
history, 5
urban/rural, 1, 3, 4, 5, 7, 8, 10, 11, 12, 14, 15, 17, 18, 19, 22, 23,
24, 27, 28
Retention of Qualified Army Personnel, 21
Retired Persons, 11
Retirement, 17, 19

S

Scales (about issues): 10
equal rights for women, 10
change in form of government, 10
government aid to minorities, 10
government guaranteed job and living standard, 10
legalization of marijuana, 10
liberal/conservative views, 10
rights of the accused, 10
school busing to achieve integration, 10
U.S. foreign policy and Vietnam, 10

Schedule for Affective Disorders and Schizophrenia, 16
School: 1, 4, 5, 7, 8, 9, 10, 13, 14, 19, 22, 25
    absences from, 7, 8
    academic content in, 10
    activities and interpersonal relations at, 10
    after-school supervision, 8
    atmosphere at, 8
    attitude toward, 8, 10, 25
    attitudes toward school policies, 8
    behavior in, 5
    course enrollment at, 7
    course offerings at, 7
    courses taken outside of, 5
    discipline at, 8
    drop outs from, 7
    enrollment in, 7
    experiences at, 9, 25
    extracurricular activities at, 5, 8
    faculty composition of, 7
    goals, 7
    grade in, 5
    grading and testing structure of, 8
    guidance services at, 7, 8
    highest school year completed in, 1, 4, 13, 19, 22
    homework at, 8
    identification code, 7
    institutional characteristics of, 7
    instructional programs at, 7
    parental supervision at, 8
    participation in federal programs/policy relevant groups, 7, 8
    performance, 5, 7, 8, 9, 14
    policies and practices, 8
    problems, 13
    school-related activities, 7
    staff attitudes at, 7
    staff work load at, 7
    subjective value of high school experience, 9
    suspensions from, 7
    type of school child attending, 4
    wife in, 22

Secondary Sampling Units (SSUs), 28
Self Esteem, 5, 8, 9, 11, 18, 23, 25
Self Identity, 18
Sense of Community, 9, 21
Senior Cohort, 7
Separation: 25, 29
     age at, 29
Sex, see Gender
Sex Education: 5, 7, 17, 23, 27
     content, 27
     relation to chances of unwanted adolescent pregnancies, 27
     relation to onset of sexual activity, 27
     relation to use of contraception, 27
     sources of, 27
Sex Role Attitudes, 20
Sexual: 5
     activity, 5
     behavior, 5
Sexuality, 5, 17, 22, 23, 25, 26, 27, 28
Sexually Transmitted Diseases, 5, 15, 17, 27
Sleep Habits, 13, 14
Smoking, 14, 15, 17
Sociopolitical Participation, 17
Social Accounts, 20
Social Development, 14
Social Networks, 17
Social Inequality: 17
     beliefs about, 17
     intergroup conflicts and, 17
     perceived and preferred income differentials between
          occupation and, 17
     reasons for, 17
     social mobility and, 17
Social Learning Approach, 16
Social Services, 1, 3, 5, 6, 7, 8, 11, 12, 13, 14, 15, 16, 18, 19, 21, 22, 23, 27, 28
Social Stability, 11
Social Structure, 11
Social Support, 17, 20, 25
Socialization, 10

Sophomore Cohort, 7
Spanish Origin, 3, 4, 24
Standard of Living, 25, 26
        ownership of consumer durables, 25
        satisfaction with, 26
Standard Metropolitan Statistical Areas (SMSAs), 11, 18, 19, 22
Standard Listing and Screening Procedures (SLASP), 18
Standardized Test Scores, 7
Stanford Child Custody Study, 6
Statistics: 29
        marriage, 29
        divorce, 29
Status: 1, 2, 3, 4, 5, 6, 7, 8, 9, 10, 11, 12, 13, 14, 15, 16, 17, 18, 19, 20, 21,
        22, 23, 24, 25, 26, 27, 28, 29
        economic, 3, 26
        employment, 1, 3, 4, 8, 13, 26
        family, 9
        financial, 23
        labor force, 17
        marital, 1, 2, 3, 4, 5, 6, 7, 8, 9, 10, 11, 12, 13, 14, 15, 16, 17, 18, 19,
                20, 21, 22, 23, 24, 25, 26, 27, 28, 29
        mental health, 18
        poverty, 19
        socioeconomic, 4, 9
        veteran, 24
        work, 9
Stepchildren, 5, 9
Students, 24
Substance Use, 5, 7, 8, 11, 12, 15, 17, 18, 22, 23, 26, 28
Suicide, 17
Supplement, 3, 13, 14, 19, 23, 24
Survey of Parents and Children, 4

T

Teacher Ratings, 7
Telephone Interview Opinion Survey, 4
Television Viewing, 5, 7
Thematic Apperception Test (TAT), 11

Therapy Process Coding System (TPC), 16
Therapeutic Interventions, 16
Time Diary, 20
Time Trend Studies, 17
Time Use, 5, 20
Time Use in Economic and Social Accounts, 20
Time Use Longitudinal Panel Study, 20
Transcript Information, 7
Transportaion, 5
Treatment Process: A Problem at Three Levels, 16
Trends Over Time, 5
Triplets, 7
Twins, 7

U

Unemployment: 11, 18
        effects of chronic, 18
        estimates of, 3, 24
        history of, 7, 9
        statistics on, 24

V

Vaccinations, 15
Veteran Status, 24
Violence: 23, 26
        between husbands and wives, 26
        between parents and children, 26
        between siblings, 26
        by race and ethnicity, 26
        descriptive information about, 26
        in the family, 26
        state-by-state estimates, 23
        three theories about, 26
Vital Statistics: 27, 29
        on birth, 29
        on children of divorce, 29

on death, 29
on divorce, 29
on family formation and dissolution, 27
on fertility, 27
on marriage, 29
Vital Statistics Cooperative Program (VSCP), 29
Vital Statistics on Marriage and Divorce 1968-1988, 29
Voting Habits, 7, 10

W

Wage Rate, 1, 7
War on Poverty, 19
Wealth/Finances/Material Things, 1, 2, 3, 4, 5, 6, 7, 8, 10, 11, 12, 13, 14,
    15, 16, 17, 18, 19, 20, 21, 22, 23, 24, 25, 26, 27, 28
Welfare; 5, 19
    history, 5
Wide Area Screening Procedure (WASP), 18
Wives' Interview, 19
Women: 24
    married, 24
    never married, 24
    outside the labor force, 24
    sociodecographic characteristics of, 24
    working, 24
Women's Marriage and Childbearing Experiences, 24
Work: 3, 5, 9, 11, 15, 17, 18, 19, 20, 22, 23, 24, 25
    also see Employment
    attitudes about, 5, 25
    current desire for, 24
    discrimination, 18
    effects of race on work force composition, 18
    full-time, 3
    history of, 9, 19, 23
    number weeks and hours per week at, 3
    orientation, 17
    patterns, 15
    performance, 9
    previous experience at, 3, 9, 24

satisfaction with, 9
status, 9, 22
supervision, 9
time spent at, 20
wife working for pay, 22
wife working full or part-time, 22
Workers: 3, 24
distribution of workers by number of hours worked, 24
intentions as to job seeking, 24
nonfarm self-employed persons, domestics, and unpaid helpers
in nonfarm enterprises, 3, 24
occupation of, 24
retired, 24
wage and salary employees, 3, 24

Y

Young Adults: 5
aspirations of, 5
consequences of pregnancy and parenthood for, 5
experiences of, 5
family background of, 5
social, psychological, and economic well-being of, 5
sexual and fertility behavior of, 5
Youth: 5, 8, 9, 23
academic achievement of, 8
aspirations of, 5
consequences of pregnancy and parenthood for, 5
educational experiences of, 9
experiences and family background of, 5, 9
fertility behavior of, 5
goal orientations of, 9
labor market experience of, 23
military recruitment and service experience of, 23
persistence in school by, 8
personal development of, 9
sexual development of, 5